Wes Anderson

WES ANDERSON

Why His Movies Matter

MARK BROWNING

Modern Filmmakers
Vincent LoBrutto, Series Editor

 PRAEGER

AN IMPRINT OF ABC-CLIO, LLC
Santa Barbara, California • Denver, Colorado • Oxford, England

Library of Congress Cataloging-in-Publication Data

Browning, Mark, 1966–
    Wes Anderson : why his movies matter / Mark Browning.
        p. cm. — (Modern filmmakers)
    Includes bibliographical references and index.
    ISBN 978-1-59884-352-1 (hard copy : alk. paper) —
    ISBN 978-1-59884-353-8 (ebook)
  1. Anderson, Wes, 1969– —Criticism and interpretation.   I. Title.

    PN1998.3.A526B76   2011
    791.4302'33092—dc22   2010043218

ISBN: 978-1-59884-352-1
EISBN: 978-1-59884-353-8

15   14   13   12   11   1   2   3   4   5

This book is also available on the World Wide Web as an eBook.
Visit www.abc-clio.com for details.

Praeger
An Imprint of ABC-CLIO, LLC

ABC-CLIO, LLC
130 Cremona Drive, P.O. Box 1911
Santa Barbara, California 93116-1911

This book is printed on acid-free paper ∞

Manufactured in the United States of America

Contents

Series Foreword

The Modern Filmmakers series focuses on a diverse group of motion picture directors who collectively demonstrate how the filmmaking process has become *the* definitive art and craft of the 20th century. As we advance into the 21st century we begin to examine the impact these artists have had on this influential medium.

What is a modern filmmaker? The phrase connotes a motion picture maker who is *au courant*—they make movies currently. The choices in this series are also varied to reflect the enormous potential of the cinema. Some of the directors make action movies, some entertain, some are on the cutting edge, others are political, some make us think, some are fantasists. The motion picture directors in this collection will range from highly commercial, mega-budget blockbuster directors to those who toil in the independent low-budget field.

Gus Van Sant, Tim Burton, Charlie Kaufman, and Terry Gilliam are here, and so are Clint Eastwood and Steven Spielberg—all for many and for various reasons, but primarily because their directing skills have transitioned from the 20th century to the first decade of the 21st century. Eastwood and Spielberg worked during the sixties and seventies and have grown and matured as the medium transitioned from mechanical to digital. The younger directors here may not have experienced all of those cinematic epochs themselves, but nonetheless they remained concerned with the limits of filmmaking: Charlie Kaufman disintegrates personal and narrative boundaries in the course of his scripts, for example, while Tim Burton probes the limits of technology to find the most successful way of bringing his intensely visual fantasies and nightmares to life.

The Modern Filmmakers series will celebrate modernity and postmodernism through each creator's vision, style of storytelling, and character presentation. The directors' personal beliefs and worldviews will be revealed through in-depth examinations of the art they have created, but brief biographies will also be provided where they appear especially relevant. These books are intended to open up new ways of thinking about some of our favorite and most important artists and entertainers.

Vincent LoBrutto
Series Editor
Modern Filmmakers

Introduction

The films of Wesley Mortimer Wales Anderson often provoke extremes of fierce loyalty and violent antipathy and little in between. In British culture, there is a well-known yeast-based product called Marmite, spread thinly on toast, which has given rise to a useful phrase, even used by advertisers, "the Marmite test," an action that provokes a love or hate reaction. In considering Wes Anderson, there is little space for neutrality, with individuals even using the response to *Bottle Rocket* or *Rushmore* as a gauge of personal compatibility. From the lengthy gestation of *Bottle Rocket,* which was first a short (1994) and then a longer feature (1996), through to the animated feature *Fantastic Mr. Fox* (2009), Anderson has produced a highly distinctive body of work that has developed a fiercely loyal fan base.

This book attempts some neutrality in looking at the relatively small body of work that Anderson has produced thus far, considering how it works and trying to explain why it has had such an impact on contemporary filmmaking. In an era of generic and stylistic homogeneity, there are, at present, very few filmmakers whose work is instantly recognizable. The only movies Wes Anderson films look like are other Wes Anderson films. For fans, this adds to his growing reputation as a distinctive auteur; for his critics, it signals creative stagnation.

Anderson is a rare example of a modern director who has a significant input in a number of areas of production, resulting in a distinctive style, which links his films together and separates them from the work of others. He directs, writes, and sometimes produces, and takes an almost forensic approach to the look of his sets. He is one of a growing number of directors who did not hone their skills in film school, but he just took up the tools of filmmaking. He grew up in Houston and at school, staged plays and experimented with Super 8 mm films. Studying philosophy at the University of Texas, he met future collaborator Owen Wilson (who was studying English) in a playwriting course. At the time, both aspired primarily to be writers. Like the characters in Anderson's first film, *Bottle Rocket,* they had plenty of ambition but were looking for a way of expressing it. After they graduated, Wilson and Anderson remained in the Austin area, Anderson working at a public access television station while Wilson gained acting experience in local theatre. Like Max Fischer, the hero of his film *Rushmore,* Wilson had been ejected from St. Mark's School in Austin, so the irony was sweet when they were able to film part of *Bottle Rocket* there.

The subtitle of the book is "Why his movies matter." Anderson is often linked to a certain distinctive kind of filmmaking that is dominated by matters of style, particularly so-called hipsterism.[1] In some eyes, this rather indistinct term represents someone who is cultivating a persona that is cool, distinctive, and associated with particular clothing and lifestyle choices. Perhaps, by definition, anyone who regards himself as cool is probably not. However, in terms of appearance, dining habits, and particularly literary and cinematic preferences, Anderson has several points of similarity with this group. Always thin, tall, pale, with hair sometimes long and unkempt in appearance, he has the look of a more thoughtful Beck or the guitarist Simon Bartholomew from the Brand New Heavies (Anderson supposedly played bass on the reggae track in *Tenenbaums*). Olivia Williams (Miss Cross in *Rushmore*) described him as "quite physically and socially awkward...a precocious and intelligent young boy."[2] A former wearer of designer glasses, now more commonly seen with designer contact lenses, he has been known to sport a shoulder bag and if he does not openly discuss politics and his sexual preferences, he does admit to a liking for European culture, spending part of the year in Paris, part in Rome, and virtually living in one specific Italian restaurant, Bar Pitti in New York, during the writing of *The Life Aquatic.* Broach the question of influences, and discussion will encompass French (Truffaut, Renoir, Malle), Spanish (Buñuel), and Italian cinema (Fellini).

Although Anderson is dealing in a visual rather than a purely literary medium, he is still a writer, having at least cowritten all his films, which up to *Fantastic Mr. Fox,* were not based on the works of others. This has led to the development of an individual and distinctive voice, clearly different from those around him, and a concern for the style of the medium in which he works. He is a writer, however, having at least co-written all his films, which up to *Fantastic Mr. Fox,* were not based on the works of others. The relevant part of the term for Anderson is perhaps the development of an individual and distinctive voice, clearly different from those around him, and a concern for the style of the medium in which he works. At his best, this can create cinematic moments where the style seems to capture a key aspect of a character or a situation in a memorable line or image. For some, Anderson's concern with the minutiae of production matches the pretentiousness they associate with the self-conscious artiness of poetry because, of course, the same features lauded by his fans are often also used as the basis of antipathy towards his films.

However, most reviews and even more detailed articles almost always present a given view, either favorable or critical, and make the same assertions about a recognizable series of features. Often, the films themselves seem left behind in the regurgitation of existing critical positions. This book will endeavor to derive any conclusions from close readings of the films themselves and will consider to what extent the films are really as similar as reviewers routinely assume, whether his style expresses or disguises a lack of substance, whether scripts and performances are more nuanced than usually described, and whether he goes beyond merely imitating his cinematic and literary influences.

Traditional print media and academic journals have been very slow to react to Anderson's work, and some of the more interesting comments expressed so far have come from the virtual community via fan sites like http://rushmoreacademy.com. Online blogs are increasingly using film clips and image capture to compare specific scenes of moving footage, alongside written comments, in ways that open up film criticism to whole new vistas of intertextuality. Despite Anderson being a critical darling of some film journalists, this book is the first study of his work. He has passing mentions in Sharon Waxman's *Rebels on the Backlot: Six Maverick Directors and How They Conquered Hollywood* (2006), James Mottram's *The Sundance Kids: How the Mavericks Took Over Hollywood* (2006), and Derek Hill's *Charlie Kaufman and Hollywood's Merry Band of Pranksters, Fabulists and Dreamers: An Excursion into the American New Wave* (2008) but often (as Waxman's title suggests) in relation to the system and how a group of directors broke into it, overtly targeting readers who wish to do the same. Hill does have a specific chapter on Anderson, but it is only 15 pages long and predominantly descriptive in tone. Anderson is nearly always mentioned in lists and seen very much as part of a group—something he himself continually denies. It is precisely the point that he is *not* like other filmmakers that is used to both praise and criticize him. He is sometimes dubbed as part of "the New Sincerity," defined by Jim Collins as referring to a mode of filmmaking "that rejects any form of irony in its sanctimonious pursuit of lost purity."[3] It is a fairly loosely defined term that has been adopted across a range of academic disciplines but in terms of film it refers to a lack of cynicism, an embracing of immediate pleasure. It is an issue to which we will return in examining the ambiguous nature of Anderson's protagonists.

In an era of growing aversion to risk taking in filmmaking, in which scripts are often based on existing literary properties, apart from *Fantastic Mr. Fox*, Anderson's scripts are noticeable for being original (at least in the sense of being written for the screen). However, this does not mean that the scripts are original in the sense of being uninfluenced by other films or literary works. Indeed, it is debatable how original films like *The Royal Tenenbaums* actually are.

Since Anderson foregrounds his stylistic choices so clearly, viewers are sometimes more aware of aspects of film form and similarity with other Anderson films, far more than when watching films by other directors, and generalizations are frequently made about Anderson's work in relation to another director, often without any detailed substance. This book endeavors to look closely at each film on its own merits and consider how the possible purposes and effects of stylistic decisions play out in their original narrative context.

The book tries to use plot in the furtherance of argument rather than regurgitating straightforward summaries. It is aimed at discerning film viewers who have already seen Anderson's work. It may not persuade those with a strong antipathy to love his films but will perhaps help them understand a little better why they feel this way. This book is *not* concerned with the minutiae of production processes, the politicking of studio finances, or even box office numbers. It is about the films on the screen. The general organization of the chapters is chronological. Anderson's work in commercials is discussed in the chapter devoted to considering his style, since this aspect of his filmmaking does not constitute a particular phase and the commercials themselves are of most interest in relation to his influences, especially from French directors.

Chapter 1 considers *Bottle Rocket,* especially in relation to its central character and how Anderson's conception can be usefully compared to the work of Woody Allen and Quentin Tarantino, and what was gained and lost in the growth of the 1996 feature from the 1994 short version of the film. Chapter 2 looks at *Rushmore,* considering the representation of one of Anderson's most enduring characters, the hero Max Fischer, and to what extent he is admirable or purely a fantasist. Chapter 3 examines *The Royal Tenenbaums,* particularly in the light of influential texts from J. D. Salinger. Chapter 4 discusses *The Life Aquatic with Steve Zissou* in relation to the ambiguous nature of the main character and the work of French filmmaker Jean Painlevé, as an example of an explorer film as described by André Bazin, and how Zissou might be seen as a contemporary of Herman Melville's Captain Ahab. Chapter 5 considers *The Darjeeling Limited* and particularly how far the Whitman brothers really understand what is going on around them and whether the film represents a major maturing in Anderson's filmmaking. Chapter 6 covers *Fantastic Mr. Fox* and discusses the balance between human and animal values in the film. Chapter 7 looks explicitly at influences on Anderson's work from other filmmakers, especially those from a French background, and considers to what extent he develops those into a style of his own. Chapter 8 contains an important discussion of Anderson's portrayal of issues connected to race and class. Chapter 9 considers Anderson's use of framing, especially his work in commercials and his positioning of paintings in feature films, and discusses stylistic similarities between his film style and the early silent era. Chapter 10 focuses on Anderson's filmic style, including his use of music and whether this is just a collection of mannerisms or whether it constitutes something more coherent and profound, in particular his strategies for signaling his presence as an auteur. The conclusion tries to decide whether there is something that binds Anderson's heroes together and what future projects might represent for his growing body of work.

For the most part, films made for general release attempt to tell stories, not deliver themes, so trying to throw either a thematic or critical blanket over all of Anderson's work and distort the films themselves to fit this is not the purpose of this book. Each of Anderson's films is considered in turn: its strengths, weaknesses, and complexities. This is just the first step towards a more considered approach to Anderson's work.

Please note, for ease of discussion and to help distinguish between character names and some film titles, the latter are often shortened to *Tenenbaums*, *Aquatic*, and *Darjeeling*.

Take the Money and Run:
Bottle Rocket (1996)

And so it begins.

—Dignan and Mr. Fox

The "bottle rocket" of the title, heard on the soundtrack, right at the opening, represents as much as anything the energy of the conversation, which fizzes brightly and then fades out. The script, co-written by Anderson and Owen Wilson, reaches rhetorical heights of absurdity, undercut by the reality of the inability of the main character, Dignan (played by Wilson), to plan anything effectively. The shots down the length of the car with Dignan holding out a firework or his setting off rockets in a field feel like adolescent pranks akin to the mailbox baseball in *Stand By Me* (Rob Reiner, 1985). Part moody teenager, apparently depressed at the departure of Bob (Robert Musgrave), Dignan is also enjoying the opportunity to indulge himself in his own drama. To celebrate the success of the bookstore robbery, we see Dignan holding lighted fireworks from the passenger seat of Bob's car and hear Oliver Onions' "Zorro is Back" (1974), underlining Dignan's casting of the gang in the guise of unstoppable superheroes (while conveniently skipping over the morality of theft).

BOTTLE ROCKET (1994)

The 16mm short film, on which the feature is based, has several features that persist into the longer film, such as the central relationship between Dignan and Anthony (Luke Wilson), the initial robbery of their own home, and the postmortem of the job. Small features are there too, like the childish target drawings, the iconic three-shot as they practice with the guns, and Dignan's malapropism with "hypocritical." However, other material is lost, which is a pity. It opens with Dignan, played by an incredibly young-looking Owen Wilson here, and Anthony approaching their target, featured in the longer version, but here they argue about an old episode of *Starsky and Hutch* en route. These are characters who naturally express themselves in the language of televisual fictions and who take such elements of their lives very seriously (Dignan stating that the plot as described by Anthony "has the logic of a dream"). Like Starsky here ("This is he"), Dignan also speaks about himself in an elevated style in the third person at times, viewing himself objectively like some kind of mythic hero. This exchange and his later slide across the hood while wearing the jumpsuit ironically look forward to his role in the movie version of *Starsky and Hutch* (Todd Phillips, 2004). The original TV series of *Starsky and Hutch* (ABC, 1975–1979), starring Paul Michael Glaser and David Soul in the respective lead roles, ran for four seasons in which the two detectives fought crime around a fictional California town, Bay City, and introduced a series of icons into the detective genre such as informant Huggy Bear (Antonio Fargas), a red Grand Torino with a distinctive white stripe, and a jokey buddy relationship that contributed to global reruns for years afterwards.

The house robbery, as in the feature, uses some handheld shots, and we see Dignan taking coins (rather than earrings) but not in a tight overhead shot. We see Dignan and Anthony trying to buy guns from a salesman (Temple Nash Jr., playing himself) who explains some blunt home truths about weapons, perhaps a small nod to "Easy Andy" (Steven Prince) in Martin Scorsese's *Taxi Driver* (1976), who also plays a gun salesman and can draw on his own life experience (in his case in relation to drugs and celebrity). Dignan naively seems to think (and continues to do so through the film) that guns can be used just to scare people. During planning for the bookstore robbery, we share Bob's point of view as he wanders down the aisles, but here his attention is taken by self-help books like *A Road Less Travelled: A New Psychology of Love, Traditional Values and Spiritual Growth* by Dr. M. Scott Peck.

There is no actual bookstore robbery seen in the short version. As Mark Olsen observes, "The action itself is important only in that it gives them something new to talk about."[1] This need to fictionalize is seen in the postmortem scene. The robbery is no sooner committed than retold with the absurd elements airbrushed out and glossing over the fact that $183 is not a "pretty good haul." Dignan uses elevated language to create a heroic, exciting adventure that provides a bond between Bob, Anthony, and himself. However, even here there are reality checks as Bob is increasingly alarmed at the prospect of being hunted down, a key part of the narrative for Dignan. Their school-style desks lined up outside the burger bar underline the fact that we are still basically looking at three adolescent boys, persuaded with minimum justification to join in a footrace in an act of teenage rivals, not professional criminals.

Also lost are some great comic lines. In the diner Anthony initially does not understand the connection between Bob's marijuana and his interest in a book on herbs and then subsequently asks if Bob can also grow cinnamon because then he could have his own cinnamon toast. The exchange was shot for the longer version but cut from the finished film. Anthony also explains that he came out of the window from the institution (in a scene referred to but not shown) even though he had a set of keys, with the absurd justification that they might have changed the locks. This only provokes admiration from Dignan as an example of forward planning. In terms of characterization, the protagonists are very similar, hopelessly lusting after a waitress who might be described as mature at least, and the impulsive crime of breaking into a parked car that Dignan pushes Anthony to commit only yields a wallet with $8. However, Dignan's dialogue "What did I tell you!" is delivered with a sense of accomplishment, not censure, depression, or recrimination. Not all the signature Anderson elements are here, such as the distinctive use of particular music, tight overhead shots, or slow motion, that we would come to see in his body of work, but the key character types, the comic banality of language, and the absurdity of dramatic situations are all here from the outset.

Although radically shorter than the feature, there is a tenser dynamic at work here between the three leading roles. Bob calls Dignan a "son-of-a-bitch" and then asks Anthony (who does not correct Bob's assessment) not to tell Dignan because "he can't handle that kind of information." Bob's ranting complaint about their motel existence and Dignan's leadership, eventually calling him "Commander Dignan," is fantastically choreographed so that he turns away, unaware that Anthony has walked off to fetch a drink, to be replaced by Dignan himself who hears the name he is called. Far from noting the sarcasm in Bob's voice, Dignan takes this as a flattering reference and clearly finds the potential nickname attractive. Dignan manipulates experience to what he would like it to be (both robberies) and only hears what he wants to hear. A series of scenes in the short version emphasize the immaturity of the threesome. We see extended questioning of Nash about guns with progressively more childish questions from whether he has ever shot anyone to whether he has ever shot a dog and if so, what kind, and in a restaurant scene, they are told to go back and clear their tables, which they obediently do. We also have more detail about Futureman's name. Dignan explains, "He looks like he was designed by scientists. For desert warfare." Although it is a great line, the lack of explanation works too as a reminder of the absurdist universe that the protagonists, especially Dignan, inhabit.

Despite being shown at the Sundance Film Festival, the film received almost unanimously negative review cards at initial test screenings and struggled to find its audience at first. The 1994 version gained limited promotion by Columbia Pictures, and it was only after the *LA Times* posted a more favorable review that the film started to grow into the cult movie it has since become, finding a belated audience on DVD.

A LIFE OF CRIME—TAKE THE MONEY AND RUN

Anderson's heroes often take their lead from celluloid role models. In *Fantastic Mr. Fox,* Rat (Willem Dafoe) constitutes a benign version of Dafoe's gangster Bobby Peru from *Wild at Heart* (David Lynch, 1990), who also seems to have learned most of his lines from cliché movies. The opening scene of *Bottle Rocket* blends a motif of childhood adventure story, evoking Mark Twain's *Adventures of Huckleberry Finn* (1884), in which a character climbs out of a window in order to meet another, with that of a spy narrative as Dignan, sporting gloves and using binoculars and a mirror, signals to his coconspirator. This looks forward to the stupid signal and birdcall he uses during the bookstore robbery. We are in the world of childish games, of fantasy, and yet the protagonists are adults, adults unable or unwilling to grow up. When we later see Dignan's handwriting, it is clearly childish in form (as is his drawing of a human for target practice) with upper- and lowercases mixed. The absurdity of the situation is underlined as we learn that Anthony (Luke Wilson) is checked in to the hospital voluntarily and that he is indulging this escape as a fantasy for Dignan's benefit. In looking at Dignan, Anthony says, "Look how excited he is." In effect, a patient of a mental institution is pretending for the sake of someone normal on the outside, and it is actually ambiguous as to who is rescuing whom. Dr. Nichols advises him before he leaves, "Don't try and save everybody, OK?"

The burglary scene uses standard means to create suspense. Rapid cutting, handheld shots of drawers being opened, and close tracking shots behind Dignan all suggest a sense of immediacy and the excitement of the participants. What undermines this is the context. Anthony and Dignan approach the house from a bus; that is, they have no getaway car, no disguise, and most telling of all, it is subsequently revealed as Anthony's parents' house. No great research was required to learn the layout of the place and if Anthony and Dignan were caught, the owners would be unlikely to press charges. The bookstore robbery continues the ridiculous theme when, having called the manager "an idiot," Dignan is forced to apologize and ask politely for larger bags like those used "for atlases and dictionaries." The choice of this store as a target is not exactly a great one as it is quite large and carries little ready cash.

The final robbery is a catalogue of avoidable errors, underlining that Dignan's weakness is ironically where he believes his main strength lies: preparation. As previously, Dignan is drawn to the gadgets of crime, sporting a headset like a cross between a pop star and a Bond-style secret agent, using walkie-talkies and code names. From the outset, the plan starts to crumble because of the weakness of individuals (Bob comes and joins Anthony because he claims his radio is not working but really he does not want to be alone) and the absurdity of Dignan's supposedly precise planning being met with a group of bemused workers. Events descend into farce. Kumar just sits in the office, clearly unable to open the safe and uses

Dignan's real name; Bob fires the gun accidentally; Applejack (Jim Ponds) has a heart attack; and the smoke bombs supposed to disguise their escape set off the fire alarm. The van is locked and Anthony, who has the key, is stuck on the second floor due to a broken elevator. However, despite general incompetence, Dignan also shows a more selfless side here, rescuing Kumar from the deep-freeze and helping Applejack from the building. However, at the same time, his decision to go back into the building is partly his desperation to be the hero in his own narrative.

Anderson could only gain the services of James Caan as Mr. Henry for a few days but shows an ability to get the most from this in his debut feature. Although looked upon as a "Mr. Big" character by Dignan, Henry is really quite a small-time crook (thereby making Dignan's idolatry all the more pathetic). He hardly appears the criminal mastermind as described by Dignan, pouring water on Dignan's head as he stands at the door of his warehouse. By turns charming and aggressive, he berates Dignan for bringing Anthony there, and yet he defends Bob against the bullying of Futureman (Andrew Wilson) and Clay (Brian Tenenbaum), humiliating them and thereby helping to win over Anthony and Bob. He is hardly a personification of style, practicing martial arts moves without pants in a storeroom and later dressed in a ridiculous kimono at a party.

The film has similarities with Woody Allen's *Take the Money and Run* (1969), both featuring central characters who aspire to criminal greatness, particularly as armed robbers, but are undone by their own ineptitude, of which they seem blissfully unaware. In Allen's movie, the incompetence of Virgil Starkwell (Allen) is shown through an escape plan using a gun made of soap that dissolves into a handful of foam in the rain and bank tellers not being able to read the written demand he hands them. Here, Dignan's pride in his research is undermined by a slight adjustment to working rotas, building a criminal team with no visible criminal skill (Kumar) or desire to do the deed (Bob), who allow themselves to be locked out of their own getaway vehicle. Like the protagonists in *Bottle Rocket*, Virgil craves the status of being a notorious criminal. As Anderson's theatrical trailer states, "They just wanted to be wanted." Virgil even complains that he never made it onto the America's 10 Most Wanted list because "it's who you know." Although Dignan lacks the fast-talking, New York–Jewish neuroses of Allen's character, both films are co-written by their star and feature sequences in prison and with their heroes on the run (in both cases the police hardly seem interested in initiating a pursuit).

Allen is often also described as an auteur for his involvement especially as director, writer, and selector of music (although Anderson does not go the further step of casting himself in the lead role). Allen also, in his early and mid-career films in particular, repeatedly cast the same actors and faced similar criticism of a lack of development and that his earlier films were better and funnier. For both filmmakers, central characters are largely failures; families are dysfunctional; and humor is generally ironic and low-key in expression. *Take the Money and Run* may not be Allen's debut but as his second film, it still represents the start of his career and, like *Bottle Rocket*, contains many great comic lines and moments missed on its initial release. Allen also uses a distinctive typeface for text on screen, Windsor, usually white on black but not with the frequency with which Anderson uses Futura and not to the extent of all lettering within the fictional universe on screen.

Another clear influence, Mario Monicelli's *Big Deal On Madonna Street* (1958), also features an accident-prone group of hopeless robbers, whose climactic big job also fails due to a less-than-impressive safecracker (Dante, played by comedian Totò). There is a similar romantic subplot involving Mario (Renato Salvatori) and Carmela (Claudia Cardinale), the smooth progress of which is also impeded by an overprotective brother (Tiberio Murgia).

DIGNAN: A CRIMINAL MASTERMIND?

BOB: What are you putting that tape on your nose for?
DIGNAN: Exactly.

The sad truth about Dignan's character is that there is no air of mystery about him. What we see is really what we get. Perversely, this lack of guile is also an engaging quality. He is pathetic in the sense of both being ridiculous and worthy of pathos. Dignan is a control freak, setting out in a rough sketch personal goals for up to the next 75 years. When he says to Anthony that "you and I both respond to structure," it is clear that what is proposed is *his* structure. He chooses the biggest and loudest gun for himself. He shushes Anthony over terming the institution a "nuthouse" as "other people are not comfortable talking about emotional disturbances," but it is not clear that he is either. He is extremely sensitive to any criticism of his planning, picking up on Anthony's use of the word "avid" (unconnected to the computer editing system of the same name) in relation to his approach to fitness, fishing for compliments in the robbery postmortem, and assuming that Anthony is trying to undermine his authority when he asks if they really need explosives. He later has a tantrum when Bob will not listen to the plan to rob the bookstore and wants to play with the gun instead, showing Dignan's prickly nature and Bob's childishness.

It is fitting that the characters still play pinball, a game that offers apparent choice and excitement but really is nothing more than loud music, flashing lights, and the inevitable loss of your money. In order to deal with Dignan, Anthony indulges in his fantasy world, playing along with the escape at the opening. The power of childish pacts, made concrete by writing rules, is invoked and dismissed at will. Dignan dismisses Bob's departure from the team as nothing had been written down, but earlier Dignan breaks his own agreed rules, stealing the earrings he had promised to leave alone. However, his unwillingness to grow up is also engaging from his ridiculous martial arts moves with the gun to contriving a skid on his small motorbike, which then he cannot restart and has to push out of the shot. He even has the occasional malapropism. In going through the robbery plan, he claims that he is just being "hypocritical," instead of "hypothetical."

What makes Dignan particularly winning is his ever-present optimism in the face of a reality that flatly contradicts this. Anthony comments that he does not think Dignan's "happiness is quite appropriate" and this is literally true, but taking any semblances of a positive from a situation is still an engaging quality. Dignan assures Bob and Anthony that they will get the best room possible at the motel. This may be true, but it does not really disguise the tawdry state of their existence. Futureman is partly right when he calls Dignan "a rodeo clown" and "a little banana" (on account of the jumpsuit), but his assumption of superiority is only that of the high school bully. He and his photogenic friend Clay literally look down on Dignan from their van, but they have achieved little more in life, other than being considered good-looking. When Dignan explains that "I'm not always as confident as I look," it is the fact that he is blissfully unaware of the absurdity of such a statement that makes his character engaging. There is an innocence to him that prevents him from being easily dismissed as just a loser plain and simple. He confronts Bob with a platitude about living in the real world and settling problems "with bare knuckles" before Bob just punches him.

Dignan idolizes Mr. Henry completely uncritically, and he seems desperate for recognition from someone whose opinion he values. This makes him ripe for exploitation. His carrying of a photo, posing next to the source of his admiration, feels like fan worship, in which he constructs a fictitious relationship with the object of his affection. Dignan expects the picture to have the same effect on others, even though Anthony parodies his pseudo-sexual interest ("Fact: Dignan, the picture's not doing it for me right now"). The fiction that he creates about himself as being part of Mr. Henry's criminal family, extents to the pseudo-cowboy impression of "The Lawn Wranglers" when in reality, it is just a team of gardeners. This truth he only admits piecemeal and skates over why he was fired. His craving for recognition is everywhere, even present in tiny points like the symbols he uses for them in the robbery plan: he is the star, Anthony is a cross, and Bob is a zero. Dignan is drawn to the distorted criminal notion of family and morality, seeing Anthony's joining with Mr. Henry's group as "doing the right thing." In this, Mr. Henry becomes a father figure for Dignan that he seems to lack at home, even to the extent of forgiving Mr. Henry for ripping them off at the end.

Dignan is an innately ridiculous character, shouting to Anthony at the motel that they have to hide their identities and use the aliases he has created, although his choice of Cornelius and Rocky is hardly likely to help them blend in. He repeats this shouted warning not to "blow their cover" in the final robbery. The innate absurdity of the situation is reflected in Dignan's dialogue: "He's out. You're out too. I don't think I'm in either." He returns moments later, apologizing for "poor leadership" (a mantle that he has assumed without debate). He casts himself in a narrative of his own making, so that after the bookstore robbery, he is disproportionately proud of his excuse to get the man to open the store door (a lame story about losing his sweater) and describes them as "fugitives" even though there is little sign that anyone is pursuing them or that Mr. Henry would be interested in them making contact with him. He seeks a sense of belonging and recognition, reflected directly in his pursuit of the status of a criminal. He wants to be "wanted." Dignan enjoys the aimlessness of their road trip. Their supposed status as outlaws and being on the run is more important to him than going somewhere for a reason. He wants the others to feel "scared" and "celebrate the moment," but Anthony is more interested in recounting a typical day back in the institution. Dignan dramatizes the unpredictability of their situation, not knowing exactly where they are going only to be juxtaposed with a shot of their actual destination—a crummy motel.

The team as he envisages it has no place for women or romantic relationships. He claims to Anthony that he is "as excited for you as anybody is" about the relationship with Inez (Lumi Cavazos), but this is not true. Most obviously, he fails to pass on Anthony's declaration of love (and even denies that Inez loves him) but earlier, he muscles in on a flirtatious conversation between Anthony and an unknown girl and crashes in on the romantic poolside scene between Anthony and Inez. When he comments sarcastically, "Talk about a language barrier," in relation to Inez, he might equally have been talking about his own inability to express what he really thinks and feels. He is piqued by Bob's bad mood (justified by the arrest of his brother) and Anthony's distraction in pursuing Inez, both of which threaten to distract attention from his narrative with the roles he has assigned for each player. He is left to petulantly state, "I'm the leader" and expects Bob to abandon his brother rather than adapt their plan.

When Bob rejects this and takes the car, Dignan tries to strike a pose of indignation, promising revenge and that Anthony will see "a sick, sadistic side" to his character (talking about himself in the third person), but this is just another role, the spurned boss, to which he is attracted. There is no real shock here: Bob told him he was going. In the diner, Dignan takes this pose a stage further as if he was a jilted lover, only wanting an apology for his pride to be placated. When Dignan gets into a fight in the diner, he threatens to "call my gang," but in the foreground we can see that only constitutes one individual, Anthony, who is preoccupied by chattering on about love, unaware of events by the pool table behind him. Anthony subsequently tries to apologize, but Dignan does not want to be reminded of facts that relive his humiliation and that run counter to his narrative of himself as boss of a criminal gang.

The strip of plaster across his nose might have a practical value in distracting witnesses, but it is typical of his attachment to the paraphernalia of crime without thinking through what his actions really mean. Lying on the ground, shot in alternating high and low angles, Dignan talks about himself again in the third person, wondering if he needs a break in an institution. He is far more mentally unstable than Anthony, who correctly identifies that arguably Dignan has issues that might need treatment. When Mr. Henry tries to persuade Anthony to join them, his attempts at emotional blackmail ("You're breaking his heart, you know" and describing Dignan as a "poor guy" and rather melodramatically as "a man alone") are actually but unwittingly true.

THE TEAM

KUMAR: I lost my touch.
DIGNAN: Did you ever have a touch to lose?

In his interview, Bob claims, "There's a real air of mystery about me" and "I'm a risk taker," and yet he panics when police find his homegrown marijuana. He has a short concentration span, not just in playing with the gun, but he also picks up a book during the robbery and starts flicking through it. He does not really seem a worthy recipient of "the spirit award" (Dignan's suggestion) for the bookstore robbery, having to do very little and then complaining about the size of his share. Typical of Dignan living within a fiction of his own making, he interviews Bob for the position of getaway driver using a blend of the language of a high-profile, high-status corporate job and sentimental TV quiz host ("That hits me right here," he claims, pointing to his chest). However, the context deals the coup de grace that Bob is the only one with a car. There is ultimately a Hollywood-style reconciliation between Futureman and Bob, in part brought about by the robbery fiasco, although it is couched in more graphic language. As Futureman says, "Just because you're a fuck-up doesn't mean you're not my brother."

When Stacy, a friend of Anthony's sister, states, "You're really complicated, aren't you?" and Anthony replies, "I try not to be," there is a reference here to Peter Sellers's Chance the Gardener in *Being There* (Hal Ashby, 1979) with other characters projecting profundity into his extremely inane dialogue. When Stacy introduces herself as "Elizabeth's sorority sister," Anthony exclaims that he did not know she had a sister, which Stacy takes as a witty joke. This is also evoked in Dignan's work for Mr. Henry, where he claims "just because it's a front doesn't mean you don't have to do landscaping," suggesting the menial nature of the work only adds to the authenticity of his cover. Dignan is concerned about using false names while Anthony refuses to get his hair cut or dyed and is more interested in making banana daiquiris.

Anthony also echoes some of Dignan's characteristics, such as his touchiness, becoming upset at Grace's view of him as a failure, and not questioning Dignan's absurd accusation, "What has she accomplished in her life?" The key difference here is one of age. Grace is still at school. Anthony's drawing in the diner of Inez on a horse is as ludicrously childish as Dignan's targets. Like Dignan, he initiates a rule which he then makes others sign on to (the list of "things Dignan's not supposed to touch"). Later in the final robbery, Anthony's feverish drawing is revealed as nothing to do with their planned crime but a man pole-vaulting. He hankers after one of Dignan's yellow jumpsuits (possibly the very last choice of an experienced criminal seeking to avoid detection), which he seems to think is cool. However, our next view of Anthony shows him with little sense of self-awareness, advising Grace to keep busy as his three jobs look like the personification of industrious behavior. However, these are low-paid (a paper route) or hardly physically demanding (he talks of "working hard" while eating lunch on a building site). He even advises Grace to learn a foreign language, although there was little sign of him doing that when he was with Inez.

Anthony's action in looking right down the camera lens before adjusting the position of a soldier is a quintessential Anderson scene, partly pretentious, partly profound. It is a very self-conscious action, overtly symbolic, and yet within the scene the character is not performing this act to impress anyone else. Anderson's characters exist most fully in their own narratives, and here Anthony's small gesture expresses a frustration that he seems to have so little control and direction in his own life. However, as Grace's belittling comments make clear, he is responsible for this.

DIGNAN—A TRANSCENDENT HERO?

What Martin Scorsese termed a "transcendent moment" (Dignan describing how he cannot be captured because he is innocent) can also be read less positively.[2] Scorsese's terminology links him with Paul Schrader, with whom he worked a number of times, most notably on *Taxi Driver* and *Raging Bull* (1980) and which provides the basis for Schrader's study of Yasujiro Ozu, Robert Bresson, and Carl Theodor Dreyer, *Transcendent Style in Film* (1972). Here Scorsese is responding to *Bottle Rocket*'s lack of cynicism, but Dignan is about to find out that there is a world of difference between cinematic poses of toughness and the real thing. A young, good-looking man is about to experience a prison term. This may not be *The Shawshank Redemption*, but his innocence may be about to be shattered. In an early version of *Bottle Rocket*, there is a shot described which is not used in the final version of the film in which Dignan is seen after his show of bravado at the prison fence: "Dignan's expression has changed. He wasn't expecting them to see it. His eyes look cold." Scorsese describes *Bottle Rocket* as about "a group of young guys who think that their lives have to be filled with risk and danger in order to be real. They don't know that it's okay simply to be who they are."[3] However, this is only partially true. It is *Dignan* who feels like this, and the film shows us his sometimes successful attempt to impose his view of the world on the others who go along with him, not because they are convinced, but out of solidarity with their friend and occasionally won over by the force of Dignan's personality at specific moments.

Conventionally, slow motion is often used, for scenes of motion, to draw attention to what would normally remain unseen. Moments of particular drama, especially involving simultaneous actions, lend themselves to such a technique. Slow motion, a breaking of the dramatic illusion, is also used by Anderson to signal that the film is ending. It invites us to view the frame more carefully and links with previous slow motion scenes, effectively bookending the film and considering how characters have changed and what we have learned about them (and possibly ourselves). In that context, the final slow motion shot in *The Darjeeling Limited* (near, but not at the very end of the film) could almost be a joke played on the viewer, who might expect such a stylistic device to signal the very end of the film.

The use of slow motion generally has a number of important aspects. It lends movement a significance, even if the literal action is mundane. It plays with the temporal element of film, drawing the viewer's attention to the metaphorical meaning of what they are, and have been, viewing; that is, it invites a moment of contemplation. In sporting terms, the most iconic use of slow motion, the replay, is not part of Anderson's aesthetic. He elongates time within individual sequences, rather than replaying images we have already seen. The slow motion of the closing sequence here shows Mr. Henry in low angle puffing a cigar, satisfied with his robbery ruse as a means of distracting Dignan, Anthony, and Bob from the real target: Bob's house. Dignan is trapped in the building, ridiculously commanded to "freeze" while cowering in the freezer, and then we have a tilt shot as he is led out, already in a pseudo-prison outfit. The slow motion continues into the final prison sequence as Bob and Anthony visit and the camera tracks Dignan's departing form as he looks over his shoulder in a tableau of "not looking back in anger." Even now, he retains an element of innocence, refusing to blame Mr. Henry about whom he says he does not have any hard feelings (or Applejack who has mysteriously disappeared since leaving the hospital), keeping silent about the robbery in an absurd adherence to a criminal code that he has seen in films but which makes him a patsy here.

Another self-taught filmmaker emerging at the same time as Anderson, Quentin Tarantino, also found his debut (*Reservoir Dogs*) attracting some critical attention and also found some critical focus on the apparently derivative nature of his work. Neither Tarantino nor Anderson served an apprenticeship in pop videos or TV commercials but found inspiration elsewhere: Tarantino, through his hours in a video store, and Anderson, through his poring over copies of the *New Yorker*. Whereas Tarantino made a stylistic signature of juxtaposing scenes of banal discussions of pop culture with extreme violence, Anderson just gives us the banality element (such as the *Starsky and Hutch* exchange or later conversation in the diner about the growling ability of Bob's dog, Hector). Reflective of the wannabe status of the protagonists as notorious criminals, Anderson draws on Tarantino's trunk shot from *Pulp Fiction* (1994) to reveal the object of idolization is not money but guns. With earmuffs and varying degrees of hopelessness in their stances or accuracy, they hardly look like aspiring gangsters. The argument that breaks out while Dignan is discussing his plan is sparked by Bob playing with one of the guns—the thing they are really all interested in. The iconic three-shot of the men firing the handguns provides obvious poster material for the film and reflects how they see themselves. The wide shot of the animals in *Fantastic Mr. Fox,* all dressed in suits, walking in tight formation down the sewer towards their climactic meeting with the farmers, evokes the iconic walk-through sequence in *Reservoir Dogs* but tellingly here without slow motion (used in *Rushmore*'s first montage of Max's hobbies).

What separates *Bottle Rocket* from *Reservoir Dogs* is class and age. Although several of the gangsters in Tarantino's film are young, they are at least in their twenties, established criminals, and used to carrying guns and using them brutally in the pursuit of their aims. In *Bottle Rocket,* the wannabe crooks are seen firing pistols inexpertly in a field, not at point-blank range into police officers. Anderson cuts a few darker elements from earlier versions of the story, such as Anthony telling Bob about a prank with the school generator going wrong and electrocuting the custodian, and he also describes how Dignan saved him from drowning.

Apart from a single punch to Max in *Rushmore,* following a petty spat over a script, blood is a substance rarely seen in a Wes Anderson film. Until Esteban's disappearance and Ned's demise in *The Life Aquatic,* death remains as subtext (via Max's mother and Miss Cross's husband in *Rushmore*) and decidedly offscreen (Royal's death is described by a close-up on Chas rather than shown). Part of the engaging nature of the characters we see is that they seem to think they really will live forever.

More than mature though, Tarantino's characters are career criminals; they know what they are getting into. They may display pettiness about naming and indulge in unlikely exchanges about pop culture, but they know what it is like to be without money (the whole point about tipping in the opening scene). In *Bottle Rocket,* gangsterism is purely a game. Anthony and Bob go along with Dignan's plans, not because they share his romantic view of life as outlaws but to please their lifelong friend, whose fragile ego needs regular support and assent. The robberies are adventures—games with the appearance of transgression but without any of its context. Bob lives in a palatial house with a swimming pool and the greatest stress in his life is an older brother who teases him. Anthony does not suffer a genuine breakdown (that we see at least) but checks himself into an institution, much like a celebrity entering rehab. The object of Dignan's hero worship, Mr. Henry, is also a strictly lower-league criminal, an organized burglar and dealer in stolen goods, who, although more worldly than his dupes, would still be out of place in a Tarantino narrative.

Key to this difference in intent and ability is talk. In *Bottle Rocket*, Dignan inspires (or wears down) Bob and Anthony, not so much by the power of his argument but by his rhetoric and blind enthusiasm. In *Reservoir Dogs*, no one needs a pep talk; in *Bottle Rocket*, Dignan's flights of criminal fantasy become like the fireworks he holds out of the car window—something bright and apparently spectacular but only lasting a short time and ultimately fizzling out. At times Dignan's rhetoric appears to have run out of steam (particularly in the sequence where Anthony walks away from him, leaving him alone among fields in the middle of the shot). However, when Dignan says, "We did it though, didn't we?" in part this is a ridiculous inability to see the truth of an absurdly botched criminal act, but in another way, it celebrates the potential of joint action. The literal success of the robbery is less important than finding a sense of belonging and camaraderie while it was taking place. Like Allen's Virgil in *Take the Money and Run*, it is the undimmed enthusiasm, or ability to stubbornly ignore reality, depending on your point of view, which endures by the end. Dignan is not crushed. He is not lying in a pool of blood like one of Tarantino's protagonists. He is still dreaming.

2

School Daze: *Rushmore* (1998)

I don't know what you've got here, Wes.

—Pauline Kael

BLUME VS. MAX: WHO IS THE BIGGER FANTASIST?

Rushmore begins with a curtain opening and in a sense the whole film is a school play, scripted by Max (Jason Schwartzman) and whatever the apparent subject matter, Max himself is the real topic under scrutiny. An early line, cut from the finished film, has Blume (Bill Murray) stating to Max, "You've been living in a dreamworld for 10 years," which he does not deny. There is a theatrical element running through the film, not just in whether Max's behavior is genuine or posed but in terms of structure. Chronological progress is conveyed by a caption (such as the progress of time across the three acts, September to November, on a curtain). The chronological function of these time markers is largely forgotten as there is little sense of a time-pressured climax, only of relationships developing in a linear fashion. Indeed, when Dirk (Mason Gamble) tells Max that Guggenheim (Brian Cox) has had a stroke, it feels like a great passage of time but only a month has passed. It is more that Max has matured and grown up, having been forced to live outside the cocoon of Rushmore (and school more generally).

The opening lesson uses a 180-degree pan to the board and then two 90-degree pans to other math problems, these stylized camera movements both announcing a typical Anderson signature but also suggesting here that we are in a fantasy rather than a realistic scene. However, as Anderson uses this device elsewhere, its effectiveness to signal such a subtext is compromised. The slightly low-angle point of view in front of the board mimics that of the students, but a wide-angle lens makes it feel closer, like a particularly privileged student standing up close to the board, anticipating the position of Max the math genius, whom we are about to see. The teacher's bet on a ridiculously difficult problem and the prize (never having to open a math book again) should alert us to the fantastical nature of the scene, but the instant buzz that this causes draws us in. The camera passes behind the back row, suggesting the whole room is interested in the challenge, apart from one lone individual, sitting and reading the *Wall Street Journal*. In a different context, such an action might suggest an interest in the wider world, but here the effect is ironic.

It is solely a part of Max's pose of detached coolness, an idealized vision of himself as calm, urbane, sophisticated (or how he thinks such qualities would reveal themselves in a classroom). When called upon by name, he has to ask for confirmation ("I'm sorry, did someone call my name?"). For this version of Max as a dilettante, school is an intrusion into a life of leisured ease. An empty coffee cup and a pad featuring a sketch of the Eiffel Tower occupy his desk space. He slowly rises, folding the paper and putting it on top of others (there is no sign of anything as prosaic as a textbook), and buttons his jacket. Still with cup in hand, suggesting the irritation of having his morning routine interrupted by such a trifling matter, he walks to the front of the class. We then cut to the "board's" point of view, allowing closer shots of Max at an oblique angle, as he covers the board with equations, but also keeping the wider class still in view. The teacher is sidelined, forced to sit and check the answer in a book.

The gauntlet that the teacher has thrown down is designed to be impossible and thereby reinforce his position, but in meeting the challenge, Max turns the tables; the class erupts; several students rush forward to pat him on the back; and he is raised aloft as a conquering hero and carried through the class in triumph—at which point we cut to Max, sitting in a different setting, with his head lolling back, and we realize the preceding scene was just a fantasy. The effectiveness of the scene comes from the lack of fictive markers, the engaging nature of Max's character (he is charming but also clearly a deluded fantasist), and the realization that he dreams of being cool, academically brilliant, and popular because he is none of those things.

The clapping of his fantasy merges with applause in the hall, where Max is sitting right in the front row next to a much younger boy, later revealed as Dirk (his chapel partner), who is nudging him in the ribs to wake him up. In this reality, Max is not the star and he is being talked at. However, this speech is different, and it is a turning point for Max. The words of Herman Blume act as a catalyst in his views about school. Blume's key message is a seditious one: "Take dead aim on the rich boys. Get them in the crosshairs and take them down." Post-Columbine in particular, this has an eerie ring to it but even without this, there is something quite unsuitable about such a call to arms when gun ownership and school shootings are part of the national culture. There is also an element of posing and hypocrisy in what Blume says—he may send his boys to the school, which suggests trust and a belief in the system, but he himself is a multimillionaire (indeed this is how he can afford to do so). He is one of the rich elite whom he is apparently attacking. When he states, "They can buy anything but they can't buy backbone," like Max's pose with the coffee cup and newspaper, Blume is striking a pose rather than really preaching revolution.

It is debatable, for example, how much backbone Blume shows himself in the course of the narrative or indeed whether this speech, strangely written out in full sentences on a small piece of paper, which could only have lasted a couple of minutes at most, is a standard piece of empty rhetoric that Blume has delivered before. Max does not see these contradictions and is inspired by the speech (enough at least to note in his hymn book that Blume is "the best chapel speaker ever"), accepting the platitudes at face value. Both see in each other an idealized view of themselves: for Max, an inspirational future; for Blume, a glimpse of a more principled past. The name of Murray's character may have been partly inspired by Paul Mazursky's *Blume in Love* (1973) whose eponymous hero Stephen Blume (George Segal) is still in love with his ex-wife, although Mazursky's character is far less likeable, more self-indulgent, and tries to win his wife back by courting both her favor and that of the viewer in ways completely alien to Anderson's Blume.

The school director, Dr. Guggenheim, is sarcastic about the length of the speech, referring to an "encore," but Blume dismisses this as he paid for the natatorium. He personifies the arrogance of the rich, but Max only picks up on the surface features of the speech. He appears almost like a groupie, following Blume out and complimenting him on the speech, saying how much he agreed with it. He moves to stand next to Blume for a second, so that they are both looking at the school, nodding, literally siding with him in an attempt to align himself with his perceived views. At this stage it is unclear whether this casts him as just a sycophant or a character who is incredibly genuine and naive. Partly due to the flattery, Blume sums him up as a "sharp little guy." In a 180-degree direct reverse shot, Dr. Guggenheim corrects him: "He's one of the worst students we've got." Through the course of the film, the viewer is challenged to decide which of these two polar opinions is most accurate.

MAX AS MODEL STUDENT

This is followed by material about Max to help us make this judgment. However, this is not given to us through drama or dialogue but explicitly via a series of on-screen poses and captions, a device used even more extensively for the opening of *The Royal Tenenbaums* (2001). Anderson makes no apology for such overt means of narrative exposition. He pauses the dramatic momentum to tell us things that he thinks it is important for us to know, especially near the beginning of his films.

The shot of five students with Max in the middle, all walking towards the camera, has a *Reservoir Dogs* (Quentin Tarantino, 1992) feel in that we are given information about characters, who are portrayed in character-defining actions, looking cool while doing so (walking past the camera on either side rather than directly into it). As the montage sequence progresses, we realize that all the activities feature Max and create a picture of someone who is creative but also concerned with using this creativity to manufacture his own imaginative worlds (via journalism, playwriting, even calligraphy). He tends to adopt a controlling position (he is president of the French and Beekeepers' Club, conductor of the choir, and director of a drama group that carries his name). His strength is organizing (lacrosse team manager), although there looks to have been a battle of wills for the Astronomical Society, with Max as founder looking less than happy that he appears to have been superseded.

Max's fastidiousness in matters of dress also reflects Anderson's own sensibility about attention to detail. So we have Max in a red beret and tricolor sash in the French Club, a Russian hat and a pose of seriousness for the United Nations (apparently flanked by Mexico and Pakistan, suggesting they each have a club or more likely Max has sequestered others to join his), and the Yankee Races where he dons beret and goggles and looks straight down the camera lens. Max's contrary nature is suggested by captaining the Debate Club, allying himself with France and particularly Russia, countries that have been critical of America at various points in history. He does participate in sports (he is thrown in seconds when wrestling) but usually using specialist equipment, such as in fencing. His poorly attended practice, and the group of boys who swarm past him to play basketball in the same space, shows his status as a quirky outsider in the eyes of mainstream students. His strength seems to be to set up a new activity, which he can dominate for a while (Trap and Skeet Club), and surround himself with smaller and younger boys, who will not threaten him (Kung Fu Club). This is true of Dirk who can be spotted in every one of Max's clubs performing some subservient function. What is perhaps missing from all of this is a sense of spontaneous fun. Free time is ruthlessly organized, and Schwartzman adopts a fairly fixed expression for much of his time on screen. We rarely see him smile. Also absent are friends. He is surrounded by other pupils, but they are often minions to do his bidding rather than genuine soul mates. Max is fundamentally quite a lonely, isolated boy, whose frenetic school activities seek to hide this lack with only partial success.

The interview with Dr. Guggenheim continues this element of tension in Max's character. He is dressed very formally, in blazer and tie, sitting with his fingers locked, and asks to see documentation on Guggenheim's notion of "sudden death academic probation." There is also some arrogance in Max, asking about a postgrad class, as if the school should be organized around him. His blithe optimism in the face of a fairly stark fate (one failure and he has to leave the next morning) seems both naive but also engaging. At the Backgammon Club, serious discussion of the provision of languages proceeds like a group of teachers in a kind of alternative staff room. Max tries unsuccessfully for five years to have Latin canceled, but then he suddenly reverses his position and tries to save the subject after Miss Cross shows an interest in it.

In an echo of a plotline from *Se7en* (David Fincher, 1995), Max finds the person he is looking for by tracing a library book. Like Blume's words from the chapel speech, Max is affected by inspirational language, here taking this to mean that one has a duty to others to be true to oneself. Originally, Anderson used a Henry James quote: "Try to be one of the people on whom nothing is lost."[1] Out of context, this has the sense of making the most of talents but also a potential oversensitivity and a perception of slights when none exist. In context, however, it has a more precise meaning as advice to writers, that is, the makers of fiction. This leads him to Miss Cross (Olivia Williams). In typical Anderson style, we follow Max walking down the corridor towards her classroom, via forward and reverse tracking shots (from behind and in front of the character respectively). Anderson borrows a trope from an espionage narrative as the camera rises up behind him as if peering over his shoulder, and Max looks both ways before spying through a crack in the door, and we zoom in on the object of his curiosity. The camera positioning underlines the ridiculous nature of Max's subterfuge here as he is clearly visible through the glass panel.

CREATIVITY OR IMITATION?

The play that we see Max and his group rehearsing is not one of the classics but a self-penned (and highly derivative) drama featuring squad cars and drug dealers, later identified as his version of *Serpico*. Such unoriginality is easy to condemn, but an aspiring 15-year-old playwright needs to take inspiration from what lies around him. In *Tenenbaums,* Margot very obviously draws on her immediate family for subject matter, but Max opts for cinematic fantasies, emulating what he has seen on TV rather than writing from personal experience. The fact, however, that we do not actually see any television present makes this connection one that is only implied, and the fact that the audience for this play includes even very young children, for whom the content is likely to be unsuitable, also adds to the sense of anachronism, almost as if the film were set in a pre-TV era. Like Max's character more generally, viewers may find Max's fight over a missing line blurs the boundary between artistic integrity and ridiculous inflexibility. It seems that Max is most at home on stage, where he can script the dialogue and control the action. Real life does not always respond to his direction so easily.

The amount of work in Max's productions, while not attributable to him alone, does reflect his (and by extension, Anderson's) attention to detail, from the elaborate set with the model train from *Serpico* to his casting of Margaret (Sara Tanaka), in which he instructs her to take her glasses off and bring a head shot or the use of girly pinups for barrack scenes and the donning of safety glasses and ear plugs for the climactic production, *Heaven and Hell*. Like the description of him by Magnus (Stephen McCole), we have to decide if he really can be summed up by "Big show. No results."

Max is by turns pretentious and precocious. Like the young hero, Oskar Schell, of Jonathan Safran Foer's novel *Extremely Loud and Incredibly Close* (2005), also from a European (and probably Jewish) background, he even has his own business card (although Max's has virtually nothing on it, apart from an extension number at the school) and like Oskar, he is articulate, intelligent but also oversensitive (he sees Blume's offer of a job as patronizing) and lacking a sense of irony. What allows both characters to remain engaging, however, apart from the loss of a parent, is their energy, their naïveté—which leads to absurd and comic situations—and, above all, their age. We can forgive such faults in characters still at school; in adults, this is far less attractive. However, Oskar is more appealing because despite the fact that he is only nine, he spends the narrative trying to solve puzzles and understand the world around him. The claustrophobic environment of Rushmore can make Max's exploits seem self-indulgent and narrow by comparison. Dirk's mother, Mrs. Calloway, thanks Max for helping her son, to which he replies with fake modesty that he is "just trying to input some of the experiences I've accrued." The absurdity of the situation is that the only experiences he has accrued are related to the workings of the school, not about life beyond its boundaries.

Max is clearly demarcated from the mass, even among his peers, in his physical actions (standing alone to applaud the speaker), his geeky appearance (sporting a bright orange sash and carrying a radio on pickup duty), and dialogue (asking the barber, his father, to show him the back of his head). He is apparently oblivious to the innuendo-driven banter of students around him, boasting what they would do to Mrs. Calloway, for example. He seems oblivious to snide remarks about the closeness between him and Dirk. His problems get significantly worse when he tries to indulge the language of these other boys, boasting about what he has done, using a crudity of sexual language that does not come naturally to him.

Blume envies Max's apparent self-assurance: "What's the secret, Max? You look like you've got it all figured out." A strange relationship develops between him and Blume, who drives repeatedly round the turning circle, reflecting the aimlessness of his life. He seems to be trapped in a loveless marriage with two nightmarish children and sees in Max the personification of someone who has found his place in life. This is true to a degree but ironic also since the place Max has found is supposedly a preparation for life beyond its walls, not an end in itself. The contradiction of his position, of which he seems blissfully unaware, is explicit in his maxim about finding something you love (which for him is attending Rushmore) and then doing it "for the rest of your life." Becoming such an intrinsic part of the school system makes him singularly ill equipped to exist outside it.

Beneath the appearance of harmony, the Blumes are not a happy family. Murray draws on his on-screen persona more associated with absurdist humor here as he sits tossing marshmallows into the pool. Anderson pulls focus from a close-up of Blume's face to his wife in the background, flirting with an unknown man. Such public humiliation explains Blume's interest in Miss Cross and his rapid descent into alcohol-fuelled depression as he immediately picks up a beer here. Anderson creates a mini-climax, using a handheld camera to follow Blume to the diving ladder, a close-up as he drains his glass, an overhead shot as he walks onto the board, and alternating point-of-view shots as he looks right and left as people start to watch him. We then cut to a long shot as he walks back, runs up and executes a perfect cannonball, splashing guests. Underwater, with his eyes closed, he maintains the fetal position, suggesting a wish to escape and that it is only underwater, possibly even in death, that he can find peace, with also a little look forward to some of the elegiac side to Steve Zissou in *The Life Aquatic*. The Cousteau film *The Living Ocean Part 2: Exploring the Reef,* from which Max and Dirk take notes, is the standard of production to which Zissou aspires and repeatedly fails to reach. A little boy, who had come to the table to take a marshmallow, is freaked out by Blume underwater and he swims away hurriedly. This potential for scary instability underlies Blume's more conventional absurdity.

We see Max in a barber's shop and from the setting and the formal way in which Max addresses the barber (asking him to show him the back of his head), it is not immediately clear that this man is Max's father, Bert (Seymour Cassell), until Max explains that he needs a signature on a report and the two exchange a look for a few moments. It seems quite a respectful relationship, certainly compared to Blume's riotous twins. The dialogue seems oddly stilted and lacking much emotion (referring to a clipper ship captain who has been out to sea too long), but it does allude in passing to the ship seen in the case in the background of Max's opening classroom fantasy. Bert converts the mark from 37 to 87, which is hardly a subtle piece of fraud and suggests the source of Max's gift for audacious invention. However, when asked by Blume about his father, Max lies without hesitation that he is a neurosurgeon and later takes umbrage that his father "may only be a doctor," but he does not need Blume's charity. A desire to impress his idol Blume is perhaps understandable, but this is still a betrayal. Only in the final phase of the film is Max willing to acknowledge his father as a humble barber, introducing him first to Blume in the shop and then later at the play to Miss Cross and other guests.

When Max next appears, walking into the shot to light a cigarette for Miss Cross, we must suppose this is part of "the new Max," playing a part, that of the suave sophisticated lover as he adopts a studious pose in blazer and beret, reading a book. He may feel that an interest in girls is not his "forte," but he is smart enough to realize that a display of shared interests is a start. She is also reading, appears to be sitting alone, and in talking to her, he seems to be able to converse with adults more easily than students his own age.

However, he is unaware of his own absurdity (an engaging trait in itself) as he spins a story about going to Oxford or the Sorbonne and that Harvard is only his "safety." In using the assertive and possibly rude phrase "Moving on," he drags the conversation unsubtly back to what he wants to talk about (the imminent canceling of Latin). Her expression of an engaged opinion is exploited by Max as a reason to come and sit right next to her, introducing himself. There is an awkwardness here. We are looking at a teacher and a student, but they are outside a classroom context and Max clearly is interested in using the conversation to impress her. She, for her part, finds him interesting and quirky (she looks at him for several seconds as if a little unnerved by him), but he is still a 15-year-old boy, the reality of which Max only really accepts right at the end of the film. His naïveté about this situation, that this could ever be a romantic situation, is pathetic in every sense of the word. If Miss Cross's reaction was more cynical or there was a third party present, we might feel Max to be humiliated more overtly. It is only at this moment that Anderson jumps the 180-degree continuity line and we have a shot over their shoulders at the game they are watching. The scene is shot in the same way as the following dialogue between Max and Blume, suggesting a link between the three characters before they develop into a love triangle.

The saving of Latin becomes a cause to which he can devote his organizational powers, marshalling lines to construct a petition, addressing a meeting with a speech, and by force of his personality (and possibly the indifference of the opposition), he persuades the school to reverse the decision. It is a minor action and one undertaken for an ulterior motive (to impress Miss Cross), but it is still an example of a character asserting his will on the world around him (however limited in scope) and bringing about a change. He brings the dead (a language at least) back to life. It is as she feeds the fish that Max takes this relationship a step further by asking if he could be her assistant as he drops food into the tank. He coaxes her into talking about more personal matters, and she mentions her late husband. Max responds by insensitively using this as a crude way to imply common ground between them: "We both have dead people in our families," alluding to his mother. Again, this is delivered without irony or an awareness of the absurdity of what he is saying or the context in which it is said. He is in a parallel emotional state to the newborn fish and at some level she responds to this. The pair are framed in a two-shot from behind, allowing him to turn, very close to the typical choreography of a kissing scene in a romantic narrative (particularly after the aquarium scene in Baz Luhrmann's 1994 version of *Romeo and Juliet*). It also links him with Blume after his dive. They are both emotionally underdeveloped and instinctively seeking some guidance (Max's more maternal than Blume's). Max's big idea for the school (and really for Miss Cross) is an aquarium, which ironically he can only manage by borrowing money from Blume, initiating contact between them; that is, he is the means of his own emotional downfall.

The aquarium project, like saving Latin, allows Max to demonstrate his strengths, energizing those around him, as we see him directing an architect in the construction process. The tracking shot used here conveys the scale of the project he has envisaged and the energy with which he is approaching it. The difference between the money he asks for and actually persuades Blume to donate is comical ($35,000 to $2,500), but his reaction is colored by determination rather than resignation or cynicism. He presents Miss Cross with two bags of fish as a personal present, although he shows a puppyish desperation for recognition, unaware of how hopeless that is. The shots of him peering into her classroom with the camera placed inside the room reflects his emotional exclusion from the situation. He does not belong in the room, either as a student or as a romantic partner. He is literally a fish out of water here. The overhead shot of "Young Ben Franklin" revealed as an essay from a fifth grader underlines the fact that she teaches much younger children and that she is an unsuitable love object for Max. He fills her glass with lemonade and gives her a new red pen, but he reads such acts as evidence of a relationship, whereas for her they remain kind gestures.

Blume describes Miss Cross as "sweet but she's fucked up . . . She's in love with a dead guy." Originally conceived as American, Miss Cross's character needed some adaptation with the casting of Olivia Williams but adds resonance to Max's absurd aspirations to Oxford. It is debatable whether Miss Cross bears any responsibility for Max's growing obsession with her. She certainly did not initiate it, but as an experienced teacher, she should know the effect of allowing such a situation to develop. Anderson intercuts mid-shots of them both looking directly at the camera, which then shift to close-ups, suggesting an approaching climax as she playfully suggests that he is too young for her. However, her coy rejection only elicits a sophisticated response from him: "It crossed my mind that you might consider it a possibility." She could be seen as trying to let him down gently here, but she has allowed him to see their interaction as a "relationship," which she is now forced to deny. He then says that he only sees her as a "friend" and claims, "That's all I meant by relationship." He might be retreating slightly, afraid that he has frightened her off, or be redefining how they might classify their relationship in the eyes of others, even though they know there is more going on here; that is, he is provoking her into recognizing a secret, an agreement that really they are more than just friends. His pose of resignation as a spurned lover ("I understand that you're not attracted to me") seems intended to provoke a reaction from her. It succeeds in that she then says, "I've never met anyone like you," which in combination with her dismissive "You can take that for whatever it's worth," is not particularly perceptive or professional as she should realize that despite the apparent parting with a mature handshake, Max will interpret this as encouragement.

The dinner scene after Max's play makes it very clear that he does not take rejection well. Miss Cross introduces him to Peter (Luke Wilson), which is the start of a scene that is funny, embarrassing, and even touching. Max is clearly hurt but cannot hide his jealousy well, instead expressing it in a series of barbed comments at Peter ("I like your nurse's uniform, guy"). When asked about his nose, he explains that he was punched in the face, turns to Peter and asks, "What's your excuse?" Exhaustion and euphoria from the play, raw jealousy and the availability of whiskey, create a series of painful exchanges. Max indulges in childish behavior (pretending to forget Peter's name, calling him "Curly") and stating bluntly that he was not invited, as if it was only his party. However, even in the childish insults, there is some wit, replying to Peter's explanation that he is wearing OR scrubs with "Oh, *are* they?" The willingness to express passionate feelings, at least partly intelligently and articulately, is also an attractive quality as Max shouts, "You hurt my feelings...And I'm in love with you."

Ironically, Max, at the moment when his emotions are at their most raw, entrusts Blume to bear a message of apology, and Blume also develops an attraction for Miss Cross. The scene where she is teaching students to draw outside gives Bill Murray one of his great comic moments when he can indulge his skill in physical comedy to the fullest extent. We see him peering at her furtively from behind a tree and at the end of the scene he suddenly sprints away for no apparent reason, looking absolutely ridiculous. Later he stumbles over a relatively low fence in trespassing in order to peer in at Miss Cross while feigning lack of interest to Max, and the face-to-face exchanges between them (Blume and Miss Cross) are characterized by lengthy, sometimes very funny pauses punctuated by inane dialogue, such as when she offers him a carrot. In stepping away from the students in order to speak we see this as instantly more a relationship of equals, and both share first names, Rosemary and Herman, information we never gained through Max.

At the grand opening of a "new venture," an aquarium, even accompanied by a band, Max takes center stage, giving orders to an architect and facing down a bemused coach (Andrew Wilson) who is wondering what happened to his baseball diamond. Max's motivation here is to produce another project for Miss Cross, that is, to show his maturity and substance as a lover, but even with such problematic motivation, he still makes things happen. It is only when Dr. Guggenheim rushes up with a policeman that proceedings are brought to an abrupt halt, signaled by a sudden cut and a thunder sound effect. The following scene is viewed from outside as Dirk peers through a window to see Max sitting, still in his hard hat, tears rolling down his face. It is not clear whether he is crying at being in trouble, at the destruction of his dream, or at his underlying loss of Miss Cross's affections. By denying us direct access to the scene, Anderson retains more dramatic credibility for his hero.

The reason for his tears becomes clear in the following scene. He is sitting at the front of a big class in a modern building at Grover Cleveland High School and asks to address the class. His mode of speaking and behavior clearly mark him as an outsider. Rushmore neither prepares you for the wider world, nor the more egalitarian processes of a mainstream school. In the corridor, a nerdy girl, Margaret, advises him that such a speech "might rub some people up the wrong way," which totally bemuses Max. The fact that no one has ever asked to make a speech before provokes him to comment "Shame" without sarcasm. His request for a telephone pass, demonstrating his assumption that he can lead the life of assumed privilege as he did at Rushmore, is abruptly met with a blunt reply as a hand cuts off his call. When he rides out of school, he passes faded signs about searching students for drugs and weapons. This is a whole different world for Max. However, he seems to start to fit in, or at least makes an attempt to do so, at the pep rally for the Owls, making the owl gesture, chanting the slogan, and managing an impressive tumbling routine. Ironically, Miss Cross and Blume grow closer together in going to see Max—Miss Cross and Blume sit on either side of Max in a three-shot, looking dreamily at each other.

The face-off between Max and Blume descends into playground boasting. "I fell in love with her" is answered by "I was in love with her first," which is poignant as it is literally true. Like his dinner party, under pressure, Max resorts to boasting, missing the point that writing and directing a hit play or saving Latin really only carries much weight within the narrow confines of Rushmore. He apologizes to Miss Cross, but his gesture of returning the diving book from earlier is just a way to contrive a pseudo-romantic scene, reflected in his cliché dialogue (claiming to miss watching the leaves change color as if he is marooned on another planet) and in the near-kissing distance of the two-shot in which they are framed. The positioning of Max with a big "Stop" sign behind him suggests he is being warned not to proceed with this doomed attempt at an inappropriate relationship. However, Miss Cross also admits that he reminds her of her late husband, who gave her the book when she was 13 on a visit to the library, allowing Max to hope for some kind of emotional bond, albeit based on a dead man. As previously, there is the apparent agreement to be Platonic friends, but since we have seen Max break a similar resolution earlier, we may distrust his sincerity here. He may need a tutor to survive his new school, but it does not follow that it has to be her. It feels more like Max is using any means he can to get close to his idol. We see him sitting right in front of the board in a personal class by Miss Cross. First we track up behind Max, but it is only in a reverse track back with Max nodding that we see the full shot and the ridiculous position of Max sitting on a tiny chair designed for a much younger boy with actual smaller pupils on either side. It effectively encapsulates his emotionally retarded status and undercuts his delusions as a serious contender for Miss Cross's affections.

The tit-for-tat battle that develops between Max and Blume seems initially childish and comic but soon escalates out of control from a smashed bike to potentially lethal tampering with brakes. In this eruption of male posturing, the supposed object of their affection is lost from view. Inevitably, it ends in arrest for Max, via a close-up of his cuffed hands, but there is also a climax in terms of the school aspect of this rivalry. The consequences in an adolescent world have been forgotten by Max in his pursuit of revenge. Using hand-held camerawork, Anderson conveys the emotional immediacy of Dirk and his friends cornering Max, who is now categorized as a trespasser and pelted with stones. However, even here Max lies about exactly what he said about Dirk's mother. Max's obsession first about Rushmore and then Miss Cross are both unhealthy. When Blume later uses the same expression ("She's my Rushmore"), there is the sense that making any single thing, an institution or a person, your raison d'être, is not a good idea. It is only at this point that Miss Cross takes the correct decision instinctively or by accident to add some sexual bluntness to their dialogue, thereby underlining that she is no perfect ideal but a flesh-and-blood adult with a sexual history of which he has no experience.

The third act opens with Max in the barber's shop. His hair looks fairly short already, suggesting the real reason he is there is to talk to his father as it transpires that he has dropped out of school altogether. The appearance on the periphery of the narrative of Margaret, although rejected by Max, suggests that he has made an impact on her and that there is or could be a life outside the hermetic bubble of his twin obsessions of Rushmore and Miss Cross. He acts as if in mourning for his love (waving to Margaret from a window) and given time, he will reemerge into life. This section of the film, over the Rolling Stones' "I Am Waiting" (1966), represents a hiatus as we cut between Max's TV dinner, Miss Cross eating alone, and Blume in his office. Life continues but the three are thinking of one another, waiting (as we are) for something to happen.

Max's placing of Margaret's plant on his mother's grave might suggest that he has not fully come to terms with her death, which we later learn was due to cancer and may partially explain the obsessive embracing of Rushmore's extracurricular life. It also transpires that this may be one reason of the attraction for Miss Cross who is also still affected by the death of her husband, whose presence hovers over the narrative (via the book, via Rushmore, and via designs that Blume and Max have on her romantically). The barber's shop is a neutral setting where men can talk about their feelings without social embarrassment or the need for direct eye contact. Dirk seems a little like Max's spiritual heir (perhaps he has gained some of his experience as Max promised Dirk's mother) in presenting Max with an inscribed penknife—the kind of small detail Max would appreciate. We shift into a different phase of the film in which Max's movements are brought to us via Dirk's surveillance, acting as a messenger for Max himself and for the viewer. Blume, sporting a black eye, is also kept in the narrative by visiting Guggenheim and telling us via a conversation with Max in an elevator that his sons are angry over the divorce.

However, Max does not give up. He positions his mangled bike in the street and climbs a ladder to Miss Cross's window in a parody of *Romeo and Juliet*'s balcony scene. He contrives the appearance of a romantic scenario, complete with French music, and pretends to be concussed. His laconic "Ah, this is where it all happens," referring to her bed on which he lies down, has both the sense of previous sexual activity and what he naively expects will be his initiation into that experience also. We might admire his nerve, but there is also something quite creepy at work here. There is a thin line between ardent lover and underage stalker.

Miss Cross indulges him and talks about her former husband, listing Blume's faults: that he is married, that he hates himself, and that he smashed up Max's bicycle, at which point Max corrects her, insisting it was his "previous" bike, to get his story straight about how he came to be apparently injured tonight. Blume's theory that she is still in love with her former husband seems convincing. She still sleeps in his room decorated with all his possessions, including boyish model planes, and when confronted with this, she reacts angrily that Edward "has more spark and character and imagination in one fingernail than Herman Blume has in his entire body." Significantly, she uses the *present* tense in talking about her husband, and the features she seems to find attractive we might associate with Max but crucially, unlike Max, she knows Blume's "entire body" so we are not really comparing suitors of equal status. Max responds with unsubtle directness, correcting her with "one *dead* fingernail," but the scene ends in farce as he kisses her only for her to realize that his blood is fake and throws him out. His retreat out the way he came, via the window, makes little logical sense but underscores that with the pulling of her bedroom curtain, this little piece of theatre is over. When he can control all the elements of production, Max is a success; when he tries to import his theatrical sensibility into everyday life, the results are more mixed.

Dirk and Max continue their reconciliation via shared kite-flying (another example of an activity where feelings can be talked about, while direct eye contact is not necessary). A remote-controlled plane enters the scene, bringing Margaret into the edge of the frame. Max's character gradually emerges from emotional hibernation as he starts to think once more of societies, here considering allowing Margaret into a Kite-flying Society. His renewed issuing of commands to Dirk ("Take dictation, please . . .") is a positive sign. Similarly, his dreams of a Marine Laboratory help energize himself and Blume whose money he needs. He helps bring Blume out of depression via a Rocky-style training program of physical exercise, including carrying pipes around his factory.

However, Blume's motivation, like Max's earlier with the aquarium, is to gain the attention of Miss Cross. Max seems to have moved from rival to helper (or even pimp if you want to be unkind). When she does not attend the formal opening ceremony, Max (once again in his beret) talks Blume up, saying it is the kind of thing her husband would have done and that he has "more spark than expected" (using the term she had used of her husband before). This selflessness is new for Max, even if this exchange again happens on undersized chairs while small children run around (suggesting that helping

Blume might just be another obsessive project). Max's purchase of a case of dynamite and marching to Rushmore for "one last piece of unfinished business" feels close to one of Dignan's more ambitious plans in *Bottle Rocket*. The difference here though is that Max sees it through; he does not just talk about it. The narrative still has enough elements to develop into a potential tragedy but again this is diverted into farce as he shoots Magnus in the ear and then offers him a part in his new play.

Max's production of *Heaven and Hell* is a summation of his progress through the narrative. The tracking shot along the front row acts as a reprise of previous characters, even the architect, the police, a sleeping Kumar, and Max's proud father with popcorn. Like a boxing promoter, a mic is lowered to Max who dedicates the play to his mother and Miss Cross's late husband, Edward Appleby. The title of the play is a reflection of youthful hubris, but the sheer scope of recreating Vietnam in an amateur school production, Max as a Rambo-style action hero, complete with flamethrowers, bazookas, and napalm, is extremely impressive. There is a pause as Max is knocked to the ground and it is unclear at first whether he is really hurt or not. During the intermission, while actors adjust their makeup, Miss Cross brings a drink to Blume, who stands stiffly as if in physical pain. He looks a broken man, despite her gesture in stroking his face and wondering aloud, "Let's hope it's got a happy ending," which might apply to the play or the film narrative, the outcome of which remains unpredictable. It is only at the point where Max asks Margaret, playing a Vietcong girl, to marry him that the tension dissipates. Blume has tears in his eyes; Margaret's parents stand to applaud (still wearing ear muffs and goggles); and Kumar laughs heartily.

It was a production he could not do at Rushmore and when asked if that was because it was too controversial, Max replies, "No, a kid got his finger blown off at rehearsal." He has finally outgrown Rushmore, finding a place for himself outside its confines and able to still remain true to his principles. The two most important women in his life so far, Miss Cross and Margaret, are introduced to his father, exiling Max to the blurred rear of the frame. Margaret seems to match Max for earnest dialogue even at romantic moments, complimenting him as they dance that "I loved it when you grabbed onto the bottom of the chopper as it was taking off," which Max shrugs off as mere improvisation. He seems happy to refer to her as his "girlfriend" and via some space in the middle of the frame with Max on the right and Miss Cross on the left, there is the suggestion of remaining awkwardness. However, Max orders some more upbeat music, and the film ends with the Small Faces's "Ooh La La" (1973) and Miss Cross taking his glasses off, reflecting the fact that he has clearer vision now and can state, "I wish I knew what I know now." The two are in the center of the frame as the curtain closes, suggesting both that she remains important for him but that also he has greater sense of proportion about that. His preparation of music might reflect his meticulous planning or a secret hope for a dance with the enduring object of his affections.

A SCHOOL STORY

As a school story, this is a world away from what is often associated with *American Pie* (Paul Weitz, 1999) and its subsequent sequels, dominated by crude jokes and attempts to lose one's virginity. *Rushmore* is not voyeuristic around girls. Max largely ignores girls. Even before he sees Miss Cross, Margaret remains a peripheral part of the narrative, only gradually making her presence felt by the final dance as Max arguably grows up a little. The fact that she was a winner at the science show but was subsequently revealed as a cheat brings her closer to Max in his manipulative attempts to gain the attention of Miss Cross. It is not a narrative of pranks and narrow escapes (John Hughes's *Ferris Bueller's Day Off,* 1986), the intrusion of the supernatural into the everyday (Brian De Palma's 1976 *Carrie*), or the constant pursuit of ideal dates (Amy Heckerling's 1982 *Fast Times at Ridgemont High*). *Rushmore* does not focus on the typical but the exceptional, both in terms of the institution itself and its main character Max, who is very much an outcast for whom sex, sports, and drugs play only a peripheral role. Even his appearance—he is always donning the school blazer with pride—signals him as unusual to the general population outside the rarefied atmosphere of an elite school but even within Rushmore, his concern over his appearance is exceptional.

With Max's perpetual blazer-wearing and music from so-called British Invasion bands like the Who, the Kinks, and the Rolling Stones, it is easy to forget that this is actually a contemporary film. There is a strongly anachronistic look to Max's character but this is because he is such a product of an outmoded institution. He and Blume seem to both be lost in time, looking for a place in life. The music complements and helps create a sense of timelessness and also nostalgia for a previous unspecified era. This makes Max's struggle engaging but possibly easy to dismiss. If schools like Rushmore persist in 21st-century America, they are so anachronistic as to be completely irrelevant. Blume describes Rushmore as "one of the best schools in the country," but if this is true, it is questionable what this says about this particular education system. We learn that Blume's boys are at military school, perhaps their natural home, and loving it.

Whether by accident or design, Max acts as an irritant to the status quo, but it is unclear if he is at fault or if it is the system that cannot accommodate him. He does make things happen, sometimes by sheer strength of will, refusing to give up until he has what he wants, which can make him seem annoying or admirable. He may represent an extreme example of what a system can produce, but he is also paradoxically different, and his idiosyncrasies and how they both reflect and buck the system make him interesting to the viewer.

The facial reaction of Guggenheim at the mention of Max's name is reminiscent of Inspector Dreyfus (Herbert Lom) at the mention of his bête noire, Clouseau, especially when he snaps awake at Max's unsubtle mention of brain damage at his bedside: "It's Fischer!" The note of horror is lost on Max who takes it as a compliment that he helped bring Guggenheim out of his apparent coma. Jason Schwartzman's performance as Max is crucial. So central is his role (there are very few scenes in which he does not appear), that if he were not convincing, the narrative would not work at all. Anderson looked at over 1,800 potential leads before finding Schwartzman ("five foot three, 112 pounds, black hair, glasses, oval face" as described by Blume), who appeared at the audition not just in a blazer but complete with a Rushmore school badge (the kind of attention to detail that Anderson definitely appreciates). Schwartzman himself, a minor at the time he appeared in *Rushmore*, was trying to balance his acting career with his role as a drummer for the band Phantom Planet. He captured an out-of-time-ness in Max missing from his later characters, such as the work-shy geek Ethan in Dewey Nicks's 2001 *Slackers,* who also obsesses about an unattainable girl (Angela, played by Jaime King) but very much within the generic limitations of predictable *American Pie* style high school, gross-out humor.

In his name (suggestive of Jewish origins), appearance (physically small and including the wearing of glasses), and character (an articulate social outcast, ill at ease around women by reputation at least if not in actuality), Max shares similarities with a typical Woody Allen protagonist (from the early part of his career). Ultimately, Max is seen to be most suited to the intelligent but equally socially awkward Margaret, also a glasses-wearer and given to minimal facial expression and gesture (as in her tiny wave to Dirk during the kite-flying scene). Like his theatrical productions, she excels at fakery (her science project) and is a marginalized figure (often placed at the edges of the frame, reflecting her more obviously "kooky" nature). The cutting is lengthier in the kite-flying scene, suggesting that, albeit slowly, Max is becoming more mature and thoughtful. Looked at more objectively, Margaret's view that "You're a real jerk to me, d'you know that?" seems fair.

CONCLUSION

Anderson specializes in blurring the borderline between adult and child, especially dramatizing childlike adults, but in the case of Max Fischer we have the reverse, an excessively earnest adolescent. As Miss Cross says, "You know, you and Herman deserve each other. You're both little children." Characters around Max tend to fall in with his plans, and he adopts the role of teacher or instructor. As Blume asks Miss Cross, "Did Max have anything planned for us today?" The scenes between Miss Cross and Blume seem quite awkward here with strange lengthy pauses, as if Max's plans, like his own frenetic clubs and hobbies, are really a displacement activity, disguising the hollowness of lives beneath. When Max confronts Blume, he adopts the language of a spurned lover, accusing him of immorality because he is a married man. Max mixes his grubby betrayal of a rival with the veneer of sophistication, meeting Blume's wife on a rooftop car lot with tuna sandwiches before offering evidence of marital infidelity. As Blume continues his physical decline, Max invites him to join his "losers's club" in a childish act of blood brotherhood. He makes Blume have a haircut and literally and metaphorically take a look at himself in the mirror and realize what he is fast becoming. As Blume is tipped back in the chair, we have an inverted image of his face, and Max's father jokes that he should not worry and that "it's a relatively painless procedure," but such a process of self-realization is more difficult than this suggests.

3

Salinger Reloaded: *The Royal Tenenbaums* (2001)

Anthony: One morning, over at Elizabeth's beach house, she asked me if I'd rather go water-skiing or lay out. And I realized that not only did I not want to answer that question, but I never wanted to answer another water-sports question, or see any of these people again for the rest of my life.

Critic Jonathan Romney describes *The Royal Tenenbaums* as "a genuine UFO among American screen comedies," reflecting the difficulty of classifying it generically.[1] This chapter suggests one way forward is by approaching the film from a literary perspective and picking through the dysfunctional relationships as part of a family drama.

ANDERSON AND SALINGER

There is a strongly literary element in *Tenenbaums,* most obviously in the literary conceit of its construction but also in the appropriation of material from J. D. Salinger. Anthony's dialogue above evokes the rebelliousness of Salinger, but it is only a *pose* of disillusionment. As his sister points out at his protestations of exhaustion, "You haven't worked a day in your life." The opening shot, a bird's-eye point of view of a book being stamped, carrying the title *The Royal Tenenbaums* in an overtly metatextual reference in the manner of a fictitious literary adaptation in the style of a 19th-century novel. Like *Rushmore,* the progress of the plot is signaled by on-screen text, but here the literary conceit is continued with numbered chapters. The self-referentiality reaches a climax at the beginning of chapter 8 as we hear a description of a wedding and yet also see it on the front cover of the novel that the narrator is supposedly reading. The sequential process of writing and filmic dramatization are made more problematic.

Matt Zoller Seitz, in his blog entry considering Anderson's style, is one of the very few critics to push the Salinger connection any further, spotting the reference to the Tenenbaum name in "Down at the Dinghy" (1949).[2] However, Seitz both overstates the case for Anderson's debt to Salinger's *Catcher in the Rye* (1951) and misses other Salinger-specific influences. Anderson's heroes are only tangentially related to Salinger's iconic antihero Holden Caulfield. Caulfield is loosely linked to Max Fischer in terms of age, but Max is anxious to find a place within the institution, not to reject it as "phony." Max's tragedy is not that he cannot escape school; *it is that he does not want to.* There are some superficial similarities (both get drunk and both have a family bereavement in their background, but Max's life is completely circumscribed by school, whereas Caulfield is striving to understand the adult world, and his place in it, which he regards with cynicism. Caulfield is also expelled but seeks life experiences outside school (including an aborted meeting with a prostitute and an ambiguous, possibly flirtatious touch from former English teacher Mr. Antolini, which is light-years away from Max's hopelessly adolescent attempted seduction of Miss Cross).

In *Bottle Rocket*, Anthony breaks out of a mental institution; Caulfield ends up at one (from where he is telling his story); and Anthony (like Holden) has a sister with a friend called Bernice. However, Seitz distorts his material a little to make it fit his desired reading. The family dynamics are quite different (the Caulfields idolize one another). Seitz suggests Anthony dotes on his sister, but actually we only see Anthony in one scene with her, in which he endures her perceptive questioning rather than showing much affection. Moreover, Salinger's Bernice is an object of desire for Holden, a brief dance partner and unlike here, dull in conversation. Seeking to find a match for Holden, Seitz elevates Anthony to the position of hero in the film's narrative. Although it opens with his escape, he is very much a passive echo of Dignan (whose fragile ego is the real reason for Anthony leaving the institution).

Salinger's *Franny and Zooey* was first published in the *New Yorker*, the magazine about which Anderson was obsessed as a teenager, and underpins Anderson's film. The basic narrative follows the breakdown of the heroine, Franny Glass, partly reflected in an unsatisfactory relationship with her boyfriend, Lane, and a closer bond she shares with her brother, Zooey. Both Salinger's work and Anderson's film are essentially family sagas. The background of the Glass family is given to us in a lengthy footnote, which Anderson converts into filmic terms via the opening montage, on-screen captions, and voice-over. Salinger's book, like Anderson's film, features an unseen narrator, although his identity (Franny and Zooey's brother Buddy) is clear, whereas Anderson keeps this figure anonymous (although literally voiced by an actor—Buddy's profession too).

Seitz also overstates Anderson's use of small but precise details in the appearance of characters, which are character-defining. This is certainly present on book covers, the chapter-heading illustrations, or Richie's paintings, especially of Margot, and there is something of Lane's self-satisfaction that he alone understands Franny from being able to spot precise details about her appearance, in Anderson's fastidious approach to the props with which he surrounds his characters, such as Richie's pepper shaker, which he carries everywhere in his top pocket. However, Seitz's lists of character-defining clothing misses the key point here that it almost never changes and, indeed, when it does it is the removal of clothing that signifies character change rather than change being subtly reflected in a costume alteration.

This is clearly present but is a factor in most fictional films and novels, taken to further extremes in Jane Austen or in particular, the cartoonishness of Charles Dickens. Anderson certainly pays attention to small details with the attention of a set dresser but other directors, such as David Fincher, do this too. What is distinctive about Anderson is the amount of detail that he tries to pack into the frame and its purpose, the visual impact, rather than figures like Fincher who spend hours on set design for its impact on performance, such as high-quality facsimile newspapers from the era in which *Zodiac* (2007) was set, the early 1970s, even though these remain out of shot in scenes in the newspaper offices. Like the names, which cannot easily change (except self-consciously as in *Aquatic*), the look of characters tends to remain fixed (Margot wears the same apparel and makeup throughout) with a few notable exceptions as when the twins wear black at the end or Richie shaves off his beard, exorcising his previous self, before attempting suicide.

Specific situations from *Franny and Zooey* appear in the film. Seitz spots the clear parallel between Richie's meeting of Margot (Gwyneth Paltrow) in a mink coat at the bus station and Lane waiting for Franny at a train station, and in the latter case, his immediate recognition of her as she steps down to the platform, particularly due to her sheared raccoon coat. Both Zooey and Margot, in their respective narratives, are seen reading and smoking in the bath and are likewise interrupted by their mothers, both attractive older women who find their intelligent children hard to understand and who interrogate them about what they are doing with their lives. Mrs. Glass talks about finding a psychiatrist for Franny (echoed in Raleigh's minor role with his protégé Dudley), and there is mention of a suitable man being on a boat, requiring a telegram to be sent (as with Richie at the start of the film narrative). We see Zooey shaving before a mirror in a moment of revelation (about the influence of their elder brother Seymour over the family and Franny in particular) but not about himself as with Richie. Like Richie and Margot, siblings Franny and Zooey have a profound conversation about their innermost feelings, while lying down (one pair in a tent, one on a bedroom floor), thereby avoiding direct eye contact. Even though the Glass family pet is a fat cat rather than the dog in *Tenenbaums,* Salinger's name, "Bloomberg," is echoed in "Buckley."

The backstory of Salinger's narrative seems similar to *Tenenbaums.* A family of prodigiously talented children, lacking a father, gain national notoriety (in *Franny and Zooey* by appearing on a radio quiz show). They may be more precocious than the clear-cut genius status ascribed to Margot, Richie, and Chas (Ben Stiller), but child prodigies they definitely are. The lives of Franny and Zooey, like the Tenenbaum children, have also hit a spiritual buffer in which they shy away from the compromises and hypocrisies of adult life. Like the Glass family, the Tenenbaums, when they converse at all, often do so in a way that those outside the family might find pretentious or even difficult to understand. Whereas Zooey asks what is behind Franny's troubles, prompting some introspective comments from Mrs. Glass, Anderson gives us a filmic flashback via a montage to convey visually the information in the investigator's report on Margot. The suicide of Franny's older brother Seymour (in "A Perfect Day For Bananafish" from the 1953 *Nine Stories* short-story collection) lurks beneath that narrative and erupts in Anderson's film in Richie's act and Eli's final crash (whether as serious attempts to take their own lives or as a "cry for help"), and the Glass children like the Tenenbaums, include twin boys, Walter and Waker, and are also of mixed Jewish and Irish ancestry. The setting also has similarities. The Glass house is in Manhattan and although not huge, Salinger's description of its elaborate interior, particularly the walls, which are covered with pictures and photos documenting the achievements of the children, evokes Eric Chase Anderson's elaborate artwork, often only glimpsed on freeze-frame.

There is not an exact like-for-like correspondence (Franny's hair is jet-black as opposed to Margot's mousy blonde), but there are similarities in characterization. Franny feels like a prototype Margot, pale, thin, eating very little, usually smoking and having a passionate interest in the theatre (reflected in performing precocious little plays at home), which is suddenly dropped. She is also literally bookish, seen carrying a book (not of self-penned plays but *The Way of a Pilgrim*, a religious Russian text). Like Margot, she has a fragile mental state and often seems close to some form of breakdown. Mrs. Glass describes Franny as "a run-down, overwrought little college girl that's been reading too many religious books."[3] Salinger states that "it was as though, at twenty, she had checked back into the mute, fisty [*sic*] defenses of the nursery," and there is something of this in Anderson's film in the speed with which Margot moves back into the family home and in the numerous locks, keeping unwanted guests from her bedroom.[4]

Franny and Zooey form a sibling bond that excludes others, even within the family. As Zooey states, "We're freaks, the two of us, Franny and I."[5] Like Richie and Margot, they are a close, exclusive club of two, although not pushed to the point of incest. There is, however, a hint of this in Salinger's description of Mrs. Glass's scrapbooks on the children's achievements, which lie in a pile "in almost incestuously close juxtaposition."[6] This also has implications for the characterization of Mrs. Glass who at times appears to view her children as material to be archived and then shown to anybody present in the house, even the occasional part-time cleaning woman. In this context, perhaps Etheline is less a proud mother than a negligent parent. It is ambiguous exactly how much responsibility she should bear for the dysfunctional nature of her family. Lane has some of the insecurity of Eli Cash (Owen Wilson). Eli's sending Etheline his college grades and latest reviews is reflected in Lane's desire to read Franny his latest literature paper, and like Eli, Lane declares his love but only in passing and without much conviction.

There are even particular echoes in the dialogue. Franny declares to Lane that she has missed him, but "the words were no sooner out than she realized that she did not mean them at all."[7] Rather than emphasizing a world-weary emptiness to their existence, this is *inverted* in Anderson's film to reveal a positive, life-affirming aspect of the character of Royal (Gene Hackman) so that the voice-over states, after Royal has claimed that the past six days were the happiest in his life, that "immediately after making this statement, Royal realized that it was true." The key term here is "after." The impetus for such an emotional declaration is false, but the feeling running beneath is discovered, to the speaker's own surprise, to be true.

There is a moment between Richie and Eli, when Eli says, "What did you say?" to which Richie replies, "I didn't say anything." This is consistent with Eli's drug problem, but it also creates the kind of pregnant pause that appears in Alan Ball's *American Beauty* (1999), when Mrs. Fitts (Allison Janney), Ricky's strange mother, has a similar exchange with her son, also in an empty domestic space. Anderson is dramatizing the hollow, dysfunctional side to the American dream in several of his films (especially *Bottle Rocket* and *Rushmore*), so such an allusion is fitting. However, it also alludes to the kind of almost telepathic communication possible between siblings in Salinger's fictional universe (even those ironically not related by blood, like Margot) from which Eli, ever the outsider, is excluded.

There is a pretentiousness about Salinger's characters, not just overtly as in the figure of Lane who calculates every action for its effect on others but the Glass children too. Buddy's tendency to pace around reflects a melodramatic tendency that some viewers may find in the Tenenbaum household. Some viewers may even find an echo of this in Anderson's directorial style. On the DVD extras, we see him looking for the "beat" in performances, extending the dramatic moment a little (in Gene Hackman's speaking on the intercom or the landing of Mordecai on the roof).

Other comments by Seitz also need challenging. The Tenenbaums are certainly dysfunctional and deemed to be clever but compared to the Glass family, the Tenenbaum siblings are quite inexpressive. Only Margot's early genius is communicated via verbal expression and that is still more pithy than loquacious. Richie cannot articulate his feelings about anything, Margot in particular, and Chas's barked orders do not quite square with his supposed business empire, the reality of which is never really convincingly conveyed (perhaps suggesting its scope was actually quite modest as a child). Unlike the Glass family, they do not seem at ease with the parts they have allocated themselves in life (not that Salinger's characters are happy exactly, but they recognize the limitations of themselves and the world in which they operate) and are unable to take the larger decisions made by Salinger's characters—going to war, staying married, committing suicide. Salinger's characters *commit* to people, ideas, or actions; Anderson's stand around and talk about committing.

What is missing, however, which Seitz admits in passing, is a sense of self-awareness. Salinger's characters are aware of their own absurdity, a capacity singularly lacking in Anderson's narratives. It is the very fact that Max in *Rushmore* is *not* "a tortured adolescent" as Seitz describes him, which makes him an appealing figure. Max proceeds apparently completely unaware of his academic position (such that his "sudden death probation" comes as something of a shock). He does not really grow up or look outside himself in anything other than the most limited of forms. At the close, he still dances with Miss Cross and although he has moved schools he is still putting on the same plays that he would have staged at Rushmore (if he had been allowed). In effect, he has just transferred his Rushmore sensibility to another institution. His relationship with Margaret seems more forced upon him by circumstances than choice, and there is no positive sign of how he will fare once outside the confines of school (a world about which he still knows very little).

Like Anderson, Salinger creates characters and whole fictional worlds cut off from everyday reality, partly by circumstances and partly by the willfulness of his characters who focus unremittingly inwards on the minutiae of their lives. They do not act or speak as characters we might meet in everyday life and seem suffused with a sense of melancholy. However, for Salinger they do this not as a retreat from the social world but as a reaction to it and what they see as its "phoniness." This does not work in Anderson's films as all the protagonists are to a greater or lesser degree openly "phony"; they are all playing parts of their own making. *Tenenbaums* is full of fantasists who use a range of displacement tactics to avoid engaging with the reality of life—marriage, sex, and smoking (Margot); tennis and travel (Richie); business, routine, and expressions of anger (Chas); and financial and personal chicanery (Royal).

HAPPY FAMILIES

ROYAL: There are no teams.

It could be said that Etheline (Anjelica Huston) contributes to the dysfunctional nature of the family. She provides a structured program of cultural events for her exceptional offspring, including karate, ballet, and Italian, which might be seen as nurturing and encouraging. However, her giving of money to Charles without a quibble or allowing Richie to put up endless pictures of Margot (carefully created by Anderson's younger brother, Eric) could also be seen as indulgent and leading to them becoming spoiled. On the other hand, coping with one so-called genius in the family would be difficult, but three truly is exceptional. She has written on the subject (we see a book entitled *Families of Geniuses*), but whether she is a real expert on the subject or is only casting herself in this role in the light of her personal experience is unclear. She does seem to be a calming presence in the midst of all the eccentric behavior around her and certainly in comparison to Royal's machinations, she seems serene and a character of some integrity, whose true worth is only recognized by Tenenbaum too late to win back her love.

She is an attractive woman who has had a line of eligible suitors, defined in montage and by stereotypical names, including a British explorer, a Japanese architect, and an American film director. Her confession to Sherman (Danny Glover) that she has not had sex for 18 years suggests that she is hardly promiscuous and reflects the power that Royal had over her (or conversely that he put her off sex completely). Royal seems to reach a kind of rapprochement with Etheline as they walk through the park together, but at this stage he is still trying to win her back, so his compliments and more responsible behavior in taking an interest in his grandchildren are all suspect. We do, however, see glimpses of the man she fell in love with years ago. Although his motivation is dubious, his crediting her with bringing up the children and expressions of shame at his own behavior both seem fair.

In keeping with the literary nature of the film, the characters are partly introduced by their status as authors, via a typical Anderson overhead close-up of the book itself (we see Etheline signing hers) or their appearances in articles, such as a close-up of a magazine front page, a headline describing Richie's "Meltdown," and accompanying sound effects of a tennis match and polite applause. The cutaway to Eli Cash's second novel, *Old Custer*, is complemented by distinctive sounds from a cowboy film. Later, after Eli is spied by Royal sneaking out of Margot's window, we cut to a close-up of an article on Eli with the headline "The James Joyce of the West" and a ridiculous picture of him holding up dead snakes. His later use of Apache-style makeup for his dramatic death-crash and his bizarre lasso lessons in rehab suggest little progression in his character. Raleigh (Bill Murray) is defined as more of an expert in his field but here too there is the sense of a craving for status and notoriety. His cover for *The Peculiar Neurodegenerative Inhabitants of the Kazawa Atoll* features two children, one of whom appears to be covered in leopard-style spots, suggestive of a courting of media attention and exploitation of subjects as much as scientific validity (of the books shown, only this one passes without musical accompaniment). Sherman's *Accounting for Everything: A Guide to Personal Finance* encapsulates his role as the personification of reliability, risk-averse, trustworthiness.

Chas is characterized by his setting (an office, described by text on screen as a "Work Center") and his body positioning (standing initially and then in a second shot, sitting on a shelf next to a fax machine). Anderson manipulates the perspective in this sequence. The oversized appearance of old-style office technology, often placed in the foreground, contrasts sharply with Chas, emphasized by putting him in the background. The handheld camera used for Chas's emergency drill conveys the sense of immediacy with an accompanying siren and flashing light, the absurd nature of which only gradually becomes apparent. The identical tracksuits and Chas's hectoring about their slow time in evacuating the building may distract us initially from considering why he is doing this, but we are immediately provided with backstory via a posed shot of Buckley in a cage with the smoking wreckage from the plane crash in the background. Thus, their lives are lived in a state of perpetual panic, and immeasurable fears about safety dominate Chas's life, causing him to move back into the family home and declare that they should introduce a sprinkler system. Although his behavior in some ways is the most extreme of the three siblings, he alone has a genuine traumatic reason to feel this way and seems more mature than the other two, having established his own family, separate from the centrifugal power of the Tenenbaum dynasty. Chas's overprotective nature is firmly established not just by the drill but by the scene back in the Tenenbaum residence when he goes out of the boys' room only to return seconds later and lie down on the floor rather than leave them alone.

Chas flatly rejects Royal's overtures of friendship and requests to spend time with his grandchildren. In this, Chas seems more a caricature of anger in failing to give a reasoned, or even emotional, response. It is true that Royal abandoned his family, but he is supposedly dying and is trying to make up for lost time. Here the characterization of Chas draws on Ben Stiller's on-screen comedic persona as someone given to outbursts of sudden and manic rage. It is a party piece that appears in the self-explanatory character Mr. Furious in *Mystery Men* (Kinka Usher, 1999), more recently in *Greenberg* (Noah Baumbach, 2010), and even in the TV show *Friends* (1997), where he plays Tommy, a minor character whose outbursts of homicidal anger are only witnessed by Ross (David Schwimmer). The inflexibility which leads him to turn Royal's lights out at precisely 11:30 as if he is at summer camp is a manifestation of a deep-seated psychological instability. We do not see him before the loss of his wife, but it seems he has suppressed his natural impulses to grieve, and this erupts in his draconian regime over the twins. He finds emotions hard to talk about and is unsettled by Richie's expressions of love.

When Royal brings the boys back from their impromptu day of rebellious activities, Chas takes Royal into a small cupboard in order to berate him. However, Royal is oblivious to Chas's shouting and, indeed, shouts back, expressing for the first time in the film that he thinks that Chas is having a nervous breakdown and that he has not recovered from the death of his wife, to which Chas can only respond by petulantly turning the light off. As Royal leaves in disgrace later, he advises him to take it easy on the boys as "I don't want this to happen to you"; in other words, they will eventually rebel against him and cast him out as the adults are doing to Royal now. Alone in the cupboard, filled with the detritus of family life, board games in particular, Royal muses on something he finds, just out of the shot and lifts up a boar's head, with a triumphant "There you are." A symbol of family honor is ironically juxtaposed with a character representing the deep dishonor of the family (Royal). However, as events transpire, it seems that Royal is the one who understands the dynamic of his family best, and perhaps because he knows his own disreputable character and is seemingly unable or unwilling to change it, his action in absenting himself may be seen in retrospect as for the greater good of the family.

The twins, Ari and Uzi (Grant Rosenmeyer and Jonah Meyerson, respectively) with identical haircuts and red Adidas tracksuits, seem like freakish versions of their father who controls every element of their existence, even their appearance. The brutal training program that he has set out for them on a rooftop climbing frame, complete with sit-ups, humanizes Royal's surreptitious (and potentially creepy) approach to them. Like Max in *Rushmore,* the Tenenbaum children are all eccentric and clearly exceptional to those around them, symbolized by Chas's breeding of Dalmatian mice. Like *Rushmore,* the film also raises the question as to whether being exceptional is a blessing or a curse in a society which does not really know how to respond to such individuals. Within the film world, there is no judgmental distinction made between playing tennis, writing plays, or buying and selling stocks.

The opening sequence in *Tenenbaums* threatens to bury the audience with an avalanche of information, something which Anderson does not shy away from. It also plants unexplained facts, such as Margot's loss of a finger, Richie's abandoning of his tennis career, or the effect of Chas's wife's death, which are elaborated on more fully in the course of the film. Each one carries a secret, and it is only when all of them are revealed that they can break out of the emotional inertia in which they seem trapped. The catalyst for confronting these secrets, as well as the resolution of the conflicts which they express, is the arrival of Royal. What energizes the narrative is not a change of heart in Royal or, as Richie suggests, that he is "lonely," but a deterioration in his financial position. Having lived in the Lindbergh Palace Hotel for 22 years, he is forced to leave, and we are told in compressed form about his fall from grace as a prominent litigator to first being barred and then imprisoned for malpractice.

Royal's denial of the notion of teams in shooting Chas with a BB gun might seem to run counter to ideas of familial loyalty but in another sense he is right. The children have to learn to be independent, something they never really achieve. His version of "tough love," living from one's wits and resourcefulness, is less important when you have inherent gifts, but it is telling that early in the narrative, when all three children are faced by adversity, they retreat to the family home. Emotionally, they remain retarded (for which Etheline should perhaps take some responsibility). There is a shared sense of arrested development as the siblings all wear the same clothes from a given point back in the past (Richie in the remnants of his tennis whites, Chas in a tracksuit ready for an emergency, and Margot in her Lacoste dress and fur coat). The fact that their rooms are still apparently as they left them

(Margot's clothes are still on hangers) suggests they never really left home. It is true that Royal is bluffly insensitive but that is only perhaps by contrast with an oversensitive element in the children. It is this sense of adventure and risk that Royal seeks to develop by his interaction with his grandchildren and from their enthusiastic responses, it seems he is right to do so. It is perhaps an underlying tragic element of the narrative that although he is granted time to share this important message with his grandchildren, it is too late for his own children to benefit from it.

Pagoda (Kumar Pallana) acts as a spy in the enemy camp, framed in the background of a shot of Etheline and Sherman, discussing marriage and speedily relaying information to Royal. Anderson draws on Hackman's on-screen persona as a tough *French Connection* style, sometimes maverick cop to give him some noirish dialogue ("I've had my share of infidelities but she's still my wife...no damned two-bit chartered accountant is going to change that"). This is delivered to a passive Pagoda, who does not respond to its absurdity in a park meeting that draws on tropes from espionage and thriller movies. Later, Royal tells him by phone to "await further instructions" and once he is in the house, Pagoda provides a steady supply of information and fast-food deliveries. The backstory of the friendship between Royal and Pagoda is given to us as the twins are shown a form of street gambling (as Richie was). The exact nature of this is not spelled out here, but on their return to the house, Royal tries to calm Chas down by assuring him that any blood on the boys is "only dog's blood," as if that is less disturbing. Pagoda apparently saved Royal's life from a stab wound suffered 30 years ago in Calcutta, but a potentially heroic story is shifted back into familiar absurd-ist territory by one twin asking who stabbed him, at which Royal points at Pagoda and says simply, "He did." It is fitting that a figure as infuriating as Royal should inspire anger in those around him, but it is also a contrary mark of his charisma that he still inspires loyalty (albeit of a love-hate kind) in Pagoda after such a length of time. It means that when Pagoda stabs him in the course of the film, we might understand that it is more of a wake-up call for Royal than a serious attempt to kill (and possibly that Pagoda remains an incompetent assassin).

Margot's door, covered with locks and notices and a forbidding knocker, suggests a secretive nature that has withdrawn into itself, in large part as a result of her father's emotional unavailability. Routinely introduced as ad-opted, Margot cannot feel that she is anything but an outsider. She is seen as precocious from the outset, and her 11th-birthday play has much in common with Max Fischer's ambitious productions. Royal's judgment that the play represents "just a bunch of kids, dressed up in animal costumes" is clearly insensitive to the hard work of his own child (albeit adopted) and shows a lack of imagination in what the play was trying to do, but it does also liter-ally state a truth about any dramatic production. Although Margot claims to be depressed at the mention of Chas moving back in, sibling rivalry surfaces immediately and she asks why *he* is allowed to do that, implying that she would like to as well. Perhaps it is important for Margot to stop playing and grow up a little. Her subsequent withdrawn behavior, symbolized by habitual smoking, might be a direct consequence of Royal's lack of recognition, but he might also have been right to try and make her question fictionalizing life rather than actually living it.

Margot's coldness towards Royal when his scam is uncovered is only really a continuation of the unemotional character we have seen up to this point and a reverse of their previous positions. In referring to Sherman, he reminds her, "He's not your father" to which she retorts, "Neither are you." Fatherhood seems to be something Royal wants to claim, but he has not displayed any sign of this towards her up to this point. The private investigator's background file on "Tenenbaum, M." provides a further block of information for the viewer, again presented via explicit on-screen text and typical action or a virtually posed shot. So we see Margot begin smoking at 12, run away from school at 14, and marry secretly at 19. Subsequently, the report focuses on her sexual history, including a lesbian relationship and kissing a man who turns and is revealed as Eli, suggesting they have known each other quite a while. Despite the dramatic revelations, Raleigh's only reaction at the end of a procession of images showing Margot's fairly promiscuous life, some of which occurred while she was supposedly married to him, is "She smokes?"

Richie's series of hobbies, shown in single shots and examples such as his interest in falconry, may remind us of Max, especially the kite-flying. Richie's rooftop aviary represents another place of withdrawal, and his freeing of Mordecai the hawk to the accompaniment of the Beatles' "Hey Jude" reflects his desire for emotional release. Richie is literally drifting aimlessly on a cruise liner, going nowhere, listing the places he has been to ("both poles, five oceans, the Amazon, and the Nile"), given to dictating intimate telegram messages, absurdly through a third party on board ship. He is the only one of the three who has achieved a level of global fame, posing for a picture as he gets off the boat, and an old poster is turned around angrily by Chas, suggesting an element of jealousy that he has such recognition (and a known nickname, "the Baumer").

The potentially incestuous nature of his feelings for Margot, whether she is his real sister or not, makes the progression of that relationship problematic, and the narrative shies away from it. Richie seems absorbed by Margot's plays, the content of which we do not see (the play at the end is written subsequently), to the point where he seems more interested in reading her works than actually talking to her (even though they now live in the same building). He seems happy to live in a tent, reading her plays and surrounded by images of her in a rather creepy pseudo-shrine. Although the sports commentators are bemused by the sequence where we see Richie's breakdown on court via old TV footage, the connection between his erratic behavior and the cuts to Margot in the crowd next to her new husband are clear enough.

The revelation of Margot's past snaps something in his nature as we see him, via jump cuts, finally remove the vestiges of his tennis uniform and shave. He has been literally hiding behind his beard (and sunglasses) and this is the first time in the film that we see his face clearly as he looks in the bathroom mirror and resolves to kill himself the following day. We see flash-cuts of his previous bearded self, his birds, and the iconic sequence of Margot stepping off the bus towards him. We do not have a firm sense at this moment of whether he will go through with the act, but the motivation seems to be the unattainability of Margot and possibility that she is not the person whom he thought she was. Found by Dudley, Richie has to face the embarrassment of being captive in a hospital bed, surrounded by his family, quizzing him about what he just did. Chas in particular is bluntly direct (possibly showing some inherited characteristics from Royal) asking about why he did it and whether the note he left was "dark," to which Richie wearily replies, "Of course it was dark—it was a suicide note." Richie's premature exit from tennis and cutting of his Björn Borg–like hair and beard reflects Borg's retirement at 26, followed by rumors of suicide attempts.

Richie breaks back into the house in a gate-swinging maneuver, a gesture that is a mixture of romantic drama (think especially of the end of *Pretty Woman,* Garry Marshall, 1990) and displaced sexual attraction as he enters the tent where Margot is lying. Richie confronts her about Eli and she admits that they mostly talked about him and "I guess that was the attraction, if you know what I mean," suggesting that Eli is just a socially acceptable conduit for her reciprocal feelings for her brother. It is the first indication that she also has feelings for him and after some emotional frisson between them, they kiss, lie back together, and the music (motivated by the record player positioned within the tent) suggests momentum towards a sexual episode. However, this raises the difficulty of incest, from which Margot (and Anderson) shies away, as she states, "I guess we're going to have to be secretly in love with each other and leave it at that" and leaves the tent.

Richie is the one who restores the boar's head to its position on the wall, suggesting that it had either fallen or been taken down when Royal left but now he has a role once more within the family, even if he has disgraced himself. Rather than a prodigal son, he is a prodigal father, not easily given to mending his ways but at least contrite for his mistakes and therefore worthy of forgiveness. Richie has always been the sibling closest to his father (he shows some of Royal's ability to manipulate others in appearing to offer a "listening ear" to Margot). He is the one who goes to visit Royal in his new lowly job as a bellhop, suggesting Royal has evolved into a slightly more humble figure who realizes he must work hard, not just for money but to regain the trust of his family. The two exchange confidences and Richie explains why he choked in the tennis match and asks Royal's advice, the first and only time this happens in the film. In his state of new humility, Royal is flattered to be asked but admits he never understood either Margot or indeed any of his family. Even here, Royal vacillates back and forth between saying he should "Go for it" with Margot, as incest is not such a taboo as it once was (truly bizarre advice for a father to give as at that moment he has forgotten that she is adopted) and then undercutting himself with "Don't listen to me."

The position of Eli Cash as a wannabe Tenenbaum is made quite clear from the outset, as we see him watching the family from the building opposite and desperately wanting to be a member of this dysfunctional group. He appears at Margot's party and is treated as an extended member of the family by all except Royal who seems unaware of who he is. Cash's name is suggestive of his mercenary nature, and his opening appearance as an adult on the credit sequence, posing in a cowboy hat, establishes him as a figure who purports to have a link with the West that he does not really possess. The tracking shot up to him as he reads from his latest work gradually speeds up as he reaches a supposedly profound climax, but from the extract we hear at least, it seems as if he is commercially, rather than critically, successful, compromising the credibility of the professorship he holds. We see him during a phone conversation, denying that he is a genius but in such a way that he is inviting the person with whom he is speaking to contradict him. His craving for status and recognition is encapsulated in his sending of clippings (possibly echoed in Anderson's scrapbook of *New Yorker* articles) and even school grades to Etheline for approval, something Margot finds hard to believe. Etheline says that he "likes the encouragement," but Margot's expression suggests that she sees this as the mark of an egotistical self-publicist.

He betrays Richie's confidence in passing onto Margot the secret that Richie loves her. It is both a betrayal of a friend and a potentially upsetting thing for Margot to hear; that is, it is an example of Eli placing himself in a situation where he should not be just to give himself the grandiose position of messenger. When Richie confronts Eli about this betrayal, Eli is under the influence of mescalin, urinating behind a curtain, and is framed with a pile of what could be computer games or porn and can only justify himself by saying the situation is "odd."

While being interviewed on a TV chat show, Eli's behavior becomes more eccentric as he is asked about the failure of his first novel and he starts to talk to himself, repeating the word "wildcat" before walking off the set. It is unclear if this is purely the result of drug use or whether he is trying to cultivate an enigmatic and controversial public persona. Everything about Eli is a pose, symbolized by his walking stick topped by a stuffed bird's head. His grandiose claim to Margot that "I'm not in love with you any more" is immediately undercut by her more caustic, "I didn't know you ever were." He claims she was never interested in him until he started getting "good reviews" to which she retorts, "Your reviews aren't that good." He seems to have the last laugh with the comment "But the sales are," but this commercial success is not really valued by the Tenenbaums. The recognition that he craves is as elusive as full membership in a family to which he is not related by blood ("the family" is ironically the topic of discussion of Eli's chat show). He cannot be a Tenenbaum any more than he can be a credible artist. When Richie confronts him during a drug deal, Eli states explicitly, "I always wanted to be a Tenenbaum," but the emotional resolution of the moment is rendered absurd as Eli's apparent fetching of his belongings becomes an escape as he climbs out of a window and runs off.

It is unclear whether Raleigh, a member of the family by marriage, is a complete charlatan and just using Dudley as an academic trophy, his means to recognition, critical and possibly commercial fame. The veracity of Raleigh's work seems ambiguous. Dudley's completion of a puzzle, supposedly to match Raleigh's, only results in something that is nothing like it. The only validation of his theorizing is rather lost in the fine comic moment in which Raleigh lists Dudley's symptoms, including acute sense of hearing, only to be interrupted a second or so later from the deep background where Dudley questions whether he is really color-blind. The boy almost develops into an appendage of Raleigh's, following him everywhere and even trying to cheer him up by asking, "Do you wanna play some games or do some experiments on me or something?" At a loss about what to do over the death of his wife, ironically Raleigh confides in the one person who really loves Margot, Richie, whose powerful, jealous feelings are readily apparent from his action in punching out a glass panel of his aviary. Raleigh is clearly hurt by Margot moving back home and then the revelations about her sexual history, but his old-fashioned description of that as "cuckolding" him only underlines the age difference between them.

Despite Royal's skepticism and Chas's antagonism (which is not so much personal as directed against anyone outside the family), Sherman seems a positive force for good. His timidity, couching his proposal in a long-winded phrase about tax, marks him as someone who is shy but genuinely caring about Etheline. As Royal finally declares, "He's everything I'm not." He is reliable, present, responsible, and appreciative of Etheline's qualities. Conversely, he also lacks the reckless charisma that Royal manages to charm people with, albeit often temporarily. Sherman's physical timidity in the park, lurking behind a tree while carrying two large paper bags, casts him either as a romantic with a picnic planned for Etheline or more likely, a less showy version of Royal-as-spy. This latter role might initially make him seem ridiculous but unlike Royal, he does seem to have Etheline's best interests at heart, and it is through his dogged skepticism that Royal's facade as a dying man is exposed.

Sherman acts towards Etheline in an open and gentlemanly manner, but it looks as if the emotional pendulum of the narrative is swinging back towards Royal as she rejects a date with Sherman, and Royal and Pagoda have a celebratory meeting (with cigarettes, alcohol, and a take-out meal) in the tiny games cupboard. At this stage, Royal uses a boxing metaphor to describe how he has "got the sucker on the ropes." However, Sherman is no "sucker." When he arrives at the hospital, his first reaction is not to score points or engage in bickering but simply to ask, "How can I help?" which in combination with his physical clumsiness, somehow catching his tie up in his glasses, makes him particularly engaging at this moment.

There are relatively few deleted scenes, apart from a few with Eli and some semi-clad women, presumably increasing his status, in his own mind at least, as something of a sexual trophy, but this aspect of his character would distract from the Tenenbaums, Margot especially (whose character would be diminished if Eli is just a womanizer). Eli originally was to have a wife and children (one of whom was called Stetson). A pre-sex dinner between Etheline and Sherman is also cut, which is probably unnecessary, although we lose Sherman's awkwardness in catching his napkin on fire.

A SIMPLE PLAN

SHERMAN: I don't think you're an asshole, Royal. You're just a kind of
        a son-of-a-bitch.
ROYAL: Well, I really appreciate that.

Royal's plan of faking a terminal condition seems heartless, but its implementation does have a certain genius about it, using Dusty (Seymour Cassell) as a doctor (with a credible bedside manner and a pager supposedly calling him back to the hospital which really tells him about shifts at the hotel) and fake medicines, including Tic Tacs (held up later in close-up by the more skeptical Sherman).

The scene on the street where he jumps out and surprises Etheline with the news is challenging as Anderson shoots it in one long take, including some tracking, further movement, and important marks at which Hackman has to stop and Huston must walk out of the shot and then come back in. In terms of performances too, although Hackman is quite dismissive on the DVD commentary of how demanding the role was, Huston has to credibly shift rapidly between shock and genuine affection, and we have to see Hackman change his mind *twice* in the light of gauging her reaction. Hackman refers to this scene as "full of craft" and "full of emotion," the kinds of scenes he feels he plays best. The effect of the exchange should be to create confusion, reflecting Etheline's feelings, but not ridicule. Films rarely switch back and forth like this, and Anderson risks the goodwill of his audience if he gets this wrong. Hackman is uneasy about the concept of roles being written specifically for him as he feels this is always based on someone's idea of him, rather than the reality. However, it is a credit to Anderson's persuasive powers and the strength of the script that Hackman was persuaded to take the part anyway.

Royal's ability to manipulate others, such as feeding the twins lines to repeat to Chas and mentioning his dead wife, is more dramatically engaging than morally reprehensible. He admits to Richie that he is "not very good with disappointment," and he does ask Chas whether he still has the pellets in his hand, but when Chas snarls a yes, Royal actually laughs, suggesting he regrets little of the detail about how he brought up his children. He chastises Margot for her treatment of Richie in her two-timing relationship with Eli and states she used to be a genius, which she denies and then instead of reaffirming his compliment, he qualifies it, "Well, that's what they used to say," as if he had never believed it either.

Royal refers to his children as "my darlings" but has had no contact with them for 22 years. His behavior may seem unforgivable but what redeems him, partially if not completely, is the crass insensitivity with which he energizes the family. He offers to take the twins to see where their grandmother is buried and after some questions about who Rachel is (Chas's dead wife), he blithely suggests, "We'll have to swing by her grave too." The film is peppered with great throwaway lines from Royal, like "which one are you?" to the twins (although at least this does show he sees them as individuals, unlike Chas), to his admission to Richie he had a lot financially riding on his aborted tennis match. At the end of the montage explaining how Chas got him disbarred, the charge of stealing from his 14-year-old son is put to him, at which he pauses and then laughs. It is this persona as an unapologetic rogue that energizes the film but makes its speedy resolution slightly unsatisfying as it hard to accept that the Royal we have seen up to this point would suddenly give up and meekly sign divorce papers. Indeed, in the scene where he confronts Sherman and Etheline on the steps of the house, we half expect the papers to be fake or that he will not mail them or that he is still trying to win Etheline back. Richie's suicide and his admission that he loves Margot might bring Royal to his senses (he claims, "Now, I get it"), but this seems unconvincing and, indeed, he seems a more interesting character as a liar and schemer.

Sometimes comic lines and absurd situations come together with some great comic timing too, such as Eli emotionally confessing, "I always wanted to be a Tenenbaum" to which Royal mutters, "Me too," or Royal wailing, "I wanna die" just before accepting a cookie from Pagoda. After spotting Richie boarding a bus, Royal casually observes, "I'd have to say, he didn't look half bad for a suicide." To use the services of a friend posing as a doctor is one thing but to make up an entire hospital is quite audacious. As he leaves later, he seems to have half-believed his own fiction, claiming to Richie that he had felt like a different person since he was "close to death." Royal's attempts at an explanation to Etheline ("I do have high blood pressure") and his covering for Pagoda, initially denying that he was involved and then instantly qualifying himself, to "not that involved," are the marks of a charismatic liar, who as a viewer you almost want to succeed but in the context of a social situation, just creates havoc as his grandiose falsehoods come crashing down. The final "killer" argument that destroys Royal's facade as an ill man is that Sherman knows what stomach cancer looks like because his wife had it, bringing the argument squarely back to matters of integrity and family loyalty. We have the stark contrast between a man who looked after his dying wife and another who would pretend to be dying to court favor with his estranged one.

HAPPILY EVER AFTER?

MARGOT: You probably don't even know my middle name.
ROYAL: That's a trick question. You don't have one.
MARGOT: It's Helen.
ROYAL: That was my mother's name.
MARGOT: I know it was.

The wedding feels more like a contrived climax, now that Royal's scheming has melted away, and the erratic behavior of Eli, represented by his face paint, although in some measure prepared for in the preceding narrative, is a rather heavy-handed attempt to introduce one last obstacle to full narrative closure. The crashing of Eli's car into the building, even if under the influence of drugs, has a Ballardian feel to it, as if Eli is seeking to fuse with the very bricks and mortar (and possibly dead bodies) of the Tenenbaum family. It is a very strange episode and tonally out of keeping with the rest of the film. It is played for laughs in that it is only Buckley who is squashed, and Royal is further rehabilitated by saving the boys (in a stunt we do not see), thereby reconciling him with Charles. However, the crash might equally have resulted in human fatalities, and this is not a narrative that can easily accommodate outright farce (also seen in the slapstick chase of Chas and Eli, pushing a priest down stairs) and the potential loss of human life. Key here perhaps is the split-second pause before the chase happens as if we are weighing up what kind of a film this is. If an angry Chas catches Eli who has just threatened the lives of his most precious boys, there could be a scene of real violence; if not, then we have a ludicrous chase through the house, ending in Eli's jumping over a fence into the embassy gardens next door.

The reintegration of Chas's character is also signaled by his noting that both he and Sherman are widowers (as Max Fischer might say, they both have dead people in their families). Chas's act in also jumping over the fence is less a pursuit of Eli as an escape for himself. He has nowhere left to run. Both men, shown in bird's-eye view, lie back looking up, in actual fact only feet from the rest of the cast but escaping into a moment of calm reflection, in which they *both* admit they need help.

The scene ends with a sweeping tracking shot along the set, taking in small snippets of conversation, underlining character development. The actual fact that Etheline and Sherman were due to marry has been almost completely forgotten as if it is the least important factor here (the ceremony is briefly referred to as occurring some weeks later). Richie asks as the priest is being loaded onto an ambulance if they have a substitute; Eli is describing the accident to a policeman, who recognizes him and becomes quite starry-eyed; Royal is asking the firemen about the breed of a spotted dog they have; Dudley is putting a helmet on Raleigh; a doctor (Dusty still in the guise of an imposter) is examining Richie's eye, telling him to page him if it spreads to the other eye; and the sequence concludes by coming back to Royal and Chas as the father gives a gift to the son, to replace the dead Buckley and to show sensitivity to Chas's childhood interest in spotted mice. The rapprochement between the two reaches an emotional high point shortly afterwards when Royal dies of a heart attack in an ambulance and only Chas is there at the moment of his death. The sequence at the wedding is a blend of running gags (Dusty's actions) and a nod to films containing lengthy tracking shots like Jean-Luc Godard's *Weekend* (1968) also focusing on cars and having characters drift in and out of the shot. Like slow motion, it draws our attention to the filmmaking process. It is a logistical party piece and does not engage with the snippets of supposed drama we see in each character grouping.

The final elements of the film, like the opening, happen rapidly, in montage style. Her creative block apparently broken, Margot writes a new play, *The Levinsons in the Trees,* a thinly veiled dramatization of the dysfunctional Tenenbaum family, featuring identical twins, an adopted daughter, and a tyrannical father. Although this could be read as an opportunity to settle old scores or as a reflection of imaginative poverty (we are told it ran for 10 weeks and received "mixed reviews"), we see Royal in the audience laughing heartily, suggesting he can recognize himself. Richie is a tennis coach at the 375th Y; Raleigh and Dudley are on a tour marketing "Dudley's World," an academic product that they both have a stake in promoting. Eli is in rehab in North Dakota, and even here we see him showing other inmates one of his lasso tricks, and Chas now appears behind Royal and the boys, also content to embrace risk on the back of a garbage truck.

The epilogue features Royal's funeral, shot in slow motion as the mourners exit the family plot. There are no speeches; the twins (now in black tracksuits) fire a salute, and we learn that Royal left them a set of encyclopedias. The script on the epitaph reads "Died tragically rescuing his family from the wreckage of a destroyed sinking battleship." The camera slowly tracks in to focus on the name on the gate. Royal does rescue the family in a way, perhaps not in an act of wartime heroism but in making good the mistakes of his past. It does sum him up accurately as a character who wanted his family to think well of him, be a kind of hero for them, and in the final analysis, presents himself as someone who found fictionalizing life more interesting than meekly accepting a more prosaic view of reality. Like his earlier wish that an imposing gravestone were his, he creates his own fiction to the last. He has successfully started the process of social reintegration for Chas, made Margot and Richie face up to their feelings, and effectively expelled Eli whose influence on the family was mostly negative. He has allowed Etheline to find happiness, and most important of all, he has taught the twins the importance of risk, adventure, and maybe even being creative with the truth. As much as Sherman's character has positive elements, if he had taken this role, would we have been engaged in a family narrative in quite the same way? The title suggests that the family are formed in Royal's image, for better or worse. It is a celebration of the liar, the loveable rogue, the prodigal father, and perhaps the one concept that unites all three: family.

The film does raise some questions about the best way to raise children, especially those designated as having unusual abilities. Royal asserts that it is important to encourage some "recklessness" in the twins ("taking it out and chopping it up") so that they are not "scared of life." Etheline says she thinks that is "terrible advice," but Royal denies that she really feels that way. Hence we see him spirit the boys away for a series of irresponsible activities, shown in condensed montage form, sprinting past "No running" signs and jumping into a pool, racing across streets against "Don't walk" warnings, horse riding, carting, throwing water bombs at taxis, committing petty theft, and riding on the back of a garbage truck. It is unlikely that such events would all happen in one afternoon and the implication is that either this is a series of occasions or that it is the combined symbolic impact of such slightly rebellious, potential activities that are important.

There are some great comic moments, such as the choreography of Sherman falling into a trench at Etheline's archaeological dig. A serious emotional moment (Sherman is trying to say that he can offer just as much as her previous boyfriends) is undercut as Etheline keeps talking, oblivious to Sherman's sudden disappearance. The timing of the fall and the maintenance of eye-lines, is deceptively skillful, so that we believe Sherman really did not see the hole or that Etheline is unaware of his fall. Like Guggenheim's recovery scene in *Rushmore,* there is a Clouseau feel to this slapstick, evoking Peter Sellers's staircase stunt in Blake Edwards's *The Pink Panther* (1963), one of Anderson's early favorite films.

Anderson would go on to adapt Roald Dahl's *Fantastic Mr. Fox* (2009). In another Dahl story, *Danny the Champion of the World* (1975), the eponymous hero states the lesson that Royal is hoping Chas will learn: "A STODGY parent is no fun at all. What a child wants and DESERVES is a parent who is SPARKY."[8] From this perspective alone, Tenenbaum is redeemed.

Cinema Paradiso:
The Life Aquatic with Steve Zissou (2004)

With a budget of over $50 million, *The Life Aquatic,* with its explosions and on-location shooting, represents a change of scale and potential control that Anderson could exert over his concept. Based on a one-page story, "The Jaguar Shark," which Anderson wrote many years previously, involving the hunt for a mythically rare beast, the film takes existing tendencies in Anderson movies, such as microscopic stylization, to an extreme, and in the process failed to find its audience and also left the bulk of critics disappointed. Typically, the film is seen as indicative of a lack of development on Anderson's part and featuring a static narrative. However, the real underlying problem is a further, more extreme example of another typical Anderson feature: the centrality of the dysfunctional hero. Although the film appears to be an ensemble piece, all the characters ultimately only matter as they relate to Zissou (Bill Murray). This hamstrings the narrative, preventing it from digressing too far from him, but it also makes it more complex than most commentators have thought. How viewers respond to Zissou largely dictates how they respond to the film as a whole.

Like the shots of Cash in *Tenenbaums,* the opening scene features a track up in low angle to a speaker, cutting to the reverse angle behind the speaker to show an expectant audience, suggesting the outward forms of academic credibility and that we are dealing with a speaker of some eminence and gravitas. The reality is that both Cash and Zissou are showmen, dazzling their public with works that appear to have an academic credibility they actually do not possess. The on-screen titles, "Adventure no. 12 'The Jaguar Shark' (Part 1)," feels more like a library cataloguing system, suggesting a long list of similar events rather than anything distinctive or original. What we see, however, is presented as unusual. On-screen Zissou pulls a map down like a 19th-century explorer still concerned with categorizing the known world. As an explorer, he may not be using the tools of 20th-century media, but Anderson (and by extension Zissou the filmmaker) is creating frames-within-frames, using planes of meaning within individual shots. Thus, we have a contrast between the map in the foreground and the sea visible outside the boat to which Zissou points. Later we see Zissou watching rushes from this film, and the camera cuts to a shot literally framed by the back of the boat. Very early in the film, we see the filmmaking apparatus on the boat and realize that the recording and filmic representation of Zissou's adventures are possibly more important than their scientific value. This sense of extremely careful framing permeates the film, reinforcing the impression that we are unsure how much experience is direct and how much contrived for Zissou's own film.

The question of the validity of the Esteban incident hangs over the whole film. Even Jane (Cate Blanchett), whose opinion we come to see as level-headed and objective, feels "aspects of it seemed slightly fake." If we really believe that one of Zissou's oldest friends was suddenly killed right in front of him, then our view of Zissou may include some sympathy and cast the film, and in particular his dealings with Ned (Owen Wilson), as part of a process of mourning. If the Jaguar Shark really exists, then he has found, somewhat fortuitously perhaps, a large unknown mammal with dramatic destructive capacities. The problem is in both these cases, we have no body, no film (he says he dropped the camera), in short, no evidence for what Zissou says. Since we see him a charming liar elsewhere, it is tempting to cast this as a setup, albeit a rather tasteless one. His shouted description of the creature from the sea, appearing as subtitles in the film-within-a-film may seem stilted and false or possibly the result of shock and reflect the need to record what he has seen. The close-up of his face is useful for the dramatic power of the sequence, but the "crazy eye" effect of rapid decompression which Klaus (Willem Dafoe) refers to seems genuine (even if the term itself is fictional). This uncertainty about the status of the shark is expressed by his rival Hennessey (Jeff Goldblum) after the screening, when he asks, "Does it actually exist?" However, Zissou's answer is couched in the language of a filmmaker, or creator of fictions: "I don't want to give away the ending." Perhaps this provides the viewer with a motive to remain engaged, to solve this particular mystery, but although there is an answer at the end, by that point the issue has been largely overshadowed by other events. Like the bond with Esteban (Seymour Cassell) himself, suggested by the spark that leaps from Zissou's finger to the screen which he reaches to touch when she is on television, the emotional validity of the shark attack is stated rather than shown.

TEAM ZISSOU

It is debatable to what extent Team Zissou is really a team. In some ways Zissou is a colonial chief in his kingdom, particularly in his exploitative use of interns, never learning their names (even when one is wounded) and only talking to them to order things for himself, such as a latte after steal-ing Hennessey's coffee machine. Ned later informs Zissou that the name of the only loyal intern is Nico, whereupon Zissou promises him an A but also squeezes him on the shoulder where he was shot. He gains a mea-sure of revenge in giving the mutineers a grade of "incomplete," dressing this in apparent generosity for not failing them. We see them struggling with heavy equipment, and when an intern falls down the stairs in the raid on Hennessey's lab (itself implying he expects them to follow him in com-mitting quite a significant criminal act), rather than expressing any con-cern about the individual, Zissou calls out that they should be sure to get a backup. There is little sign of any training going on. Simply being on board and having the privilege of acting as Zissou's personal slaves is apparently reward enough. It is unclear to what extent Anne-Marie (Robyn Cohen) is there solely as eye candy; her appearance topless, apparently evoking no response from Zissou, suggests that the presence of females on board is for sexual recreation rather than to play an important role in a scientific inves-tigation. His attempt to warn off Klaus (Willem Dafoe) might be for Jane's protection or so that he can have less competition for her attention. A shot tilts down quickly to Anne-Marie and then pans left back to Ned, as Zissou throws out a question about the distribution of handguns, which creates the sense that interns are almost always within hailing distance if a fact needs to be checked or a Campari fetched for Zissou.

Eleanor (Anjelica Huston) is described as "the brains behind the opera-tion," but apart from knowing the Latin names to classify species, it seems more that she is the money behind the operation. Zissou is still attracted to his ex-wife. As he comes out of the auditorium, he watches her for a moment as she sits eating, looking out at the harbor beyond (and, we subsequently see, the boat where the after-show party will be held). She is portrayed as a beautiful, willowy woman, given to slow, languid movements (that show the blue streaks in her hair to good effect) that seem to keep him in thrall. Zissou tells Ned later that she is a "rich bitch raised by maids" but that does not stop his lusting after her (and her money) when he follows her (the handheld tracking shot adopting his point of view) through her luxury villa where she is dressed in a leotard, accompanied by her young, attractive "research as-sistant." She departs from the expedition rather dramatically with "I don't want to be a part of whatever's gonna happen out there," evocative of lines by Etta (Katharine Ross) in *Butch Cassidy and the Sundance Kid* (George Roy Hill, 1969), except she relents fairly soon to offer financial help and a rescue boat later. She does assert that just because she agrees to fund the rescue of Bill "it doesn't mean you've won me back," but she clearly does still find him attractive, particularly when he is being dynamic and energiz-ing the crew.

Ned is something of a departure for Owen Wilson, particularly in his roles for Wes Anderson. He is not an absurd character with delusions of any sort, except perhaps being accepted by the man he believes to be his father.

He represents a core of decency and goodness and perhaps not surprisingly, juxtaposed with Zissou's bluff manner, he can seem quite insipid and less interesting dramatically. In a deleted scene, he even asks Eleanor what a "dirty weekend" is, which stretches credibility just a little too far. Like other Anderson characters played by Owen Wilson, Ned is obsessed with small, arguably superficial detail and naming in particular. Here this is made a little more complicated because the name in question, the one that Ned wants to use for Zissou, is "Dad." The problem for Wilson is trying to adjust suddenly how audiences perceive him and that this innocence may well be read ironically by some viewers as stupidity. He reacts to Zissou's attempts to warn him off Jane, that she cannot be a lesbian because she is pregnant. He is still however like Eli Cash, desperately seeking some kind of recognition and acceptance as member of a group. Thus, early on he shows off his Zissou Society ring, and the pipe smoking may be what he thinks is the pose of a hardened sailor to win Zissou's favor. He does have something of the naïveté of a younger Zissou (as described by Mandrake at least). He cannot contain his sense of wonder at the sight of the jellyfish on the beach. Jane's reading aloud of a six-volume novel to her baby seems an eccentric action, but Ned actually wants to stay in her cabin and listen, linking him explicitly with the baby (and a maternal element in his relationship with Jane) and thereby missing his turn on watch, allowing the pirates to board without warning.

Despite being in some ways a more serious departure for Owen Wilson, Ned is described on the film of the shark expedition as "energetic," "spirited," and "useful"—typical elements of Wilson's characters in Wes Anderson films. We see Ned's reply from the Zissou Society, framed and hanging on a wall, stressing the importance of youthful teen worship or its continued importance for his sense of identity (he has had it for 17 years). What was a fairly standard letter (the final note states "Dictated but not read") from a virtual corporation has a deeply personal meaning for him. It addresses him as if he was a crew member on a shared voyage and thanks him for naming a bug after Zissou. On parting with Jane, she gives him 50 stamped cards, suggesting extreme neediness on his part but also perhaps on hers, as if she cannot easily break this umbilical bond. She kisses him good-bye but on the forehead and says she "almost feels like my heart's getting broken." That "almost" casts this as a near-miss in terms of relationships rather than a full union of equals.

Drakoulias (Michael Gambon), complete with an overtly vampiric name, provides a contrast with the claustrophobia of life on board ship by the use of languid cutting and being placed in larger, more opulent sets, dressed in darker colors, especially browns and purples. This color scheme, the presence of Gambon as a potentially difficult man of some power, and the tracking shot through the wall between office and antechamber outside all evoke the progress through the restaurant in Peter Greenaway's *The Cook, The Thief,*

The Wife and Her Lover (1988). However, such unpleasant character expectations are soon dispelled by the roguish response to Ned's offer of inheritance money: "What sort of expression is the lad wearing on his face?" It is logical that Zissou's financial alter ego should reflect some of his characteristics in the manner of larger-than-life producers, such as Dino de Laurentis or Carlo Ponti. Bill Ubell, the bank stooge (Bud Cort) is dressed in beige nylon, explicitly contrasted with the yellow and blue of the Zissou uniforms, portraying him as a stereotypical moneyman, dull and uninteresting.

ZISSOU AS BRAND MANAGER

Zissou's explanation for not acknowledging Ned earlier ("I hate fathers and I never wanted to be one") seems weak. He admits that he had read the story of Ned's paternity in newspaper reports five years ago and assumed that the facts had been checked; that is, he ignored him because it would be inconvenient to him, marking him as a moral coward. Zissou's attitude to Ned is also made more complicated by Ned's status as financial savior as well as possibly blood relative. Zissou offers him the option of using his surname and his choice of Christian name (the incredibly pretentious "Kingsley Zissou"). This could be read as a father accepting paternity for his son, but it feels a little bit like an exercise in branding, especially since the name on offer seems alien. Ned politely replies, "I think I'll stick with Ned for now."

The ordering of correspondence cards is typical of Anderson heroes, concerned with the small-scale details, like Max Fischer's business card (that actually contains no business at all). The extent of the Zissou brand could be seen as suggestive of a communal spirit and a shared goal or slightly sinister, indicative of an urge to appropriate any object (or person) that comes into contact with Team Zissou and maximize potential for commercial gain. While clearly not as mentally unstable as Patrick Bateman, the protagonist in *American Psycho* (from Brett Easton Ellis's 1991 novel, directed by Mary Harron in 2000), who frets about every tiny detail of his business card, Zissou needs to have his sense of identity constantly reinforced by the trappings of his fame and to leave imprints of his brand everywhere on his immediate surroundings. There is certainly something strangely narcissistic about the boat, containing a Zissou pinball machine, a range of Zissou dolls, glimpsed next to the TV, and the notion that the crew are happy to spend their time watching tapes of previous adventures. Joining the crew means that you get to wear a red cap and a customized Speedo. The first sight of the crew on the beach features the men in matching Zissou pajamas. Eleanor asks Zissou what he intends to do "with" Ned, to which he replies that "I believe in this boy," but the implication is this is due more to the admiration, verging on hero worship, he gets from Ned.

Zissou's uncertain relationship with Ned is reflected in how uncomfortable he is being called "Dad," which he dismisses as just "a nickname." Zissou responds to Ned's suggestion of "Stevie" as in the right direction ("the basic idea's OK but not that one"). In the awkward dialogue with Eleanor, Zissou claims that accepting Ned as his "actual…biological son" is "very difficult." He inhabits such a solipsistic universe, even when he tries to be selfless, he cannot help but deflect the conversation back to himself ("What happened to me? Did I lose my talent? Am I ever gonna be good again?") echoing the hopeless safecracker, Kumar, in *Bottle Rocket*. It is a strange conversation, almost as if both speakers are only talking to themselves, which in a way they are. The interlocking rhetorical questions convey the sense of privileged characters who are not used to thinking beyond themselves, especially Eleanor, whose musing that they should have had a child together suggests that Team Zissou's expeditions are a form of child substitute. Zissou's attention to detail over his branding, down to some custom-made Adidas training shoes or having badges with grades on the shoulders of the wet suits, reflects the whole enterprise as closer to an adventure club with clear demarcations of status, like the Boy Scouts. Mentioned but not seen until right at the end, Ned's redesign for the Zissou insignia includes an *N* for himself, a belated acknowledgement by the brand.

ZISSOU AS AGEING LOTHARIO

Zissou: Obviously you think I'm a showboat and a little bit of a prick…but then I realized, that's me.

The film also shows Zissou's dilemma as a public persona, worshipped by legions of young fans. Both Ned and Jane admit to being one of these, Jane firmly in the past tense, and Zissou adopts the iconic pose used for posters (like the ones she used to hang on her wall). In a moment of honesty, Zissou says that he never felt quite like the hero depicted but then ironically tries to use this admission, to make advances to her.

Ned also competes for the attention of Jane and like Blume in *Rushmore*, Zissou talks dismissively of his interest in her to try and throw his rival off the scent. Later there is an elaborately composed sequence in which we cut between a porthole shot from within Jane's cabin looking out at one of the dolphins and then cut to a reverse shot with Zissou looking through a different kind of porthole shot as he is passing the room with the monitors and can see the footage on screen. The dolphins that he earlier castigated are effectively allowing him to spy on his rival.

Walking uninvited into Jane's cabin to confront Ned seems insensitive, and the conversation soon descends into childish squabbling in which both Zissou and Ned seem too immature to be a suitable partner for Jane. Zissou admits that "I had a thing for her" but claims he had warned Ned off. Ned replies that this warning was delivered to Klaus, which provokes more bickering and eavesdropping. Jane meanwhile explicitly states that Zissou is too old for her (not that she does not like him at all), and also there is some inversion in the swearing with Zissou now adopting the more decorous "f-ing" and Jane using the complete word. Zissou and Ned are openly absurd love rivals, and Zissou demands a word outside with Ned, code for a fight, and the two trek through the theatrical cutaway set in a long take. However, up on deck, in an antithesis to a Hollywood fistfight, Zissou smiles before punching Ned unexpectedly and then complains when Ned punches him back while wearing a Zissou ring.

Jane's first appearance suddenly on the beach instantly appeals to both Ned and Zissou mainly due to her angry plain-speaking and (quite credible) English accent. The circumstances of an Englishwoman not being picked up, being cold and wet and angry does seem a little like the arrival of Emily (Helen Baxendale) in *Friends* (who first appears in "The One With Joey's Dirty Day," Season 4, 1998). Zissou expects the interview with Jane for *The Oceanographic Explorer* to be just a "puff piece" with "stock dialogue," but instead she instantly throws him a loaded question about this being his last voyage. She reacts angrily to his accusation about her journalistic integrity, stating quite clearly that she alone was interested in this article (another blow to his inflated ego) and that she is paying her own expenses. Unfortunately, Anderson has her cry here and later in the film too, which does weaken her dramatic credibility and make it possible to dismiss her judgment stereotypically as based on hormonal imbalances due to her pregnancy (oddly so since Blanchett was really pregnant at the time). Her later plea for him not to pursue the shark also plays into this role of helpless female, given to emotional outbursts, leaving the men to take on the heroic action. She was getting somewhere in her probing questions of Zissou and to have her suddenly crumble like this and backtrack ("I'm sure you'll make a terrific father") is a lost opportunity. Clearly, there are parallels between Ned and Jane, who are both looking for a father, but this works more effectively in the case of Ned. Jane's troubled relationship with the father of her child, a married editor, is only present via strained phone conversations and the notion that she is drawn to Ned as a more suitable candidate (although this is closer to a mother-son relationship). His later gift to her of a shell he showed her earlier, now made into a necklace with peppermint dental floss, reflects his immaturity but also why Jane does not reject him so bluntly as she does with Zissou.

Zissou's attempts at seduction seem clumsy, interrupting her interview and questions about his mentor Lord Mandrake with a blunt "Wanna go up in my balloon." Such equipment seems to be used more for pseudo-romantic trysts (he tries and fails to kiss her) than any scientific function. Indeed, as the crew pay out the line, one man comments that he likes Jane's hair and although another agrees, he admits "Zissou called her first," suggesting a prime pastime, perhaps the prime function, of the whole enterprise is the seduction of women. There is a nod to the balloon ride in Federico Fellini's *City of Women* (1980), designed to demonstrate male sexual prowess, suggesting that Zissou sees himself as a version of Fellini's womanizing hero Snaporaz (Marcello Mastroianni). The strategy of the balloon, having a woman as a captive audience, might seem effective right up to the point where Jane rejects him and the conversation has to carry on and overcome this awkwardness. Unlike his tattoo ("Deep search") at that precise moment, he is pursuing something extremely shallow.

However, he later seems a slightly broken figure in asking her not to make fun of him, claiming, "I just wanted to flirt with you" and promising that someone will come and fix her door.

ZISSOU—THE PIRATE KING?

The pirate episode stands out from the rest of the film, generically and in terms of dramatic jeopardy. It is the first time in a Wes Anderson film that there is a serious threat to human life and the first time that we see an Anderson character kill, albeit in self-defense as an enraged Zissou throws off his ties and shoots a pirate dead. It marks a significant change as it potentially undermines the predominant tone of quirkiness. If real suffering and potential death are at stake, then the trivial and superficial actions and dialogue that seem to dominate elsewhere are no longer cute, just self-indulgent.

The gun battle with many shots fired but virtually no blood and the idea that a single man with a pistol can overpower a heavily armed and ruthless gang smack of the kind of cartoonish and fantastical violence of the TV series *The A-Team* (NBC, 1983–1987) accompanied by Iggy and the Stooges' "Search and Destroy" (1973). Handheld camerawork conveys the immediacy and fear of the situation and whispered, partially incoherent dialogue of hostages, rapid cutting between blindfolded figures (especially Zissou), and cutting in on that axis even more quickly while using flash-cuts of Ned (shots literally seen by Zissou a moment before but now used as a powerful mental image) all create a building sense of climax as Zissou erupts in a moment of instinctive (and paternal) rage in the only action we have seen him take thus far for the good of another. The use of the close-up from the Esteban incident with Zissou's crazy eye suggests his unstable, irrationality as his anger boils over and he actually bites through the rope binding him. His first piece of dialogue in the calm after he has driven the men away implies that it is Bill's courage that was the motivating factor, but more prominent is the drive to protect what is his (his ship, his son, and even his career).

Santos (Seu Jorge) has some dialogue here, although his function is still basically choral, asking about the strange light in the sky, motivating Zissou's description (citing Mandrake) "as if the natural world's been turned upside-down." What has been disturbed is the generic nature of the film but only temporarily as the burial ceremony for the dead pirate descends into farce as Zissou gives the order to throw him over the other side and just cover up anything marked as Hennessey's. Zissou's familiarity with the alarm system suggests this is not the first time he has broken into Hennessey's lab, and his theft of the cappuccino machine is a comic parallel to the subsequent serious piracy episode. Zissou's hubris in wanting to cast himself as an adventurer, a pirate of sorts himself (proudly describing the huge amounts of "treasure" kept in a vault), directly leads to the attack on his own ship and the danger into which he has put himself and his crew.

The planning of the counterraid to rescue Bill has the veneer of heroism but it is also colored by financial motives to free the source of funding. Absurdity rules, from the naming of the "Ping Islands" (also possibly referencing the brand of leisurewear clothing) to Zissou's assertive claim "I know the place" only to point to the wrong spot on the map. Prior to the raid itself, we see Zissou advising with the cutting of sound ("Try track 3"), strongly suggesting that he is aware of the filmic impact of events as they happen and how they might be recut and edited at a later stage. Zissou, as linchpin of the crew, is not just director of the show but its main star as well.

The decrepit interior of the Hotel Citroen where previous luxury now seems part of the jungle prompts Zissou to inform us that he spent his honeymoon here, in an image of the wreck of his emotional life. A 90-degree pan takes us to a line of figures emerging from the water, led by Zissou brandishing a speargun. However, these are not Navy SEALs. Wearing their distinctive red caps, blue suits, and attacking in broad daylight, the group are strictly aspirational heroes. Their seemingly unstoppable progress is indeed stopped by Zissou tearing leeches off his body (he proves to be the only one) and the so-called assault on the hotel only proceeds once they have taken a light reading. The men advance in ridiculous moves, redolent of paintball games or learned from action films. Handheld camerawork suggests a sense of drama and imminent action but this too is halted as once inside, Zissou splits the men into two groups at which Klaus has a mini tantrum because he is not named in the first group. It seems like a more absurdist version of Quentin Tarantino's characters bickering about names in *Reservoir Dogs*, with no one wanting to be Mr. Pink.

Zissou's sudden dropping out of the shot in falling down some stairs evokes Sherman's similar mishap in *Tenenbaums*, but here the incident is used for a piece of self-indulgent dialogue (once Zissou has asked whether the moment was captured on film). He describes himself, still lying on the floor, as "a washed-up old man with no friends, no distribution deal, a wife on the rocks, people laughing at him, feeling sorry for himself" (perhaps aware of the irony of his own words by this point). He may be a little concussed (he talks about his wife, not his marriage being "on the rocks") but even so, the moment seems unconvincing. At the same time as parodying "Hollywood moments" of outpourings of feeling, we seem expected to also share the emotional intensity of this situation. However, Zissou is not a Lear character who is brought low and given a modicum of self-knowledge. Ned may offer him a hand up and tries to find a compromise nickname that he can accept, but "Papa Steve" seems ludicrous and also Zissou's promise not to ignore him again for years is hollow as he literally cannot. His admission that "I want to communicate my feelings for you but I think I might start crying" taps into the kind of emotional language of romantic comedy. It is very difficult to maintain a dominant tone of detached, quirky irony and then expect audiences to engage emotionally with characters to the level where tears are expected. This kind of tonal seesaw does not really work, especially since the crew subsequently find what looks like a graveyard, which could represent the fate of executed hostages.

The apparently empty hotel, which almost accidentally reveals its quarry leading to a gunfight, feels like a further absurdist allusion to Tarantino in the demise of Vince (John Travolta) at the hands of Butch (Bruce Willis) in *Pulp Fiction* and whose presence is only identified by the flush of a toilet. The subsequent discovery of Hennessey, thanks to the three-legged dog Cody, leads to another unconvincing shoot-out, with guns sounding very much like blanks and as with Zissou's earlier outburst, there is a similarly unbelievable victory against overwhelming numbers and odds. There is some humor in Hennessey being unsure if he is actually being rescued, the hostage-takers themselves who look less than professional, some playing cards (one is even seen in a gimp mask), but there is a darker subtext too (the mask might remind viewers of the hostage situation in *Pulp Fiction,* leading to sexual violence and bloody revenge). Hennessey is immediately shot and although he survives, there is still an awkward tonal and generic mix between action film, absurdist farce, and the potential for something darker, which is present but shied away from.

We seem to be some long way from the tone of a typical Anderson movie as the front entrance explodes and a chase sequence ensues. However, like Max's *Heaven and Hell* this is all in the style of a theatrical production, with little sense that lives will really be lost. Ned and Klaus rush to help but their progress into the hotel is impeded by the revolving door, producing a Chaplinesque shuffling routine to get into the building. The instruction from Zissou to Ned and Klaus to "hold the bridge" against their pursuers is pure cinematic cliché (a scene we do not see in full), and the resolution not to shoot a child, Cedric, on the beach but instead "send him a red cap and a Speedo" is a parody of such moments of contrived sentiment. However, after the scene where Zissou trips, Anderson cannot expect to parody such conventions one minute and then use them the next.

They seize a boat and apparently manage to recapture the safe containing Ned's inheritance money. However, in a Marx Brothers style conceit, Santos's attempts to open the safe are juxtaposed with a shot of the huge hole in the other side so that Ned and Zissou can look at each other in close-up, effectively in another porthole shot. The setup is pure slapstick and does not bear logical examination as it seems highly likely you would see the larger hole before spending too much energy on the door. However, it is also quite a powerful image of Zissou's pursuit of financial gain, only to find Ned almost by accident. The sequence, like its action-film predecessors, ends with an explosion as we have a crash zoom to the boat as it blows up and a cheery wave from Eleanor and some dolphins who have come out to meet them. Again, this is action *A-Team* style with bullets hitting no one (apart from a shoulder wound for Hennessey), no loss of life, and order restored. Anderson is quite critical of himself on the DVD commentary for the action scenes, but it is the script and basic switching back and forth between generic codes that is problematic and risks forfeiting viewer engagement.

The helicopter crash itself has some effective elements. Ned's repetition of his childhood wish that he could breathe underwater becomes grimly ironic. The rapid cutting between smoke in the cockpit, oil on the windshield, a cracking sound, a high-angle shot from the character's point of view (reminding us of Zissou's attempted seduction of Jane earlier) and slight slow motion as the sea rushes up all effectively convey the speed and sudden loss of control of such an event. Zissou's warning "This is gonna hurt" and his reaching out to put a protective arm across Ned are consistent with a character accepting the start of a new paternal relationship, tragically far too late. A red-screen flash-cut and the cutting of sound as they hit the water convey the cold and shock of the crash, and the sudden cut back to the image of Ned waving at the film premiere could be the cliché of his life flashing before his eyes, or more likely an example of a powerful key memory flashing through the synapses of Zissou's brain (as in the brief loss of sanity as he burst out his bonds and fights off the pirates). The blood splashing up on the camera suggests a wound out of sight and although the time in reaching land is cut, it is clear as Zissou carries Ned ashore, he is already dead. However, in retrospect, Zissou may take some blame for using what turns out to be dangerous equipment and a less than fully qualified pilot in Ned. Although he is finally vindicated by the appearance of the Jaguar Shark, he is prepared to bring 10 people down in the submersible, rather than the recommended 6. Perhaps this is a sign of support for the man and his dream, reflected in the moment of pure Hollywood, as each one slaps him on the back, but the risk factor, with ageing equipment here, is considerable.

The burial is brief with a slow zoom into a coffin (flanked rather eerily by members of Wilson's own family), which after a few perfunctory words from Zissou, is tipped overboard. Unfortunately, having played this scenario for laughs with the earlier dead pirate, it is difficult not to connect the two events. The camera follows the coffin down through the water, past a submersible and a close-up of Eleanor's watching face, smoking at the porthole. At the subsequent wake, Zissou admits that it is the only time Eleanor cried (suggesting that her actions in the sub are based on grief, not lack of interest), but then he qualifies this with a gag, "except when she got her arm caught in a deck winch." Sentiments around grief and expressions of love are almost instantly undercut, making such scenes problematic. Even when Zissou asks her if she would have adopted Ned and she agrees, she still notes in a rather detached fashion that he was 30.

There is something clearly childish in Zissou, not just his sense of humor, but emotionally like the Tenenbaum siblings, he seems to have found the move into adulthood problematic. In talking to Jane about the baby, he declares that 11½ is his favorite age. Eleanor's confession to Jane that Zissou is infertile, suggesting that this might be caused by living half his life underwater, casts him almost as some kind of hybrid creature, unable to function fully on land and most at home in the water.

REALITY VS. FANTASY

ZISSOU: Can you hear the Jack Whales singing? (There is the boom of a horn.)
NED: It's beautiful. I wonder what they're saying.
ZISSOU: Well, actually that's a sludge tanker.

There is a balance through the course of the film between the real and the artificial, from the cross section of the ship to Henry Selick's animation work and even in Blanchett finding out she was pregnant when she fainted during a fitting for a prosthetic stomach. There is a deliberately non-naturalistic element to large parts of the film, such as individual shots like Ned with his pipe on the deck of the ship, framed like Popeye, or the whole dramatic construct that once on board ship, we do not have a rolling deck effect to maintain the facade of a boat at sea.

The setting is mythic—clearly European but not necessarily Italian. Fictional names like Port-au-Patois suggest a generic sense of Mediterranean climate, landscape, and culture as well as a tongue-in-cheek linguistic joke. This also includes film culture—there are clear allusions to Fellini, most literally in employing hair stylist Maria Teresa Corridoni who worked with Fellini—and use of the Cinecittà studios near Rome. However, the fact that the largest studio at Cinecittà was still too small for a single shot of Anderson's immense theatrical cross section of the *Belafonte* (even using a very wide-angle 28 mm lens) reflects how his vision is not easily contained within its filmic references. There are clear allusions to *8½* (1963) in showing the frustrations of a director trying to make a film, but Zissou is much more than a filmmaker. It is about the blurring of edges between explorer and filmmaker, the fictional nature of documentary making, and of course the nature of one dysfunctional group of characters, where notions of family are displaced onto a group of misfits bound together in a common vision, more than by flesh and blood. In that vision, there is one key individual (as with Dignan, Max, and Royal) standing in for the director, the visionary energizer who makes things happen and who (like Zissou and the shark) ultimately delivers what he has promised if people only show faith in him. Anderson seems fascinated by these extrovert clown figures but he himself does not appear to work in that way.

Henry Selick's animated creatures add a dimension of unreality, or heightened reality to the film, since most are based on real animals. In tune with Anderson's overall aesthetic, the creatures are each on screen for a few seconds only and bring an element of quirky humor, such as the bugs, which flip over, on Eleanor's welcome mat. The multicolored creature in a plastic bag brought by Werner, only just saved by Zissou holding it aloft when the fight breaks out, suggests his interest in the unusual but in a very prosaic way, like a prize won at a fairground. The so-called sugar crabs the team stop to watch on the beach are played for laughs with Zissou unable to tell if the creatures are mating, underlining his ignorance of the animal world and possibly his own species too. Typical is the puffer fish that emerges from the sunken aircraft, providing a moment of surprising strangeness for the divers who seem more intent in filming each other than the wildlife.

The shots of Zissou (editing footage) and later Eleanor looking out from a submersible also do not quite match, perhaps deliberately, underlining that we are looking at an effect, partly in homage to *Yellow Submarine* (George Dunning, 1968). The animation of the descent of the submersible seems deliberately non-naturalistic with some fish attached to a rudder as the vessel dives down into a trench, in a fairly primitive attempt at using bait to capture their quarry. There are a mass of creatures during this climactic sequence, including octopi, fish, and even one of Hennessey's research turtles, intercut with individual characters looking out.

When the Jaguar Shark appears out of the dark (via Selick's huge eight-foot puppet, one of the largest stop-motion figures in film history), we are invited to admire the ingenuity of the filmmakers as Eleanor declares, "It's beautiful."

The conception of underwater otherness and of Zissou's character, treading a fine line between scientific researcher and commercial filmmaker, is strongly evocative of one French filmmaker, Jean Painlevé, whose work was brought to a wider audience with the publication of *Science Is Fiction* (2001) and an accompanying DVD in 2007 (also by Criterion who distribute Anderson's work). Where much conventional underwater photography is concerned with making the everyday strange, Painlevé's films (like Anderson's) work in the opposite direction, taking what appears fantastical and normalizing it, translating it into the everyday. He interprets animal behavior through the prism of human relationships and his work, like Anderson's, celebrates the quirky, the bizarre, and the eccentric. Like the questions over paternity in *The Life Aquatic*, Painlevé is interested in unusual examples of how animals reproduce, particularly around the role of the male in the birthing process, questioning gender roles in films like *The Love Life of the Octopus* (1965), *How Some Jellyfish are Born* (1960), and *The Seahorse* (1934). These species provide part of the magical backdrop for Anderson's film (at the film premiere, on the beach where Kate first appears, and as the subject of one of the deleted scenes).

There is a similar sense of whimsical humor in Painlevé's work, often anthropomorphizing footage (think of Anderson's turtle turning to look and appearing to wink at the submersible) via tongue-in-cheek narration and even an attempt at stop-motion animation in *Bluebeard* (1938). Like Anderson, there is a strong European influence (perhaps not surprising, bearing in mind his French origins), but he specifically worked with Georges Franju on *The Blood of Beasts* (1949) and Luis Buñuel on *Un Chien Andalou* (1929), being in charge of the ants. Painlevé (he lent cameras to Godard) also uses intertitles; variations in film speed, including slow motion; and like Anderson, uses innovative and distinctive soundtracks, including experimental electronica and jazz, to accompany his work. This is a tendency picked up by band Yo La Tengo, who in a strange predating of Mark Mothersbaugh's score for *The Life Aquatic*, used projections of Painlevé footage to accompany live concerts of their electronic-ambient music (as seen and heard on their DVD *The Sounds of Science* from 2001).

The film ends, as it began, at the Loquasto premiere, creating a sense of closure. *Aquatic* is ultimately about the shooting of a film, not the film itself, including its critical reception. The questioner from the last time, Ned, now stars in the film and a character from the film, Jane, appears in the audience with her new baby, now sporting a red Zissou hat. Similarly, Zissou is absent, sitting on a red carpet, this time next to a statuette, suggesting the success of the film we have seen being made. Werner reappears and sits next to him. Zissou gives him an insignia ring, marking the boy as an heir to Ned, and then Zissou proceeds to pick the boy up and carry him on his shoulders down the steps in slow motion. The line he says, more to himself, than the boy, "This is an adventure," suggests the strongly symbolic value of the boy; the child is father to the man, and Zissou's work, his film, becomes like his offspring as well as a tribute to Ned. The final credits continue over a daytime harbor scene as one-by-one Zissou's crew join their captain as he strides purposely along, a motif associated both with musicals and gangster movies, particularly "the building of the gang" scene. It is also a reference to *The Adventures of Buckaroo Banzai across the 8th Dimension* (W. D. Richter, 1984), which also featured Jeff Goldblum and as in *Banzai*, a dead character (Ned) reappears, casting the sequence as a dream or wish fulfillment. Werner is still dressed in lederhosen but now in the blue of Team Zissou, and the crew also now wear a blue uniform, making them look more like medical staff and a little closer to the professional operation of Hennessey's crew from earlier.

ZISSOU—SCIENTIST OR FILMMAKER?

NED: I'm just a character in your stupid film.
ZISSOU: It's a documentary. It's all really happening.

Mandrake's description of Zissou ("He has an almost magical connection to the life of the sea. He speaks its language fluently") is not really the character we see on screen. Like Royal, Zissou is a rogue, a liar, and a teller of tales. He claims that he still has Ned's letter, written when he was 12 (and we cut to an overhead shot of the letter sitting on a desk), but this seems highly unlikely and is only mentioned in the helicopter right before Ned's death. The old man who asks for Zissou's autograph on a series of film posters shows us melodramatic adventures, dealing with the lurid and the monstrous in exotic locations, with little discernible difference between his titles and those of monster movies, particularly from the 1950s, *Island Cats* (with creatures bearing markings like the Jaguar Shark), *Shadow Creatures of the Lurisia Archipelago,* and *The Battling Eels of Antibes.* This suggests perhaps that Zissou knows the hunt for the Jaguar Shark is also a fiction and may end in death too. Zissou signs three posters and then tells the man to forge the rest, cynically undermining the very process that he is involved in.

The relationship of Zissou to Jacques Cousteau is a little problematic. Cousteau was a pioneer in the field of underwater photography and filmmaking whose TV documentaries inspired a generation of explorers and marine scientists. He appears in earlier Anderson films, as a black-and-white picture on the wall during the party in *Bottle Rocket* and the library book in *Rushmore,* connecting Max to Edward and thereby to Miss Cross (in Max's mind, at least). Here, the final on-screen dedication to Cousteau during the credits is a combined acknowledgment and disclaimer as The Cousteau Society was not involved in production, and Cousteau's name is bleeped out of the DVD commentary. However, there is clearly a link, edging more towards homage than parody. The ubiquitous red caps (even worn at the premiere) and the grizzled appearance of Zissou, especially with a gray beard, are visual evocations of Cousteau himself, who was both a serious scientific figure and also a popularizer of marine science, bringing it into people's homes via his books, lectures, and most of all, his films and TV programs. The death of Ned in a helicopter accident parallels the tragic accident of Cousteau's own son, Philippe, in a flying accident and even the names are similar (two syllable, French-derived, common "ou" sound). There is mention of "Cousteau and his cronies" inventing the walkie-talkie (actually it supposedly was the aqualung, in collaboration with Emile Gagnan), but Zissou has developed this with "a rabbit ear" so they can "pipe in some music."

The planning of the expedition seems unprofessional as Zissou spreads a map on a Ping-Pong table, still with bat in hand, and uses a toy boat to chart progress. We see Zissou look up and cut, without comment or reaction, to Marie sitting topless with a camera, suggesting she is part of Zissou's "set decoration." The focus of planning however is the shooting schedule, complete with color chart; we are on a film set within a film set. Under a series of blue notes, headed by "Stunt work" Eleanor crosses out "Sky-dive into volcano" as a visual gag, underlining that the kind of film that is under discussion is all about the pursuit of spectacle and drama. Experiments with dynamite on the beach, made more dramatic by whip-pans back and forth as crew members scurry for cover, remain unexplained. Zissou's precise need for such explosives are, like Dignan's, for the creation of gratuitous spectacle. The shots of the team running on the beach seem like the *Rocky*-style montage in *Rushmore,* that is, apparently serious exercise taking place for no clear, specific goal. It is more an opportunity for Ned to peel away from the group just to give Jane a shell he has found. He is shepherded back to the group by Zissou on a bike like an old-style boxing trainer.

A striking feature of Zissou's whole approach is its paradoxically extremely unscientific nature. He talks of being "at the academy" with Hennessey and yet relies on his wife, not just for money but to identify and catalogue the species they encounter with Latin names. On arriving at the beach, Jane (a journalist) corrects his mistake in identifying the jellyfish as men-of-war (not exactly a rare species). Zissou's reaction is how it will affect the film, not his scientific error ("I guess, we'll have to loop that line"). Introducing the boat, he describes a set of rooms as "where we do our various science projects and experiments and so on," the dismissive tone suggesting that it is less significant than the onboard film production facilities, which are far more extensive. This allows Zissou to manufacture his own version of reality, while he is on the move. He mentions the work they do going down to an "observational level," which involves lying down and watching the sea life passing by, which seems more of a "chill-out zone" than the site of scientific inquiry. The library is referred to but in relation to its housing the complete first edition of *The Life Aquatic* magazine. Overall, it feels like a blend of a rich man's playground and an indulgent personal museum or shrine to all things Zissou.

In the sequence in the "Explorer's Club," signaled by on-screen text via a close-up on a plaque, again it is unclear if he is a real scientist or an adventurer. Coming after his role as Raleigh in *The Royal Tenenbaums,* viewers may feel there is a certain "carrying over" of characterization, that he too may be something of a charlatan, albeit a more charismatic one than Raleigh. The Explorer's Club is both a physical place, for drinking and egotistical gossip, and a metaphorical concept in which he is linked by association with other pioneering figures.

Zissou's reputation is definitely on the wane, signaled by the group of figures gossiping about him at the club, suggesting that there is an element of fickleness about his fortunes, akin to the lot of a filmmaker, rather than a scientist (as he says to Jane, "Man, I just don't have any stature anymore"). He is at the mercy of critical reaction to what he produces, rather than anything of intrinsic scientific value. He is like an ageing rock star in need of a big hit to restore his fortunes. This also feeds into doubts about the validity of the initial incident with the Jaguar Shark as it just seems convenient timing that he is presented with an opportunity to produce a dramatic film and silence his critics. He may initially seem paranoid, assuming the other members of the club are talking about him but as their description becomes more precise, it is clear they are. He is described as "creepy," taken to wearing an earring and accused of trying to seduce one of the speaker's 15-year-old cousins.

Like Chas in *Tenenbaums,* unaware that loss is a situation and an emotion felt by others, Ned explains that his mother killed herself to which Zissou responds, "You know my best friend got killed," which could be almost an instinctive mirroring of train of thought, but it does sound almost like playground boasting, and the apparent outpouring of affection may be a reflection of possible culpability for the man's death. Later, when Eleanor tells him about the death of their cat, he chastises her for the bluntness of her expression, suggesting that he is attracted to the pose of victimhood, but when Ned asks what kind of cat it was, Zissou snaps back, "Who gives a shit?"

The fact that he has an island of his own, even if it is not filled with state-of-the-art equipment, is further evidence that Zissou is more playboy than scientist (he magically produces a bottle of vodka from a pocket, which eases the news of the death of his cat). The island, with its absurd name ("Pesce spada" or "Swordfish") is more an affectation of an adventurous lifestyle that he cannot really afford than a serious scientific base (as we see later in contrast with Hennessey's high-tech setup). Since he confesses it was paid for by Eleanor's parents, it could even be said to be a remnant from their marriage since, strictly speaking, it is debatable whether he should be there at all. He admits that they also paid for "two of my worse movies," suggesting that he has many to choose from in this category and that he has been bankrolled for some time by family connections. On the other hand, it is also an indication of what directors have to do to get a film made. The montage of activities on the island includes Zissou holding a fish up, which might seem to have some scientific value until a killer whale leaps into the frame to snatch what we see now as a tidbit, casting Zissou as more ringmaster of a circus than serious scientist.

Ned is called out to the beach while it is still dark and finds Zissou and his crew, more of a film crew than maritime professionals. This is clarified by Zissou who describes the former careers of crew members, including a substitute teacher and a bus driver. Since Klaus puts the camera down in protest and shock, it is not clear at this point if Zissou is telling the truth or just insulting his crew. This remains a slightly open question until we see that Zissou's crew are neither expert filmmakers nor even particularly competent sailors. In the opening sequence, Santos, supposedly a safety officer, is seen tossing a flare into the sea and later, a crew member designated as "Instructor" eats a banana, while Ned nearly drowns behind him and has to be given mouth-to-mouth resuscitation. The sudden appearance of Hennessey's huge ship in the shot (conveyed by a 95-degree whip-pan), ludicrously unseen by the *Belafonte* crew, provokes Zissou to bark "cut."

There is some crossover between the eccentricity of Zissou and Murray himself, who also acted as court jester on set, trying to keep spirits up on a lengthy shooting process in often difficult conditions. On the DVD, Owen Wilson describes Bill Murray as displaying "not the most aerobicized build you've ever seen but that kind of is part of the charm." An obsessive baseball fan, Murray had a clause placed in his contract guaranteeing him a live feed of all Chicago Cubs' games at all times. However, for Murray, playing a troubled character was not an entirely positive experience. In accepting his Golden Globe for *Lost in Translation*, Murray (possibly only half-joking) referred to the *Belafonte* (and by extension the whole production) as "The Death Ship."

What Zissou definitely is, is a knowledgeable filmmaker. It is the production of an engaging and powerful film narrative that guides his actions far more than any scientific curiosity. At the same time as apologizing to Eleanor for not being at his best "this past decade," he is brutally flicking away a colored lizard from his hand. He has no patience with observing patiently and testing animal intelligence, looking in disgust at the screens and declaring, "I'm sick of these son-of-a-bitch dolphins." In a deleted scene, we see him negotiating a price with Hennessey for "a rat-tailed envelope fish," which along with Selick's special effect of a bizarre-looking creature, casts Zissou in the guise of freak-show host for whom wildlife is just commercial property.

However, even under duress, he remembers to say "cut," and when a difficult moment has passed his first words are to check whether something was caught on camera. He berates Klaus after he stops filming when Ned agrees to join the crew ("That was a goddamn tear-jerker"), making it unclear if he was acting with the camera in mind all the time or just responding swiftly afterwards. As soon as Ned regains consciousness after nearly drowning, a light-meter reading is taken right by his face. After the gun battle, his first order is "to get some cutaways of this miracle" and only secondarily to put out the fires on deck. The whole ultimatum delivered on deck is really a dramatic gesture for Jane's benefit as much as an attempt to win back the hearts of the crew. His self-obsession comes to the fore as he almost throws a childish tantrum at the fact she missed what he describes as "one of the most dramatic things that's ever happened on this boat." There is a sense of him striving for attention romantically, filmically, and even financially. He is made to look absurd by stating that events on deck were off the record and then complaining that she was not there to record them. She describes his reaction at her departure as "histrionical," but he claims that he gave her "a Goddamn showstopper up there," judging her by his own standards, imagining she will be impressed by material that can be used in a dramatic media production.

Like Anderson himself, Zissou takes photos during the production (here of Ned in front of a castle), as a personal record and for continuity purposes. Even potential catastrophe is packaged for entertainment, reflected in the absurdly named "Mutiny on the *Belafonte*" (standing in for *Bounty*). Where viewers might expect some eloquent speech to bind the crew together, Zissou asks rather plaintively, "Do you not like me anymore?" The whole voyage is literally an ego trip; it is their affection for him as clownish entertainer, which is seen as their motivation, not any pursuit of scientific knowledge. Despite the indignity of the state of his ship, underlined by the text on screen "Towed into Port-au-Patois Harbor," like the first appearance of Jack

Sparrow (Johnny Depp) in *Pirates of the Caribbean* (Gore Verbinski, 2003), Zissou maintains a ridiculous facade of pride in approaching land as captain of a ruined vessel, here ringing a bell and calling land ahoy. In a later scene, he stands like a man of substance, a tribal chief, in a speedboat (codriven in part by Santos, playing Friday to his Robinson Crusoe perhaps).

ZISSOU AND BAZIN

The title of Jean Thévenot's book, mentioned by André Bazin in *What Is Cinema?* (1967), is relevant here. *Le Cinéma au long cours* (*Filming in Far-Off Lands*) describes what Zissou is doing. Ironically, we witness an explorer, theoretically a figure concerned with making locations more widely known, exist in a largely existential, imaginative realm. Precise geography is not specified. Like Zissou, Anderson's next project is dependent to a certain degree on audience reaction to his current film. He, like the animals he is seeking and filming, is also fighting for survival.

In the sequence "Trapped in the Ice," we see a typical Zissou film, supposedly from his glory days. Dramatic on-screen captions initially suggest a sense of daring adventure, but what we see is Zissou attempting a ludicrous high dive into a small square of water cut in the ice. Like Murray himself, Zissou excels at maintaining morale on set and in this whole sequence, like a circus clown, Zissou entertains his crew and generates the material for the shot; that is, it is a film about *him*. He appears to hear a distress cry and subsequently saves a small furry creature, which apparently was thought to be extinct, but whether this is a real animal is unclear (it would seem unlikely that a ferret-like creature would live there). The elements of the action, a cuddly creature, a vulnerable baby, indeed a vulnerable species, all seem factors designed to ratchet up sympathy for Zissou. The quality of the film stock (like the opening film-within-a-film) giving colors a saturated look, the mugging to the camera, and the posed nature of the whole shot (based around a dive into a pool, rather than careful observation of a wild creature) all place this sequence generically within the home-movie subgenre. Indeed, the gratuitous thrill-seeking might have echoes of MTV's *Jackass* (2000–2002) or *Nitro Circus* (2006–present). Klaus's sad "that's what he used to be like" might imply that Zissou was a caring human being or a successful manipulative filmmaker. Zissou's dyed-blond hair and Klaus's ridiculous Mohawk suggest this was from a period of misspent youth, now looked back on with some nostalgia. Bazin talks of a decline of the exploration film "characterized by a shameless search after the spectacular and the sensational."[1] This is Zissou's whole raison d'être.

Bazin traces the rise and fall of sensationalism in exploration films, due logically enough to the difficulty and danger of gaining such footage. Added to this in more recent years should be the advent of whole channels, such as the Discovery Channel, devoted specifically to this kind of subject matter, largely robbing it of its power to surprise and shock. Bazin suggests one compensatory form developing, which we see in *Aquatic* "when the members of the exhibition and their reactions to the task in hand constitute a kind of anthropology of an explorer, the experimental psychology as it were of an adventurer."[2]

Bazin also notes the growth of exploration films as not existing solely in a commercial vacuum but usually accompanied by a series of lectures. In *Aquatic,* the pseudoscience still appears in the lectures, in the existence of an elitist club, and on a chat show, but this is more a part of a global marketing exercise to generate funds for the next expedition. Bazin traces the growth of "the provision of a cinematic report as an integral part of the expedition itself."[3] In *Aquatic,* the position feels reversed: the expedition exists to justify the film. Zissou's real elusive prey is the perfect adventure film, particularly as Bazin expresses it, "to imitate the inimitable, to reconstruct that which of its very nature can only occur once, namely risk, adventure, death."[4] Ironically, despite being constantly aware of whether the camera is running, Zissou misses Ned's sudden death, a piece of real unscripted drama.

If the Esteban incident is contrived, then it raises the ethical question to what extent it is acceptable to fake documentary footage for greater dramatic impact and, indeed, what constitutes real events. This possibly references Robert J. Flaherty's 1922 *Nanook of the North,* where material was enhanced for dramatic purposes (with actors made to carry anachronistic spears rather than guns and renaming the hero, really called Allakariallak, who is falsely described as dying from the harshness of his lifestyle).

The problem with seeing the film as an account of grief is not just that the film is peppered with gags and absurd names or the debatable status of Esteban's disappearance and of Zissou's real feelings for Ned but also in Bill Murray's persona, especially as seen in Wes Anderson films up to this point, associated with comedic roles, including a certain witty, world-weary cynicism. This could make the climactic scene in the submersible more touching as a sudden reality of the emotional truth of his character or it might seem devalued by the cheap fakery associated with his professional life. Zissou's redeeming feature is the honesty he displays towards his crew, admitting to hating dolphins, apologizing to his wife (although he is asking for money at this point) and his awareness of his own absurdity.

ZISSOU AS AHAB

MARIE: We're being led on an illegal suicide mission by a selfish maniac.

Zissou's overtly antiscientific motivation as an overbearing captain, seeking revenge on a large sea creature, seems to place him alongside Ahab in *Moby Dick* (from the novel by Herman Melville, 1851; filmed by John Huston in 1956) or Quint (Robert Shaw) in *Jaws* (from Peter Benchley's 1974 novel;

by Steven Spielberg in 1975). However, such parallels are easy to overstate. Dyalan Govender claims that Anderson uses Melville's device of lengthy sententious digressions, and there is something of Melville's use of lists and encyclopedic information thrown at the reader, but in Anderson's work this relates solely to his characters and explicitly *not* to the real world, the world beyond his fiction, which only exists tangentially as far as the film is concerned.[5] Moreover, for Zissou, the pursuit of the shark is really "a McGuffin" (Alfred Hitchcock's term for a motivational red herring), reflected in the supposedly scientific element of his work, which is purely a facade that allows him to chase women, live the life of a playboy, and *make films.*

Zissou does approach his role as filmmaker more as business than art, but the broader point that Govender is reaching for, that the hero's actions reflect the dominant capitalist culture, is too vague to be meaningful. Trying to read Zissou as Ahab just distorts the material. In the pirate rescue Zissou acts in a sudden manic manner, but this apparent sudden release of heroic potential is also ludicrous. In subsequently pursuing the pirates, Zissou's choice of the shortest course is based on laziness, and the idea that there are "unsafe waters" allows him to evoke pirate narratives of a bygone era. It is not like sailing into uncharted waters. The pirates themselves are not mentioned until they appear, and although they are clearly not swashbuckling figures with cutlasses, the ease with which Zissou single-handedly sees them off is a direct cinematic throwback to the kind of heroic fantasy figures played by Errol Flynn in such films as *Captain Blood* (Michael Curtiz, 1935).

Govender claims Zissou is "wracked with self-doubt, and extremely self-conscious," but Murray is more convincing at conveying the nonchalance of his character than emotional engagement towards Jane, Ned, or his crew about whom he seems largely indifferent (albeit in a comic sense).[6] Govender claims that Zissou's struggle is primarily internal, but we really do not see this. When Zissou starts to talk about himself, having embarrassingly stumbled down the hotel steps, this is just another stock cinematic character (the hero giving us a moment of sentimental reflection), not a scene of genuine revelation. To see Zissou's reaction to being challenged as a move to introspection overlooks gestures like throwing his earring away, which seem more like childish petulance (and a self-deprecating performance for Ned's benefit) at his brand being eroded. The track up to him as he makes this outburst and Ned's unspoken action in retrieving and returning the ring, which Zissou pops in his top pocket, might suggest Zissou is indulging in an act of egoism, a pose of injured pride. Similarly, to see Jane as the catalyst for Zissou's self-doubt overstates her role. She is little more than a cipher (primarily placed to deliver anachronistic chronological pointers, like her cumbersome recording equipment, her inability to swear, and her carefully pronounced English accent). We do not really have much in the way of objectivity surrounding Zissou. He shows us the club and tells us about Mandrake (who is merely a picture in a frame and cannot tell us himself what he thinks), and he is the director of films like *Trapped in the Ice* (and possibly even elements of the Anderson film we see—the crews are often mixed on board).

Zissou's own film version of the pursuit of the shark ends with a reprise of the official Team Zissou pose. However, less a mark of character change in Zissou, this is more a mark of Anderson self-consciously referencing Owen Wilson and his costars in *Bottle Rocket*. Anderson, and his proxy filmmaker Zissou, are able to place themselves and their fictional works at its center. To the last, Zissou and Anderson are self-aware makers of fiction. Govender claims that "the characters come to terms with their nature as characters in a film within the film narrative itself," but *they do not.*[7] Zissou keeps developing their parts, such as designating Klaus as group leader.

Unlike Royal in *Tenebaums,* Zissou is not really trying to be a father. He plays around with the opportunities this offers for rebranding (giving Ned new stationery) and toys with new names for himself and his son, but Zissou's feelings towards Ned are complicated by his awareness that this could be used on screen as "a relationship subplot" and observing, "There's chemistry between us." He seems to be without scruples in using any potential material, however personal, in the pursuit not so much of a mythical shark but a mythical film, the perfect documentary (which in his eyes would be as much about drama and emotional engagement as scientifically illuminating). Co-writer Baumbach, who also appears on the fake chat show, says he and Anderson would have referenced Moby Dick "had we read it" as a rebuttal to critics seeking to impose literary influences on their work.

Zissou obviously loses Ned, just at a moment when they might have started to build a new relationship, but Zissou is also mourning the loss of his wife, whom he still apparently cares about (and whom he seems to have a chance of regaining) and Jane, with whom he has tried to flirt and failed. His tears at the end are in part for the vindication of that loss, a store of grief about a series of failures that overwhelm him at this point. In *Broken Flowers* (Jim Jarmusch, 2005), Don Johnston (Bill Murray) is a midlife character confronted with the possibility of having fathered a son but unlike in *Aquatic,* Jarmusch has his hero pursue the possibility as part of a mystery narrative. Both narratives end with the paternity question unresolved, but Jarmusch allows Murray's character to show some glimpses of feeling which seem genuine (at the graveside of a former lover), a dimension which Anderson largely denies Zissou. The tears in the submersible come too late to make us doubt that this is just another self-aware cinematic moment, framed as a group shot to the camera.

5

Brief Encounter or Strangers on a Train? *The Darjeeling Limited* (2007)

> Train journeys are about possibilities. They denote a change
> in state. When you arrive, you are no longer the same
> person who departed. You can make new friends en route,
> or find old enemies...you might even discover love.
>
> —Vikas Swarup in *Q & A*

The Darjeeling Limited is a departure for Anderson in a number of ways. It is geographically and culturally the farthest from America and therefore deals with a sense of foreignness as much as it tells us about the culture of the three protagonists. It has also been seen as marking a new maturity in his filmmaking, deepening ideas from earlier work but still recognizable as a Wes Anderson film. The film is based around the notion of a journey, not with a specific destination in mind (not one that is openly revealed anyway), planned by Francis (Owen Wilson) as a means to explore an emotional goal, a bringing together of three brothers. Like *Bottle Rocket*, the three leads are all young men, one of whom is played by Owen Wilson, reprising his character traits of officious organization and the prickly need to be the leader of the group, and the film dramatizes notions of emotional illiteracy between family members, male ones especially. It is the journey rather than the destination that is important, and the picaresque plot only really takes off when digressions break from Francis's rigid plan.

THE HOTEL CHEVALIER

The Darjeeling Limited can be viewed perfectly well without *The Hotel Chevalier* as its prologue; it is not necessary to understand the plot or characters of the longer film. However, if it is so dispensable, it is questionable whether it just seems self-indulgent. Shot before *Darjeeling,* it is literally a prequel and serves as an appetizer, a short before the main feature. It has the feel of a very extravagant DVD extra or a trailer for the longer film (which in a sense was how the film was used, shown at Cannes). However, viewing the two together on DVD does allow the viewer to have a deeper understanding of the emotional background of Jack (Jason Schwartzman). The Hotel Chevalier is referenced in headed notepaper as Jack reads from his short story, suggesting it is a place of contemplation and rather earnest composition. The bathrobe we see him wearing here, looking a size or two too big for him, is what we see him wearing later in the main film; in other words, he has stolen it.

It seems that this meeting between Jack and his girlfriend (Natalie Portman) is more important for him than for her, although it is ambiguous whether his actions are solicitous or duplicitous. He walks around, tidying up a little, and later runs a bath (which we assume is for him but turns out to be for her). He puts music on and softens the light before opening the door to her. The exact chronology of the narrative seems odd. The presence of an MP3 player means it must be contemporary, but Jack's choice of music, which is thereby also motivated, Sarstedt's "Where Do You Go To," evokes a 1970s, slightly anachronistic and "cheesy" sense of style. The song seems central to the inspiration behind the film (Anderson played it in the background while reading an early draft of the script to Schwartzman over the phone).

The mise-en-scène contains some curious objects, such as what appears to be a mini-shrine, music boxes on the table, and art books and even brushes lying around, suggesting an artistic dilettante, but how much of this is just a pose by Jack is unclear. We do not know initially how long he has been in the room (he says he does not know exactly but more than a week). In fact, these are Anderson's own personal possessions. The film was funded by Anderson personally (no actors were paid), and Jack here is an Anderson surrogate, a character adrift as Anderson was after the failure of *Aquatic,* holed up in Schwartzman's Paris apartment. Jack's fiction is a thinly veiled biography, and his apparent inability to create anything original strongly implies that Jack needs a new life experience to import into his writing (a criticism that might be leveled at Anderson too).

The generic markers here are also ambiguous. If this is a romantic comedy, we have a fairly needy lover in Jack and few overtly funny lines. There are small hints of a thriller. The girl, when she comes in, puts a small package in a case, shot from directly above, suggesting perhaps that he is on the run (the lyrics mention a "painting that you stole from Picasso"). Her question "Are you running away from me?" suggests a chase narrative but the answer "I thought I already did" is closer to absurdist drama. Her statement about it being time for him to come home casts him in the light of a runaway schoolboy. Partly through the music, Jack's rather camp dressing gown, and the mixed generic markers, it almost feels like a Doris Day romantic comedy. However, there are darker elements here too. They start to undress one another almost as if by habit rather than passion. She has bruises on her arm and upper thigh, and the questions about sleeping with other people provoke a long pause before her negative answer. This has the feel of a relationship that has run its course. Her declaration "Whatever happens, I don't wanna lose you as my friend" is answered by "I promise I will never be your friend." The symmetry of the dialogue does not disguise the fundamental incompatibility of the two statements (and by implication, the two characters). In the main film, Jack reads the first part, but the other brothers are unaware of his "answer"; that is, it is left as a romantic gesture, not the crushing rejection, which it is here.

He invites her to see his view of Paris, and the volume of the romantic music rises on the soundtrack, emphasizing particular key lines like "I want to look inside your head." However, the overall impression is of two people at a distance, still drawn towards each other but unable to understand one another fully. In typical Anderson slow motion, Jack puts a gown around her as she poses naked and they walk out onto the balcony. However, the focus is of a side-on shot of the couple, not their view. Only after some seconds, do we pan 90 degrees to the view, another hotel opposite. Jack's invitation to see the view was delivered without sarcasm, and the implication is that this is the Paris of rich guests in hotel rooms.

A RACE AGAINST TIME?

The opening of *The Darjeeling Limited* is a strange sequence but perhaps only in retrospect. The speed of cutting and movement through the frame do not give us time to consider what we are watching. We might assume that initially we are part of a chase sequence or the meeting of an important narrative deadline, but actually both are false. Bill Murray's character plays no (substantial) part in the remainder of the film, largely forgotten as soon as we are on the train. It is simply a cinematic device to draw us to the train, acclimatize us to a non-Western culture, and perhaps showcase typical Anderson stylistic features. Character is not preeminent here as we do not know why he must reach this particular train. If anything, he seems more like a parody of a Westerner, desperate to escape an alien culture at all costs.

A zoom picks out a car racing through an unknown town. The urgent music, the speed of the car, and the narrow nature of the streets all suggest this is some kind of chase sequence. The outboard shot of the car, with the camera positioned like someone hanging out of a window, adds to the notion of speed and excitement as well as giving us more rapid shots of the car and the street as it flies by chaotically. A reverse shot of the inside of the car, showing a clock, confirms that this is a taxi, and there is a time pressure as we have a whip-pan to the driver. A head-on shot, from within the cab not through the windshield gives us a closer view of the unnamed passenger (Bill Murray) looking round anxiously. Tropes from chase sequences, such as a low angle of the car from behind as if from the point of view of a pursuing car, exaggerate the speed of motion through the streets. A variety of camera positioning—with shots through the back window, through the windshield, and a static side-on shot as the car passes—suggests the presence of a pursuer or an unseen deadline. Although this is not quite *The French Connection* (William Friedkin, 1971) or *Bullitt* (Peter Yates, 1968), it does still draw on the same range of stylistic devices, without any sense of parody.

It is only when Murray screams to the driver to stop that we realize there is no pursuer and the motivation is destination-related. This makes his histrionic behavior seem less justified and indicative of someone poorly organized or used to ordering social inferiors around (especially as he dashes off without paying). Handheld camera work, first from his point of view and then immediately behind him, continues this notion of headlong, chaotic motion. After only seconds at the ticket counter, he mumbles "that's my train," and we pan to him running out onto the platform, and as Murray comes closer to the camera, our point of view pulls ahead slightly and then cuts to a shot from behind the running man, suggesting he is not going to catch the moving train. Eventually, we have a close-up of a Darjeeling sign, the first nod to a sense of geography, and the camera comes closer to Murray's face and his eye level, suggesting the great personal importance to him of catching this train.

Suddenly, another runner appears in the frame and draws level. We have thus moved from a chase movie to a race-against-time scenario to a sporting contest. Like the climactic slow motion scenes of Hugh Hudson's *Chariots of Fire* (1981), the gradual appearance of Peter (Adrien Brody) creates an elemental, one-on-one race to a notional finish line. Brody gradually catches up and overtakes Murray, also throwing his case on board before reaching the train himself. The highly self-aware style suggests we should be reading this metaphorically (possibly as a man being replaced by a younger alter ego), but without more concrete information about who these figures are, we cannot do this and in retrospect the whole opening sequence just seems self-indulgent. On the train, Brody looks back in a mid-shot to see Murray slow down and give up, but Brody's expression gives us no clue whether he feels sorry for the older man or a sense of victory. If Murray was disorganized, what are we meant to think of Brody who arrives later? Are trains really so infrequent that dangerous maneuvers like this are necessary? Or does it reflect a desperation to escape a culture to which they feel they do not belong?

It provides a powerful contrast with the opening chase sequence in Danny Boyle's *Slumdog Millionaire* (2009), which also uses rapid cutting and a range of camera angles and film speeds but does so to introduce a key part of the film, the slums of Mumbai and the central relationship of the brothers Jamal and Salim. No such establishing motive is present in Anderson's film. The boys in Boyle's film are running for a very real reason: they will be beaten by security guards if caught; both men here have no real reason to run, and unlike the boys, show no pleasure in the chase. *Slumdog* is not stereotype-free. The Americans who are persuaded to leave their car and see the riverside scene only to return to find their car stripped respond with offers of financial help for the boy who is beaten for this crime (an action they cast as symbolic of American generosity). Later, in *Darjeeling,* there is another scene where the Whitmans run to catch and jump on a train, this time the three brothers, minus shoes in Francis's case. In *Slumdog,* we follow *the boys* who steal shoes from outside a sacred building (the Taj Mahal), but here the narrative is focused upon the Westerners-as-dupes.

Similarly, in *Darjeeling* the rooftop shot from the train provides a spectacular view of the landscape, but we do not see anything of the real owner of such a point of view, that is, those poorer passengers, traveling *on* the roof that we see in *Slumdog* (as in the scene where Salim lowers Jamal to steal food through a window before tumbling off the train). Anderson's film uses an Indian crew, but Indian actors only appear in minor roles such as Rita (Amara Karan) and the steward. It is resolutely a Western view of a mysterious, unknowable culture. Both films focus on relationships between brothers, but in Anderson's film, this lack of knowledge leads the brothers to see the country as purely exotic and in sensual terms, understanding nothing of the spiritual significance of what they experience, despite supposedly being on a "spiritual journey."

Slumdog also has a scene of characters trying to jump on a moving train but there, Jamal, Salim, and Latika are seeking to escape brutal gang boss Maman, who threatens to disfigure them; in other words, there is real jeopardy. Here, all the danger is self-created. Anderson's film even has a cow being passed on the street, a cliché that Boyle endeavored to avoid. The fact that Murray's character remains anonymous strongly suggests we view him as a type rather than an individual, a symbol of the forces of Western capitalism rushing through the Indian landscape, failing to understand much of what he passes through (and therefore he misses his train). Once on the train we have intercut forward and reverse tracking shots and small jump cuts between carriages as Peter makes his way down the chaotic corridor, until he finds his reservation, one of three. If he has a reserved seat, the rush to catch the train can only be motivated by his lack of punctuality.

A SPIRITUAL JOURNEY?

FRANCIS: You're the two most important people in the world to me. Never said that before but it's true.

It may represent an expression of genuine feeling but Francis's assertion here raises the question that if it is true, *why* has he not said it before. Jack later wonders "if the three of us could have been friends in real life." It is difficult to see Francis as possessing particular emotional depth or such a departure from previous Anderson protagonists. In particular, he shares several characteristics of Dignan from *Bottle Rocket*. His appearance in the doorway with a heavily bandaged head and nose suggests both his tendency towards the dramatic entrance and his paranoia about people talking about him, and of course, it is a reference to Dignan's preferred method of disguise. Like Dignan, he lets slip the occasional malapropism (expecting their mother wants to see them "on some primordial level").

As a control freak given to mapping out every detail of an experience, Francis could be Dignan's older self (or more uncharitably, reflects limited development in Owen Wilson as a writer or performer). They both like to make up (and subsequently change as it suits them) the rules of their mini society. As Francis says, "On a spiritual journey, it's crucial that we don't splinter into factions or not include somebody who has advice and may know better," that is, him. Like Dignan (especially in the deleted scene in the car where he asks Anthony and Bob if they are scared), Francis dramatizes their adventure by describing Jack's heart as "ripped to shreds" and his own face as having been "smashed." He is calling for collective unity here, but this very call is expressed by using confidences and secrets, which has precisely the opposite effect. As in *Bottle Rocket,* we have three characters who keep secrets from one another and show little sense of trust (Bob expects to be cut out).

Francis's vaguely defined and cliché-ridden notion of a spiritual journey is immediately undercut by the banality of his listing of their daily routine (including waking up and showering). The level of excessive organization of the minutiae of other people's lives suggests an emptiness in Francis's own and that he tends to "steamroller" others into submission by presenting them with a weight of detail that they cannot be bothered to resist, symbolized by the presence of a laminating machine, used to make the schedule look more professional, and an underling, Brendan (Wallace Wolodarsky), to carry out his bidding. Initially, this character is only talked about, suggesting that he may be a running gag, a reference to a hard-pressed individual who never actually appears on screen (Francis says with ominous finality, they "will never see him" but we do later).

His account of the accident that produced his facial injuries seems both self-dramatizing (Anderson using a slow zoom in on his subject here) as Francis enjoys retelling a fiction that places him at the center of the narrative. However, although this is literally "a near-death experience" as we realize later, it was really a failed suicide attempt, undermining Francis's claim that his first thought was of his brothers. Like Eli's crash in *Tenenbaums,* both using the same method, and Richie's wrist-slashing, we do not know if this is a serious attempt to take his own life. In the case of Eli, we see the crash at least, whereas it is only described here by a far-from-impartial source. He is a hypochondriac, claiming his ankle is broken, and he is not honest about the real object of their journey. Thus, like Zissou in *The Life Aquatic,* there is a

question mark hanging over the validity of the motivation of the main character, which makes sustained and unqualified engagement more difficult. Like
Zissou and Max, Francis wonders, "I don't know what else to do," but unlike
them (Max at least), this expression of apparent despair is really a calculated
piece of egotism. Like Dignan, Francis also enjoys the assumed status of family elder in loco parentis. "Did I raise us?" he asks, apparently rhetorically,
but his own answer, the afterthought ("kind of") hardly sounds like a ringing
endorsement. Later, Peter says he expected to be divorced without children
and muses "maybe it relates to how we were raised," in a pointed comment
at Francis's earlier fishing for compliments.

Jack's attempt to seduce Rita again under the watchful eye of the bearded
steward pushes the narrative tone towards farce. Even the fight scenes are
ridiculous as Francis and Peter struggle to find room in the cramped compartment and fall out of the shot. The juxtaposition of physical force with
dialogue as the characters shout they love each other, the pepper spray used
to break up the fight but which makes the situation worse, and the chase
down the corridor that ends with Jack running into a glass door are farcical
to the point of being cartoonish so that when we have the tilt shot up from
Jack's concussed point of view, it is not surprising that we have a star design
on the ceiling at that point.

The brothers live vicariously, modeling their actions on their cinematic
idols. As they walk through the carriage, Jack in his full-length yellow dressing gown, Peter in boxer shorts, and Francis in a white suit, twirling a cane
and his face bandaged, there is some of the absurdity of Billy Wilder's *Some
Like It Hot*'s cross-dressing here, especially when the train stops for no apparent reason and Francis declares, "I guess the train's lost." In a parody
of romantic train departures like the one in *Brief Encounter* (David Lean,
1945), Jack says his farewell to Rita, asking her if she was "maced too," but
she claims to have been crying. Like Dennis Hopper, Peter Fonda, and Jack
Nicholson in *Easy Rider* (Dennis Hopper, 1969), they sit round a campfire
and Francis tries to portray the letter from their mother in the guise of some
kind of adventure with an exhortation to "get high," but this feels more like a
beach party as they sit with their flaming torches. Francis's order to take their
feather, walk away from the fire, blow on it, and then bury it breaks down
almost immediately and has the feeling of a fraternity initiation rite than anything truly meaningful. Very close to the exchange between Ned and Zissou
about the Jack whales, Francis romanticizes the landscape, wishing he could
hear a distant train in contrast to the more prosaic response of Peter and Jack,
who agree it would just be "annoying."

Francis pretends to be wise but is probably the most stupid of the three,
mistaking Brendan's alopecia for being albino. Francis has to interrupt his explanation about his mother's strange behavior and his plan to rescue her with
"Why are you laughing?" apparently unaware of his own absurdity. Francis,
like the patriarch Tenenbaum's dismissal of Margot's plays, is insensitive to

the artistic expression produced by other family members. When Jack asks him if he wants to read his short story, Francis just asks, "How long is it?"

Jack's writing, like Eli's in *Tenenbaums,* seems little more than a cliché-ridden, thinly veiled autobiography. The very fact that he has to assert "the characters are all fictional" suggests precisely the opposite. Later, Francis compliments him that "you remember everything so clearly," recalling another uncomfortable car journey (to their father's funeral) in which Peter leaned out, possibly due to being so close to Francis. The use of the Whitman name suggests a classic American writer but also questions whether they deserve to be seen as part of such a lineage.

Tensions between the brothers surface quite rapidly. Francis insensitively blurts out that he does not think Jack's relationship will last, as if his opinion was asked for or needed and also suggesting that he does not *want* it to work. Like Dignan, he plans detailed schedules, never gives up, and attacks anything that threatens his assumed superiority in the group with almost Freudian jealousy, exacting a promise from Jack not to contact his girlfriend without checking with him first. Francis later expresses thinly veiled jealousy as Peter suggests that he was their late father's favorite. Seeing Peter shave with their father's razor provokes Francis to declare, "I just don't want you to get the idea that you're better friends with him than we are or something weird like that" (as if his outburst is any less "weird"). Francis becomes progressively more annoying, ordering for them, a long-established habit, representing his high-handed tendency to assert control over others, which antagonizes Peter in particular. However, later Francis allows Peter to order this time, and he asks for exactly what Francis had suggested, which shows Francis does know him quite well. Peter's habit of pushing up his glasses to take a closer look at something (Murray's departing form or the first sight of Francis) clearly annoys Francis, who takes them off, but it seems that they represent a bond with their late father, symbolizing a sense of sublimated grief. Jack notes, "I think he's still in mourning."

Paul telling Francis about his wife's pregnancy is the first example of the sharing or withholding of secrets (suggested by Anderson's use of a familiar two-shot but from behind). The dynamic of the three is constantly shifting based on an ongoing exchange of information, as when Jack tells Francis about Peter's baby. As soon as Paul goes to the toilet, Francis starts whispering to Jack about Paul taking things from their father that do not belong to him, such as his glasses and later his keys. When Francis is absent from a scene, Jack wonders what his face looks like under the tape and Peter wonders whether he is brain-damaged; in other words, two often gossip about the missing member of the trio. Jack reveals that he has his own ticket as he suspects Francis has a secret plan that he has not told them about. Peter subsequently reveals this to Francis, the first of a number of betrayed confidences, adding pressure on Francis to deliver visible results along with his rhetoric about their spiritual journey.

This element of sharing secrets creates a network of knowledge with only the viewer being omniscient and brings the narrative a step closer to farce. However, it seems as if real enmity is festering just below the surface of the narrative, rather than comic irritation as Peter declares, "I'm not staying with just me and him." Rather than a force of familial cohesion, ironically it seems Francis's overbearing nature acts as a catalyst in splitting the family further apart. Francis's ferreting through Jack's luggage, shot in a reflected image of a mirror on a cabinet door, reflects his duplicitous nature and the fact that he wants to hold the passports of the others, preventing them from leaving. The use of secrets and betrayals as turning points in the family dynamic is given dramatic energy by gossip. We see Peter and Francis watching Jack from a train window as he (in his ridiculous yellow dressing gown) calls his ex-girlfriend, expressing bitchy comments about the woman (whom they barely know).

THE RIVER

However, all of the absurdity of the familial relationships is lost in a brief action-related episode. It is tempting to see this as a family pulling together when real disaster strikes, but there is also an element of playing out a fantasy here. Like the pirate attack in *Aquatic,* here the riverside accident and attempted rescue shift the narrative into action adventure, in which the dysfunctional brothers can metamorphose into action heroes, putting their own lives at risk in order to save others. Casting themselves as heroes in this unfolding drama helps to give meaning to their empty lives. Here, there is more tragedy as a boy dies, but like Ned's accident, death is swift and apparently random. Each brother has a potential life to save, but Peter declares, "I didn't save mine." Anderson's style shifts here, as in *Aquatic* with hand-held camerawork, and as with Ned's crash we have a camera in the water, muffled sound perspectives, and a jump in continuity as Peter is seen behind the other two and then suddenly appears ahead. We hear a heartbeat come up on the soundtrack, increasing the dramatic power of the incident, and then the distortions normalize once the adrenaline of the scene fades.

There is a strange section of the film after this with awkward, long pauses as the brothers find themselves in an alien culture where they do not speak the language or know anything about how it works. Into a shot of field and goats, the father carries his dead son. Slower cutting shows us primitive dwellings, a courtyard with walls, which are blue, and rooms in deep shadow that house watching women. We are not given any more information that we can easily process than the brothers; we are given little sense of the geography of the house or whether the brothers are being greeted as heroes or villains. Slowly, the camera tracks back and down to reveal a group who offer them some tea.

The overhead shot of a baby in a cot makes a stylistic link with the shot of Peter's case, reminding us that he will soon have a baby too. The images of Jack sitting with children, threading flowers, Peter sitting with a baby on his lap, and Francis shaking another boy's hand are the closest the film comes to suggesting a connection between its Western protagonists and the indigenous population. This connection requires a catalyst of something beyond themselves, activating an apparently instinctive philanthropic impulse. The connection is informed by the brothers' understanding of loss and the difficulty of expressing grief (the camera tracks right to show a grieving father with his head in his hands with no musical accompaniment at this point). Peter wants the family to understand "I almost had him"; that is, it is important to him that they know that everything possible was done to save the boy (although it is unclear whether that is for their benefit or his). They are helped onto a crowded bus as tourists, but then this action is cancelled as they are invited to get off again to attend the funeral as honorary family members.

At the funeral, we see Peter, then Jack, then Francis walk out of a hut, filmed in slow motion, which in combination with the Kinks' "Strangers" gives this sequence the slight feel of a Sergio Leone western (which include ritualistic, slowed-down scenes around death and burial). The lyrics clearly audible here ("Where you going? I don't know. I've killed my time") reflect the slightly lost nature of the brothers' progress (captured in the refrain "So where do I go?"). Asked on the bus where they are going, Francis replies that they were on a spiritual journey but "that didn't really pan out." The brothers join the funeral procession, including tractors and cows and taxis decorated with flowers, but throughout we look on, as the brothers do, with little sense of understanding what we are seeing. As the father lays out the body of his son, he looks off-frame right and we cut to a three-shot of the brothers *also* looking off-right. At moments of emotional intensity, Anderson is prepared to break continuity conventions, implying the world is out of kilter here.

The detective report in *Tenebaums* gives us a condensed slice of Margot's backstory, but the following episode here constitutes Anderson's first attempt at a dramatic flashback, a scene from the past recalled in the present. We cut from the trio, here all dressed in white, to a parallel situation in Western culture, where they all wear black, which from the appearance of the brothers, we assume, is their father's funeral. All three are in the same positions but now Francis has no bandages; Jack has no moustache; and Alice, Peter's wife, is sitting opposite. Francis's insensitivity is still in evidence as her opening remark is "I can't believe you just said that." The need to pick up their father's car galvanizes the trio, setting them apart from Alice who drives on and suggests that at moments of particular crisis, they do stick together. When they confront the garage owner, extremely tight shots exaggerate panning movements to heighten the sense of tension, especially around Peter, whose act in pointing out the red car they want seems almost as much for the viewer's benefit as the owner's. There are a number of shots here directly to the camera but not addressing the audience directly as they are intercut with a reverse shot of the person being addressed, creating a symmetry of editing practice.

There is symmetry too in framing as momentarily, Jack is on the right, Francis is on the left, and Peter is in the middle of the shot, trying to drive the car away. There is a sense of distance, however, of the owner in the foreground, in sharp focus reflecting a stronger grip on the realities of the situation, explaining "Not ready, right?" and the blurred figures in the background, not accepting the facts of the situation. Sound perspectives add to this sense of distance with radio heard inside the office where characters discuss the car, the keys for which Peter strides in and just takes. There is something powerful in Peter's desire to see justice done for a dead man and the illogicality of trying to steal a car that will not drive. Francis looks out at the bizarre scene of Peter trying to start the car and Jack putting on his father's shirt. They push the car out of the garage and after a confrontation with another driver, whom they face down by standing together, they are forced to push the car back; in other words, their show of solidarity is focused on absurd or inappropriate actions. It is only when they reach India and rescue the boys that this unity has any valid purpose. Here, shows of aggression are hollow—Peter runs back into the garage and hugs the owner.

A graphic match takes us from the car with Francis's arm around Jack back to the graveside in India. However, this feels a little forced, and it is unclear if they really have gained anything spiritually from the experience. Anderson attempts to suggest spiritual growth in the trio, particularly their presence in the river with its overtones of a baptism and in supporting the father as he faints, but Jack still asks what they should pray for when they go into a temple. Paul shows Francis a tiny vest he has bought for the baby, suggesting he has come to terms with his responsibilities, and Francis gives him back the belt he had haggled over earlier. Francis is trying to rehire Brendan because he feels he treated him badly, but there is no indication that this would not just welcome in another period of hectoring and bullying.

Jack's pretensions are perhaps slightly easier to bear if it is paternal recognition that he is really seeking (as suggested by his rifling through his case to see if his father read his dedication) rather than just the trappings of literary fame.

JOURNEY'S END

PATRICIA: There are so many things that we don't know about each other, aren't there?

The plot as well as the literal journey of the brothers seems beset by false starts as first Francis will not give them their tickets; then Peter rips his up and as for Jack, he is still walking barefoot. Once they determine to find their mother, Patricia (Anjelica Huston), they find her surprisingly rapidly, but her appearance in the narrative is too late to make a major impact on the film, although we do see the potential origin of some of Francis's annoying habits in her teacherly taking of orders for breakfast and listing new shared rules. She seems to treat them still like children, with a good-night kiss, and expecting hands to be raised to express opinions, suggesting she has never really let them grow up (reflecting Huston's character in *Tenenbaums* and a possible reading of the lack of emotional development of the siblings there too). She is happy for exchanges to remain at the level of everyday domestic organization rather than addressing deeper concerns, like why she was not at their father's funeral. They cannot understand why she is staying there, and her claim that people need her at the nunnery is not really borne out by what we see. The brothers do need to grow up but simply abandoning her family is arguably not the most responsible way to achieve this. Being reluctant to meet her children who have traveled halfway across the world and then vanishing again just as suddenly makes it hard to attribute any substantial metaphorical significance to her role.

Patricia states that "maybe we could express ourselves more fully if we said it without words." However, the drive of the film is in exactly the opposite direction: they need to verbalize more openly what has been repressed and remained unspoken. The pan from one to another around the table just seems more like an amateurish attempt at a séance or telepathy. We then have a series of images, almost as if we have an update on the dramatis personae that we have seen so far, including the bearded steward holding what might be Peter's snake, Alice with the baby, Brendan sitting in an airline seat, and even Bill Murray's anonymous businessman looking off-frame right, appearing to look at the following shot, an animatronic tiger. The intended effect of the sequence may be that these are the individuals that the brothers are seeking to reach through prayer, but the images make more sense as snapshots for an omniscient viewer than a credible notion of a spiritual connection via prayer.

Again, soon after an apparent step forward, a moment of spiritual connection, Francis makes a suggestion, underlining that actually little has changed. His agreement is just another set of childlike rules, which he can enforce, including "We'll stop feeling sorry for ourselves," not so much on moral grounds but because "it's not very attractive." His sudden leaping up at breakfast and declaration that they should complete the peacock feather ritual again seems fairly arbitrary. Outside, against the spectacular backdrop of the hillside nunnery, we pan between the three figures. However, the potential dignity of the moment is undermined by Peter and Jack doing pseudo-martial arts moves, which look more like an amateur attempt at Tai Chi. In a three-shot, they all blow on the one remaining feather and put stones on it before we zoom out to a long shot from the plain below. Perhaps many ceremonies seem ridiculous when dissected and removed from their cultural context but that is the point here. Without any sense that their actions have meaning, the brothers look like Boy Scouts undertaking some kind of initiation ritual, improvised at random and signifying nothing (except their belief that it *does* signify something). If they are on a spiritual journey, it seems that orthodox Christianity is not what they are looking for as Anderson tracks along pews full of children, singing in English, up to the brothers unenthusiastically corralled together. In a country with such a rich and complex religious history and multiplicity of faiths, such simplification seems, at best, banal.

In the final section, Jack is working on a new story of which only the end is written ("He would not be going to Italy"). It feels a little like the chronological games of *Tenenbaums* and as if a character is currently writing the very story that we are seeing on screen. There is a reprise of the first scene with a similar setting and action in running for a train, characters, and even dialogue (Francis echoes Murray's line with "That's our train"). Even the rhythm of the shot selection echoes the first scene, running figures coming closer to the camera, the camera moving ahead, reverse tracking shots, the runners shot from behind, figures running out of and into the shot, and most obviously the gradual slowing of film speed. A key difference here, however, is the tossing aside of luggage, which has been assiduously carried through the whole film up to this point. The metaphorical significance of purging themselves of emotional baggage is clear enough. We have a similar mid-shot looking back at the station, but here instead of a defeated Bill Murray, we see their abandoned cases and some bemused porters who had been part of the chase to catch the train. There are further differences on the train itself, which has a red rather than blue interior. Peter puts his glasses away (suggesting his most intense grieving phase has passed); they are served limes by a different Indian girl and are marked once more with a red spot on the forehead. Francis tries to hand back the passports he confiscated, but the other two insist he hold them, implying a greater sense of trust between them.

As they go to smoke, French music comes up on the soundtrack (Joe Dassin's "Les Champs-Élysées"), linking the scene with *The Hotel Chevalier* prologue. One-by-one we see them shot through the barred window of the train and cut to a pan down the length of the train, almost mimicking the view of a passenger sticking his head out. This might be intended to suggest the liberation of a rebellious action but feels more like an extension of the previous journey than the beginning of a new one. They may have ridden into the shot earlier like the antiestablishment heroes of *Easy Rider,* but their narrative does not end in a challenge to the status quo. They threw their designer cases away *because they can always afford to buy new ones.*

CONCLUSION

> In the end, India is really the subject matter of the movie
> as much as anything else is.
>
> —Wes Anderson[1]

If this is true, then the film can really only be viewed as a failure. It tells us virtually nothing of the country but only of the narcissistic cultural obsessions of some of those passing through it. As Ben Walters notes, in effect, the film makes India "a picturesque backdrop to an American squabble."[2] The Whitman brothers watch a country of well over a billion people through a train window while talking largely about themselves or even while outside the confines of their cabin, portraying this alien other as threatening (with talk of a man-eating tiger). The idea that the innate chaos of India renders pre-conceived notions (symbolized in Francis's laminated schedule) redundant would only work if this tipped us into a different kind of film, where cultures genuinely clashed and learned from one another, changing those involved. This simply does not happen. We learn nothing about the cause of the Indian boy's accident (or even his name) and the Whitmans can only look on in incomprehension as events overwhelm them. The focus of their thoughts remains themselves and their interrelationship. Perhaps India could be said to be a catalyst in some change to their dynamic, but this might just have equally been achieved in America.

In *The Hotel Chevalier*, Jack's attempt to order food in broken French ("How do you say grilled cheese?") feels a little like the exchange between Vincent (John Travolta) and Jules (Samuel L. Jackson) at the opening of Quentin Tarantino's *Pulp Fiction* about what "a Quarter Pounder with Cheese" is called in Paris. In part it suggests Jack is trying to integrate with the culture but his choice of dish suggests he is firmly rooted in American culture. For Mark Olsen, "Wes Anderson does not view his characters from some distant Olympus of irony. He stands beside them—or rather, just behind them—cheering them on as they chase their miniaturist renditions of the American Dream."[3] The problem is that over time, we might well welcome some critical edge to his presentation of character. Later in the journey, Francis exhorts his brothers to "say yes to everything," but this is not necessarily the open-minded, carpe diem philosophy it might seem at first. In "President Gas," the indie rock band Psychedelic Furs used the same line to express the blandness of political corruption and lack of discrimination.

6

Where the Wild Things Are:
Fantastic Mr. Fox (2009)

Fantastic Mr. Fox provides Anderson with elements ideal for his filmmaking aesthetic: a fictional world entirely at his disposal, which he can control to a greater extent than any of his previous work, and the possibility to indulge fully his penchant for characters who are quirky yet engaging and pack the frame with detail so that it not only rewards repeat viewing on DVD, it almost demands it. At school, Anderson apparently produced a puppet version of the made-for-TV movie *Kenny Rogers as the Gambler* (CBS, Dick Lowry, 1980), suggesting an affinity with Ash and Max as a precocious high school misfit who was also different (as well as reflecting an interest in James Caan, the star of Karel Reisz's 1974 film, *The Gambler*).

Even in Anderson's first animated film, where actors' faces remain unseen, he still draws upon a familiar pool of performers, including Jason Schwartzman (Ash), Bill Murray (Badger), Wallace Wolodarsky (Kylie), Eric Chase Anderson (Kristofferson Silverfox), Michael Gambon (Bean), Willem Dafoe (Rat), Owen Wilson (Coach Skip), and Brian Cox (Action 12 Reporter). What is new is the presence of two overtly A-list stars, Meryl Streep (Mrs. Fox) and George Clooney (Mr. Fox). There are even minor roles for Roman Coppola (Squirrel Contractor) and Adrien Brody (Rickity the Field Mouse). Hugo Guinness (Bunce) is new to acting, but Anderson greatly admires the work of this artist, with whom he had worked previously, having provided some of the artwork for the main interiors for *Tenenbaums*.

DAHL ON FILM

Roald Dahl has several links to film, having scripted the Bond film *You Only Live Twice* (Lewis Gilbert, 1967) and *Chitty Chitty Bang Bang* (Ken Hughes, 1968), both best remembered perhaps for their fantastical elements (a climactic gun battle inside a volcano and a flying car respectively). His short story "Gremlins" (1943) created benign versions of the aircraft-destroying creatures that appear in the Joe Dante–directed segment of *Twilight Zone: The Movie* (1983). Many of Dahl's darker short stories for adults were dramatized on television as part of "anthology-dramas," both in the United States as part of CBS's *Alfred Hitchcock Presents* (1955–1965) and in the UK as part of Granada TV's *Tales of the Unexpected* (1979–1988). *Charlie and the Chocolate Factory* (1964) has been adapted twice—first by Mel Stuart as *Willy Wonka and the Chocolate Factory* (1971) and more recently by Tim Burton in 2005, reinstating the original title and casting Johnny Depp as the iconic Willy Wonka. The first version was originally based on a Dahl script but needed a substantial uncredited rewrite by David Seltzer.

The TV movie of *Danny the Champion of the World* (Gavin Millar, 1989; original novel, 1975) has some inspired casting, allowing Jeremy Irons the rare opportunity for an actor to act alongside his own offspring, Samuel (and with a small part for the boy's real grandfather, Cyril Cusack). In *Danny*, we have the opposite of Tenenbaum, an idealized father figure, present, gentle, loving. Danny's father is an extreme rarity in Dahl's work, an entirely positive father figure. Often, a child has to look outside his or her immediate family for adult understanding, such as the eponymous friendly giant in *The BFG* (1982) or Miss Honey in *Matilda* (Danny DeVito, 1996; original novel, 1988).

Henry Selick, who had worked with Anderson on *Aquatic* was the original choice to lead the teams of animators, but he could not take up this role and moved on to *Coraline* (2009), the world's first stop-motion animation in 3-D, but did recommend Mark Gustafson as his replacement. There is actually a very direct precursor for Anderson's film in Henry Selick's 1996 *James and the Giant Peach* (original novel, 1961), produced by Tim Burton, which also uses stop-motion animation to create a fully realized fictional universe, filled with fantastical animals based on creatures in the real world and using a distinctive orange-based color palette. The smoke effect and the emergence of Mr. Fox on the bike evoke Selick's earlier effect with the rhino, involving a gray cloud of dust, introducing condensed backstory via a flashback in which James's parents are killed by a rampaging animal. However, Anderson's choice of a 3-D effect, achieved by cotton-wool, made the effect particularly difficult to manage. Primarily for budgetary reasons, Selick uses some live-action sections (the opening 20 minutes and where James goes to New York), creating an effect similar to *The Wizard of Oz* (Victor Fleming, 1939) in taking the viewer into and out of a fantastical universe via frame story with live action and also anticipating the *Tenenbaum* conception of New York as a mythic place of the imagination. Selick had worked as an uncredited storyboard artist on *Return to Oz* (Walter Murch, 1985). As if practice for *Zissou*, *James* also includes some ocean scenes (particularly including a huge robotic shark with large, sharp teeth, very similar to Zissou's Jaguar Shark).

The attention to detail and—it is probably no exaggeration to say—the love devoted to stop-motion characters by their creators are attractive features to Anderson. To hear Selick talking of his approach is reminiscent of Nick Park talking about Wallace and Gromit as real entities. This is possibly due not just to the time involved in producing a few seconds of footage but to the fact that it is literally a hands-on process, in which animators must touch and mold their creations many hundreds of times every working day.

RELATIONSHIP TO THE SOURCE NOVEL

Anderson had actually met with Dahl's widow, Felicity (known to friends as Liccy), pre-*Tenenbaums;* immersed himself in the paraphernalia of Dahl's own house, Gypsy House, in Great Missenden, a small village in Buckinghamshire, England (even staying with co-writer Noah Baumbach for two weeks); and used exactly the same writing environment (a shed out in an orchard). He carefully photographed these interiors and recreated, for example, the domestic space in the Fox home and Badger's office. In much of the promotional material for the film, Anderson plays up the links between his film and Dahl himself, thereby giving it creative and critical legitimacy, as if he is Dahl's logical heir. Anderson researched early drafts of the story with Dahl's own sketches (where he found ideas about an alternative ending in a supermarket) and claims to have been inspired by the illustrations, such as the single tree on a hill for the Fox residence, of Donald Chaffin, who worked with Dahl in the early part of his career. Most of Dahl's works were illustrated (in the mid to later part of his career at least) by the distinctive style of Quentin Blake, and perhaps animation is the only cinematic form to do justice to the imaginative elasticity of Dahl's creations.

The original story of *Fantastic Mr. Fox* (1970) is fairly slight, and the script by Anderson and Baumbach adds considerably to the basic material, to the point where this is far more their tale than Dahl's. The basic pursuit of a fox family is there, but in the book this is at the beginning and is part of an ongoing vendetta against piecemeal robbery rather than in the film where the robberies come first, thereby justifying the digging out of the family. The effect is to retain the incompetence of the farmers but actually justify their actions a little more. Whereas Dahl's hero uses cunning to escape an unprovoked attack, Anderson's film has a more humanized protagonist suffering a midlife crisis, motivating a slide back into a life of crime for *his* benefit, not that of his family. Anderson changes the attacks on the farms, which Dahl describes as miraculous tunneling adventures to over-ground break-ins, that is, humanizing Fox's methods. Fox is given a backstory as an apparently reformed thief; a more testy relationship with his wife; a troublesome dynamic with his real son Ash (greatly fleshing out Dahl's outline), who feels frustrated at an apparent interloper (Kristofferson) to that role; and a comic sidekick, Kylie, who is embraced as part of the family by the close of the film.

Dahl's tale is expanded with Ash's final idea of retrieving his father's tail as a means of proving his bravery and gaining paternal recognition, and the flooding of the burrow with cider as well as the whole meta-textual commentary of events aboveground by the TV crew. Mrs. Fox is given more depth (in the book, she is painfully passive), defending her family against Rat by wielding a chain nunchaku-style. Earlier she delivers some home truths to her husband, expressing regret that she married him (rather than displaying the hero worship of the novel) and even giving him a sharp slap, which draws blood. Her steely "if what I think is happening, is happening, it better not be," reflects a more feisty character than in Dahl's story (so that avoiding her wrath becomes one of Fox's biggest obstacles). There is even the semblance of a sexual backstory. Kylie is shocked that she might have been "the town tart," but Fox is more forgiving ("She lived. We all had"). Sexuality seems to also be part of the animal kingdom, albeit only glimpsed here (and in her regular pregnancies). That said, there is still a conservative model of gender roles here, which is close to Dahl's original story. The film may lack the sense of admittedly sometimes cloying family closeness insisted upon in the book. Dahl's Mrs. Fox cries easily, is too weak to continue digging, and during a respite in the digging, far from telling him off and slapping his face, celebrates his genius and reminds everyone that he is "fantastic." However, in the film, she still brings Fox's coffee to him while he reads the paper and is the one left to deal with issues of family discipline. We see her vacuuming, and later she is sent out of danger to be with the other animals.

The structure of the film, as with other Anderson films, uses a prologue but here it is incomplete, and it is only some way into the film that we have the mystery explained of how Fox and his wife escaped from the trap he stupidly activates at the beginning. The revelation, described rather than shown, that they just dig their way out, is quite an anticlimax, or it would be, except this narrative hook has been all but forgotten in the scheming and robberies that occupy the first half of the film. It is important that Fox is confessing to Ash—it is a father-son moment, but this is only forced upon him in the prospect of imminent death, not by suddenly becoming honest.

There are some specific relationships to Dahl's story that have been overlooked.

Quentin Blake, Dahl's illustrator for at least the last 15 years, has a picture on almost every page, meaning that every narrative episode already has a visual representation. Furthermore, some of Anderson's imagery is already explicitly in Dahl's text. Bunce is described as "a kind of pot-belied dwarf," and the line from Badger's description is also directly taken from the narration ("He was so short his chin would have been underwater in the shallow end of any swimming-pool in the world").[1] The titles of some narrative sections (such as "The Shooting") relate to specific chapter headings. There is occasional comic book style in the film such as when Fox emerges from his den. In Dahl's book, Fox's detection of the farmers is by means of a tiny rustling sound and a glint of moonlight on a gun barrel, but here we cut between his twitching ears, three trees (visually matched with the farmers) showing a change in wind direction, and the three products associated with each one appearing on screen, like a thought bubble.

Elsewhere, there are specific changes with characters who are given much greater depth. In Dahl's version, Fox's children are not even given names, let alone distinctive looks or characters. The first page of Dahl's book directly tells us that the farmers were rich but this may not seem obvious in the film as they each live such mean, narrow lives. It makes Fox's use of the term "poor" in the film seem slightly contrived and makes him seem too bound up in his own cleverness. Dahl's Rat is scared off by Fox baring his teeth, and although he has the same personalized jar of cider on the top shelf, he remains a minor character, whose opposition does not go beyond petulance (although his shrieking "Bandits" at them may have given Anderson the idea for the masks).[2]

The script includes a number of gags about language. There is some literalism here in that Fox assumes it was ancient Romans who gave animals their Latin names (hence why he suspects opossums do not have one). Exactly why the wolf would know French (unless we are to read the landscape as Canadian) is a little unclear, and Wolf's explanation that the wolf speaks neither English *nor Latin* (a dead language) betrays his ignorance in his show of knowledge. On the other hand, Wolf's knowledge of French is no more logical (throwing "Comme ci, commme ça" into his conversation at breakfast), except as stereotypical shorthand for a character who is suave and sophisticated and a small nod to Anderson's own Francophile tendencies. Dahl refers to Bunce "cursing the fox with dirty words that cannot be printed."[3] In the film, there is a little language game with taboo terms replaced with "cuss" peppering the narrative in dialogue and even appearing as graffiti sprayed on walls.

Although some of the wordiness of the film, especially the overt analysis of motive between Badger and Fox, may strike a false note, there is a similar narrative pause in Dahl's story. Dahl has Badger ask Fox about the morality of stealing, but it should be said that Dahl's version is more convincing as his Fox is talking about instinctive, natural behavior, whereas Anderson's narrative imports notions of egotistic human psychology in the style of a midlife crisis. The film is weakest where Fox starts talking about his motivation ("I guess I wanted everyone to think..."), which is unnecessary and cliché without any sense of parody. The book has an element of compromise about the ending, too, with the animals, although set to be well fed indefinitely, having to live a life entirely below ground. In a sense they make a Darwinian leap, surviving by modifying their behavior. In Anderson's film, they survive, but as much due to the commercial needs of narrative and an adult-paying audience expecting an element of self-improvement in their heroes in line with the American Dream.

INFLUENCES

There are influences from other works here, both literary and filmic. Some are minor, like the meeting at windows between Kylie and Fox, which has a slight touch of Mark Twain's *The Adventures of Tom Sawyer* (1876) in arranging an illicit adventure unknown to their family. There are some echoes of Kenneth Graham's *Wind in the Willows* (1908), an animal story set originally in the English countryside and featuring a rat, mole, and badger among ensemble roles. Although there is no Toad, Mr. Fox has some of his hubris and a similar attraction to criminal scheming, and there is a similar focus on food and communal, celebratory feasting. Badger also acts as a voice of moderation here, but Mole is less timid (with his keyboard-styled suspenders), and Rat is made into a villainous turncoat. Rat's death however is one of the high points of the film in which a Hollywood cliché is reinvigorated by the juxtaposition of pseudo-poetic dialogue ("he's just another dead rat in a garbage pail behind a Chinese restaurant") with the action of Fox, shot in low angle, gently slipping him into the sewer like a burial-at-sea or a crossing of the River Hades in the underworld. The cliché of a dying man's final words become more comic by a tolling bell and the term "redemption" (he reveals Kristofferson's location) followed by Rat's wish for cider and his death signaled by a shift to a different eye pattern (here a cross), related to but different from Kylie's vacancy (who earlier mumbles "apple juice" with a spaced-out expression).

There are evocations here of Yuri Norstein's stop-motion animation *Tale of Tales* (1979) and *The Hedgehog in the Fog* (1975). In particular, we see a related focus on animal characters, a narrative involving fear and wonder, and a juxtaposition of an animal's point of view (usually expressing naive wonder) and the man-made world. There are key differences. Norstein's figures do not speak; he is using drawings rather than puppets; and there is a strong political subtext to *Tale of Tales* in particular. However, he also uses a powerful score, featuring preexisting music (classical rather than popular), and there is a similar focus on small, furry faces (a wolf cub in particular, rather than foxes, but the look is similar), held in close-up, also looking straight out at the camera, emphasizing eyes that are big and particularly expressive.

For the attentive Anderson fan, there are plenty of references to his previous works.

Ash sports an improvised cut-out sock for a bandit hat, which does not really disguise him and is absurd in its amateurishness, reminding us of Dignan's nose plaster in *Bottle Rocket*. This aspect of the film's styling, as well as its generic linkage to Bond/caper movies, is also played up in promotional material, on DVD covers, for example, with characters all posing with bandit hats. *Rushmore* is evoked through the casting of Owen Wilson as Coach Skip (brother Andrew had played Coach Beck in the earlier film). We have a shot from outside an elementary classroom echoing Miss Cross's, a final scene of harmonious dancing as well as Blume's line during the interval about how that particular narrative will end being replayed here when Mrs. Fox states, "This story is too predictable" to which Fox replies, "Really? What happens in the end?" This is Anderson the director coyly playing with our expectations. Generically, we might expect a happy ending in a family-orientated, stop-motion animal story but with the animal/human tensions foregrounded, we might still be surprised.

Like *Tenenbaums*, we are explicitly given a shot of a source novel (here a real one), underlining the explicitly literary heritage and credentials of the film. The graphic match from the birch tree on the cover with the one revealed as part of Anderson's set stresses his fidelity to his source text (and his undertaking meta-textual research in finding the real tree, now destroyed, on which Dahl based his setting). Kristofferson under the table is a little like Margot and Richie in *Tenenbaums*, creating their own private space in the museum as runaways or later as adults in the tent. From *The Life Aquatic*, we have a high-angle shot from within a helicopter, past the feet of the pilot, and the newspaper advertisement, held up by Mr. Fox and then lowered to reveal the actual house for sale, is like the emergence of the real *Belafonte* from behind a picture. Both feature a budget-sapping, spectacular escape scene with explosions. The group shots of the Foxes, plus Kylie, emerging from a drain cover into the supermarket, reprise the group shot in the submersible, and Fox seems to know Latin, naming the animals (Eleanor's job in *Aquatic*).

Darjeeling-like trains (themselves references to extreme wide shots of a train running through the landscape in Satyajit Ray's 1955 *Pather Panchali*) are seen in wide shot bisecting the middle of the frame, both at day and night. There is a slight feel of Nic Roeg's *Track 29* (1988) here, also based on the work of a British writer (Dennis Potter), featuring problematic paternal issues and more precisely trains used as toys and as real objects within the narrative. It is a touching moment when Kristofferson's sobs momentarily temper Ash's youthful anger, and he wordlessly climbs down from his bunk bed and puts the train set on (in a still darkened room but with lights on the toy). This of course does not stop him from making cruel comments about Kristofferson's ill father (sounding very like Chas in *Tenenbaums* at this point) or spreading false rumors about him later. He has just found someone who, in some ways, is weaker than himself and bullying is a rare and very tempting option.

Anderson's film here is packed with allusions to other movies, specifically and generically. There are elements of war film in the design of the farms, with military-style hangars, suggesting the cruelty carried out on those creatures kept there, and the alarm raised at Bunce's farm features wailing sirens and searchlights strafing the yard. Fox's final escape over Bean's fence via a motorbike jump, explicitly using a handily placed stunt ramp, evokes Steve McQueen in *The Great Escape* (John Sturges, 1963). Ash's miraculous run over various obstacles, creating his own whackbat en route and releasing the rabid dog, all while under gunfire, has something of *A-Team* fantasy. The motorbike and sidecar sequences feel a little like Wallace and Gromit in

A Close Shave (Nick Park, 1995), but here Anderson uses the expressionist device of riding on a road like a forward-spinning globe with a wide-angle lens to give the impression of headlong speed. The passage of Mrs. Bean (Helen McCrory) down the cellar steps with attendant echoing sound effects is also strongly evocative of Nick Park's *A Grand Day Out* (1989). Bean's gunplay, posing with two pistols across his chest, links him with gun-toting gangsters or a John Woo action hero. He is a crack shot, hitting out the lights, but the destructive illogicality of the action is reflected in his sinister shining of his torch in the faces of the others, expecting their assent in the manner of a brutal interrogator. Badger does describe him as "possibly the scariest man currently living."

Clooney's dialogue is closer to the speedily delivered, wisecracks of screwball comedy (as in the opening exchange in which Fox persuades his wife to take "the scenic route"), but his charm is sometimes purposely undermined by the visuals, such as his excuse to Mrs. Fox that Ash is only wearing a bandit hat to keep his ears warm, when his ears are not covered by the mask. As one who plans the audacious crime of a lifetime and who is drawn into elaborate theft as a way of life, he can draw on his work as Danny Ocean in Steven Soderbergh's *Oceans* franchise (2001, 2004, and 2007), based on the original Rat Pack version with Frank Sinatra (Lewis Milestone, 1960), although in Anderson's movie there is little sense of building a team and more familial introspection. There is something of the caper movie in Fox's scheming, lack of apparent bloodshed, and the group synchronizing watches.

Rat's stock dialogue is appropriate as he is casting himself as a movie hero here—his dialogue ("You'all trespassing round these parts") in pseudo-southern dialect and his overly macho gestures (putting out the match with his tongue) are straight out of Western cliché (as well as gangster and prison movies). At the same time, in his somersaults and body posturing, finger clicking and waving of a flick knife, his alcohol-addled brain is positioning himself as a hero from *West Side Story* (Robert Wise and Jerome Robbins, 1961; adapted from Stephen Sondheim and Leonard Bernstein's 1957 stage musical). Shot in very low angle with limbs splayed akimbo, he looks like a goalkeeper about to face a penalty. Unfortunately, like Zissou, Dignan and to a lesser extent Max Fisher, Rat cannot live up to his own image of himself.

Some of the allusions are to specific movie scenarios. Fox's emergence from the sewer into an apparent ambush at a given time has echoes of *High Noon* (Fred Zinnemann, 1952), although the meeting time is brought forward to 10:00. In facing down Bean, there are overt echoes of Sergio Leone's spaghetti westerns, not only in pitting a single hero against a superior number of armed men but in the score, which earlier uses a distinctive whistling melody in the fight with Rat and is translated here to a more swelling orchestral theme. Fox's climactic listing of wrongs done him before demanding back his tail (now a necktie) with progressively closer cuts on each one, clearly evokes Russell Crowe in the final battle in *Gladiator* (Ridley Scott, 2000).

The spectacular back-lit waterfall, casting Fox almost in shadow, held in long shot, suggesting a hero isolated and alone, has the absurd but strangely touching juxtaposition of a sewer with an allusion to a key romantic scene in *The Last of the Mohicans* (Michael Mann, 1992). There is a moment of sentimentality as Fox admits to "falling off the wagon," and alternate extreme close-ups of Mr. and Mrs. Fox, looking directly at the camera, create a cliché romantic moment.

Elsewhere, the allusive quality is more tonal. In the scene with Kristofferson standing next to Agnes at the punch bowl, Ash's attempt to stand up to what he sees as Kristofferson's role as a family imposter feels like a scene straight out of a Woody Allen movie. Ash cannot sustain his pose of macho confrontation and almost immediately backtracks into insecurity and apologies ("Was I a little rude to Agnes ?...I'll apologize in a minute"). Ash's New York accent (via Jason Schwartzman), his diminutive size, and the content and setting here (insecurities about family relationships in a social gathering) evoke a stock Allen character. Earlier, some of Allen's more typical wit and intelligence come through in Ash's observation, to counter Kristofferson's complaints about Ash's spreading false rumors, that he should worry more what people think about his lengthy yogic humming.

MISE-EN-SCÈNE

Bean sees Petey "making it up as he goes along," as symptomatic of "weak songwriting" and that he "wrote a bad song." Apart from providing humor, this is ironic as improvisation is an impossibility in animation and, secondly, it is Anderson's attention to precise detail that largely precludes this. The line feels like it could almost be Anderson's own as a demonstration of what can happen without careful planning. The scene has little reason to appear where it does. Bean appears out of the dark and walks back into it after delivering this stand-alone gag.

The level of detail is forensic, such as Fox's miming of drinking champagne and throwing the glass, complete with sound effect, Ash's ear twitching when he gets angry, or actions by minor characters in nonspeaking roles, like the frenetic whackbat players, mole's break-dancing as part of the ensemble performance, or Ash's slight rolling of his eyes as Mrs. Fox takes her husband to one side to give him a piece of her mind. A personal favorite of this writer is Badger listening to his recording of the children's song about the farmers and giving a tiny shrug followed by a slight movement in time with the music. In a film with 120 sets and over 100 versions of Mr. Fox alone, nothing appears by chance (apart possibly from the sound of a boat on a dialogue recording, incorporated by Anderson as an on-screen plane). The movements of the animals in the cider flood shift non-naturalistically between being in synch and all individual, dramatizing the opposing poles in their nature. Anderson achieves the semblance of movement by his animators blowing on substances like fur and grass between takes. His usual color palette is stripped out. Gone are all semblances of blues and greens and in their place a range of glorious, autumnal orangey-browns (appropriate for a U.S. release at Thanksgiving 2009). In this respect, Mrs. Fox with her landscapes is a stand-in for Anderson, recreating the look and color scheme of the set. This makes exceptions, like the appropriately named blueberries, seem extremely blue.

The whole whackbat game does create the means by which Ash proves himself in the climax and prepares us for the pinecone grenades later, but it is really a digression (signaled by the fact the sequence was created by a separate lead animator, Brad Schiff). This feels like Anderson's version of Harry Potter's Quiddich, parodying essentially simple games like baseball or cricket, made unnecessarily complex by terminology and statistics and largely unknown outside their most fanatical fan bases with a bat that looks like a medieval weapon of war with nail-like protuberances on its edge.

Rather than being a cold experience in a recording studio, all but some lines of Rat and Mrs. Fox were recorded on an isolated farm in Norfolk, Connecticut, where Anderson took the cast and helped them really bond with their characters and each other. Sound was also recorded in a New York apartment and beside an Italian lake. Anderson often insisted the cast perform the supposed action just prior to or actually during the delivery of a line. Thus, George Clooney jumps up and down on a stationary motorbike and shouts lines over his shoulder or rolls over before delivering his trademark whistle and click. This method-acting approach produces dialogue that is sometimes breathless or overlapping but the more realistic for that (which ironically serves to counterpoint the patently more fantastical elements in the style of the film).

WHERE THE WILD THINGS ARE

MR. FOX: Who am I, Kylie? ... Why a fox? Why not a horse, or a beetle, or a bald eagle? I'm saying this more as, like, existentialism, you know? Who am I? And how can a fox ever be happy without, you'll forgive the expression, a chicken in its teeth?

KYLIE: I don't know what you're talking about, but it sounds illegal.

The film modulates, mostly successfully, between adult and child audiences, and the bubble of grown-up rhetoric is never allowed to grow too big before some kind of comic deflation. The characters drop back into their animal natures whenever they eat, snarling and biting aggressively, just to remind us of the traditional tension underlying anthropomorphic representations of animals in animation. This is a little overdone, repeated in Fox's first meal, the attack on Bunce's farm, and the final scrabbling from supermarket shelves. However, there are other small signals of a reversion to an instinctive nature, including Fox running up and off the walls twice, under pressure to come up with an escape plan, when the farmers first start to dig them out (Dahl portrays Fox in a more human light, sitting still, eyes closed, almost in a Kristofferson-like trance). Spitting carries some of this too but is more ambiguous, shifting between a natural animal trait and something human etiquette designates as antisocial. Ash does this after being told off but later Mrs. Fox does this too and then at the end, Ash describes his spitting in a list of his faults. The only prime animal feature is aggression in the argument between Badger and Fox as they circle one another, shown from each other's subjective point of view, and windmill their arms ridiculously. As in the scorpion fable, there is a tension between learned, civilized behavior and their instinctive natures. By implication, foxes are made to steal and plan stratagems that will put their lives in danger.

Mr. Fox is a little smug, as befits the traditional fox character in classical literature, such as Geoffrey Chaucer's *The Nun's Priest's Tale,* in which a fox is tricked into opening his mouth, allowing a chicken to escape. It is ironic that Mr. Fox counsels his family to "Be aware," oblivious that at the same moment, his wayward son is engaging in a dangerous freelance mission to recover Fox's tail. The repetition of the term "wild animals" in the dialogue and the whole theme of being true to one's own nature seem to bring the animal versus human dichotomy to the fore. However, there is actually a significant movement towards humanization, from Mrs. Fox's first appearance (apparently returning from a visit to the doctor for a stomach bug). Anderson may rename his tape players "Walk Sonic," but removing the word "man" does not make it any less human-oriented. The figures not only speak (fairly standard for animal stories) but use very self-aware dialogue (such as Badger's commiseration with Fox about the loss of his tail, which feels more like counseling for impotence), featuring irony, self-deprecation, and registers associated with certain human professions (such as real estate agency). This self-awareness is too knowing to be effective on occasion, such as Mr. Fox declaring, "over my dead body" to be qualified by his wife, "You'd be dead too in that scenario."

Fox's egotism is distinctly human. He vainly refers to his newspaper column in self-deprecating tones, waiting to be contradicted, and curiosity and a desire to impress his wife get them both caught in the cage that falls on them at the end of the prologue section.

Like Zissou's challenge to his crew to join him on his self-styled revenge mission, Fox declares about Ash that "I'm going to find him and I'm going to bring him back." His overt favoring of Kristofferson (not something purely imagined by Ash) is underlined when Ash is sent back from a raid and his rival subsequently welcomed as an *invited* participant. Ash's teen rebellion might seem unjustified from his opening excuses of why he cannot go to school, routinely dismissed by his mother, Ash finds himself displaced in sport (he is literally substituted for Kristofferson), romantically (he expresses some Dignan-like jealousy, calling his lab partner, Agnes, "disloyal" in being attracted to his rival), and as his father's heir (Coach declares, on watching Ash, "He really is your father's nephew"). Ash's angry reaction, ear flicking and all, seems reasonable. The pressure that Fox's apparent perfection creates is represented by his intimidating trophy, which is non-naturalistically literally present outside by the game itself. He seems to have a self-image akin to Hannibal (George Peppard) from the *A-Team,* but his master plans are not quite as flawless. He has an overly complicated plan to break into Bunce's chicken house, and he does not anticipate the electric fence or have a means to escape back over it. Fox's egotism (on being confronted by Badger, it is clear he had given no thought to the consequences of his actions on the other animals who live nearby) still persists even to the end where he literally stands on a soapbox to deliver his homily. Self-aware parody on behalf of the filmmakers aside, the fact remains that, in content, his speeches articulate pure Hollywood sentimentality.

Physically, the foxes stand upright on legs that are slimmer, taller, and significantly longer than in previous illustrations in Dahl's book. Their facial expressions, often shown in close-up and looking straight out to the audience, convey human emotions. Doubt, guilt, and love are arguably impossible in the animal kingdom, as well as related actions, such as Fox romantically stooping to pick a flower for his wife or for a split second, putting an item of clothing over a puddle during their opening robbery. They perform physical actions from the human world, such as dancing, riding a motorbike, or diving without creating any splash, or animal actions are given a human connotation, such as the baring of teeth, which is not a sign of aggression here but of embarrassment, such as the moment before Fox is swept away by the flood of cider.

There is a shifting dichotomy between the animal and the human and between artifice, which draws attention to itself and that which does not. Dahl does not duck the cruelty of the natural world, describing (albeit in one brief sentence) Fox's action in killing the chickens (as well as later allowing Fox's children to swig some cider). This is reflected obliquely as Kylie's squeamishness about killing the chickens is conveyed by Fox disappearing off-frame to dispatch the animals, represented by a few falling feathers and the snarl we have heard before in connection with food. Kylie feels more like a contemporary vegetarian ("That's so grisly. There's blood and everything"). However, Anderson also approaches head-on a key difference between sentient life and its simulacra, which is how you depict eyes, traditionally seen as "windows on the soul." As the farmers dig down to break into the foxes' ceiling, all five main characters are shown in a tight, high-angle close-up, light apparently dancing on their eyeball. The glazed expression which overcomes Kylie at regular intervals, signaled by a jump cut to different beads for eyes, is not explained at first, and the low-tech artificiality of the image and the held nature of the shot challenge us to understand it. By the time Mr. Fox reacts in this way too (but manages to make a hand signal) when he escapes the rabid dog, we realize that it is the way to express a shared rather than idiosyncratic reaction of surprise or incomprehension. Like the notion of accepting diversity connected to Ash's need to be recognized, there is the sense here of everyone's need just to freak out from time to time (although Kylie does it more than most). Hence the shared gesture of whirling both hands next to one's head to express the inexpressible, what being different means (but also in slightly different ways each time, as if to exemplify the point). Fox starts this in describing Ash but in quite a dismissive (and possibly even derogatory) way, followed by the real estate agent in referring to Kylie, then Mrs. Fox in describing Mr. Fox ("him especially," pointing at her husband without looking), then the Beaver bully in denoting Ash as "a wet sandwich," and finally, Ash does this too in describing himself after rescuing Kristofferson.

There is the Bond-like wisecracking, long associated with that particular franchise (particularly important to keep adult viewers engaged, alongside their younger charges), pointing up the absurdity of sophisticated dialogue coming from animals, such as Mrs. Fox's "Am I being flirted with by a psychotic rat?" The appearance of Kylie's titanium credit card seems like a randomly placed gag, out of place up to this point, as reliability has not featured in his character (or indeed later, forgetting the blueberries). He seems dominated by illogical fear of wolves and thunder and slow to understand what is going on (adding a "Let's eat" to Fox's imaginary after-dinner speech). If we are supposed to see him as a symbol of steady reliability and believe that he does actually pay his bills on time, we need more of this. It is his impenetrability that is emphasized more strongly, either not listening or understanding (or both) when Fox explains the significance of the lightning symbol at the electric fence.

The labeling of characters, in which names denote their essential nature, is continued here with the specific use of Latin terminology, and logically without such a label, a character has no function, no purpose in the narrative. This reflects Anderson's tendency elsewhere to create characters with broad brush strokes via names and clothing. When dealing with less complicated organisms, this seems appropriate and an ironic comment on human science's tradition of looking at the natural world in this way, classifying and labeling living beings to make them easier to understand. In this, Anderson is again tending towards making the strange (talking animals) familiar, rather than the familiar strange.

There is a sentimentality (and even a pseudo-Christian theme) running beneath Dahl's very English sensibility here, involving the notion that everyone has particular (God-given) talents. It is just a matter of recognizing what they are and valuing them (and the individuals who possess them). Everyone has value; no one is irredeemable. As Ash explains to Kylie when he asks how he can fit through the skylight, "Cos I'm little." The neat moral of the Latin-naming scene, however, is compromised a little by certain names, which are wrongly translated, or characteristics wrongly attributed, suggesting that it is just another mechanism to place Fox in the role of director again. Badger's description of his field of expertise as "demolitions expert" suggests that it is not only a matter of evolution but existentialism plus American capitalism. You really can be what you want to be. More precisely, clichés are being dramatized here. Everyone has to be his own hero (Ash's cape literally underlines his own search for superhero status) and fight his own battles (Ash's karate on Kristofferson's cage does work, and apparently self-belief is enough to protect Ash from the farmers' bullets).

A fairly common, and highly predictable, criticism is the Americanization of an English text, drawing attention to Clooney and Streep in the main roles. What was originally small-scale and particularly British in its charm is shifted into transatlantic wisecracking. It is perhaps an inevitable element of the commercialism of adaptation that English characters should be recast as American (as happens in the 1996 version of *Matilda*). However, as elsewhere in Anderson's work (such as *Aquatic*), geographical setting is more ambiguous than it may seem. The setting is a transatlantic limbo. Some viewers tend to assume this is a mistake but in such painstaking animation, it is much more likely to be deliberate. American actors are used for the animal characters but all the humans, including the farmers (and even the voice-over on the whackbat documentary), are played by British actors, such as Brian Cox as the TV reporter. There is actually quite a complex blend of influences from American and British culture. The "station wagon" over the manhole cover is an American term, but it is a British right-hand drive. Mr. Fox makes his break for freedom along a very traditional English main street with small shops (featuring a bakery, a pub, and red mailboxes). However, such features are juxtaposed alongside more overtly American references (the presence of a wolf and an opossum) and cultural symbols (a roving TV van, newspapers thrown towards houses, and an early shot of Fox limbering up to the Wellingtons's "The Ballad of Davy Crockett"). There is chronological ambiguity too. The British features are anachronistic (there is mention of a "cobbler's shop" where Kristofferson will be exchanged) representing more of a cultural myth, which may have disappeared even before Dahl was writing.

The ending, Anderson's very first to avoid use of slow motion (which perhaps just looks too self-conscious in a stop-motion medium) seems almost like a more positive reversal of George A. Romero's *Dawn of the Dead* (1978). We slowly track back out of a large supermarket but instead of leaving a scene of death, destruction, and chaos, we are bidding farewell to a scene of joyful, self-expression and security (a "dance of life" to match Fellini's at the close of *8½* and the cast of Bill Melendez's 1965 *A Charlie Brown Christmas*). Indeed, Mr. Fox toasts Romero's key theme but in a life-enhancing context: "to our survival." However, perhaps the necessity of drinking from juice cartons reflects the compromises involved in such a process, and Ash is still holding onto his individuality, waving grape juice. Perhaps ultimately, a viewer's response (in relation to Dahl's story) might be symbolized by which audience reaction to Fox's speech we identify with most. In the written version, Fox gives "a tremendous belch"; in the film, we have a self-conscious gag about an invisible champagne flute.

The Last Picture Show:
Cinematic Influences—
Homage or Divergence?

The Great Appropriator must have no style; he is merely
a vehicle for the rearrangement of images, a kind of
auteurish director who splices from the collective eye of his
cameramen.

—Kay Larson

Whenever I am getting ready to make a movie I look at
other movies I love in order to answer the same recurring
question: How is this done, again?

—Wes Anderson

Noah Baumbach jokes that viewers could find all the elements from *Aquatic* in the fabric of New York's Bar Pitti where the pair met day after day for months to write the script, and although it does not have the qualities of the climactic revelation of Bryan Singer's *Usual Suspects* (1995), there is an element of found poetry in Anderson's film, like the name of Zissou's island. Appropriation seems entirely natural to Anderson's method of working, using whatever comes to mind, such as the bald owner, Giovanni, who becomes the model for Esteban's look.

Matt Zoller Seitz raises a number of interesting comparisons between Anderson's style and a range of filmmakers. However, like the Onion A.V. Club's "16 Films without Which Wes Anderson Wouldn't Have Happened," sweeping statements become part parlor game, part willful distortion. All artists, including filmmakers, are inevitably influenced by prior works. This is entirely logical and natural and something about which Anderson himself is very open. Comments concerning Anderson, however, tend to harp on about this, as if his art is purely derivative. In *Rushmore,* Max's early show of *Serpico* is an earnest imitation without any sense that this is an attempted parody. Like his later preciousness about small changes to the lines of a play, his art is still in an imitation phase but nonetheless important for that. It is more interesting to consider why Anderson makes the stylistic choices that he does, their effectiveness or otherwise in context, and how he develops or uses intertextual influences. Anderson's films do not demand a large amount of prior cultural knowledge to understand and enjoy them, but connections are there to be made.

Bill Melendez's *A Boy Named Charlie Brown* (1969) is apparent in Anderson's work, not only in Tenenbaum's soundtrack with Vince Guaraldi's "Christmas Time Is Here" (1965) but also in giving Max a barber as a father in *Rushmore* (like Charles Schulz, creator of the cartoon character), Dirk as a Linus-like phlegmatic provider of information, and more generally the deadpan delivery and tendency to look outwards directly at the camera. Anderson's work also includes bright, childish colors, characters displaying a cartoonish drawing ability (Anthony in the diner in *Bottle Rocket;* Richie in his wall pictures in *Tenenbaums*), and a whimsical sense of humor, which viewers tend to either love or hate. According to Seitz, Miss Cross is a blend of Charlie Brown's teacher and the little red-haired girl he has a persistent crush on. However, Charlie Brown is quite different from most Anderson heroes, who lack his more realistic self-awareness that he is likely to screw up whatever chances life appears to offer him, and unlike figures like Zissou or Max, Charlie is completely unable to manipulate those around him to sustain even the illusion of achievement. The serious-minded children of the Peanuts world are diametrically opposed to the continuing childishness of Anderson's adults, and only seem to be mirroring each other. Anderson is not really concerned with childhood. His narratives are based around adults who refuse to grow up (including Max, who at 16, is a world away from Charlie Brown's peer group).

AMERICAN INSPIRATION (NICHOLS, BOGDANOVICH, AND ASHBY)

Seitz interestingly suggests that the poolside party in *Tenenbaums,* via rack focus on marital infidelity, a similar location, a final despairing leap into the pool, constitutes a homage to Mike Nichols's *The Graduate* (1967) from the third party's point of view, that of the cuckolded husband. The Kinks' "Nothing in This World Can Stop Me from Worryin' bout That Girl" accompanies Anderson's poolside scene and certainly shares a strong similarity with the opening of Simon and Garfunkel's "Mrs. Robinson." Like *The Graduate, Tenenbaums* ends with an interrupted wedding and a chase, but its generic mix, something Seitz emphasizes, is typical of any Anderson film, not just this one. Nichols may use innovative pop accompaniment and all from one artist as in *Aquatic*, but Paul Simon's songs are contemporary with Nichols's film, whereas Anderson's are determinedly not of-the-moment. In the example of *Aquatic*, the songs are not by the original artist and even sung in a different language by an on-screen character. Anderson uses Simon's "Me and Julio Down By the Schoolyard" to complement Royal's gleeful rule-breaking with the twins, but it is probably the upbeat melody and the handheld camerawork evoking small-scale chaos that predominates here, rather than any lyrical notion of him acting as a proxy teacher. Like Nichols's film, *Rushmore* features a relationship across ages with an older woman but crucially, Max is younger, still at school, casting this as primarily a teacher-pupil relationship, in which the woman most definitely does not occupy a Mrs. Robinson seductress role. Unlike Nichols's hero (and Salinger's Caulfield), Anderson's male protagonists are *not* examples of disaffected youth (even if Schwartzman reminded Anderson of a young Dustin Hoffman at the point of casting him). The younger characters of *Bottle Rocket, Rushmore,* or *Tenenbaums* may be lacking direction and unwilling to accept responsibility, but they have not yet experienced enough of life to reject it cynically. It is a feature of later Anderson films but primarily through the older characters (especially those roles played by Bill Murray). Even here, it is not so much disaffection, in *Aquatic* for example, as much as a persistent unwillingness to grow up.

Peter Bogdanovich's *Paper Moon* (1973) shares Anderson's attention to detail over mise-en-scène and the creation of self-contained fictive worlds, but precociously intelligent youngsters only occur in *Tenenbaums* for specific reasons and, indeed, the protagonists of *Bottle Rocket* are extremely stupid and Max is put on "sudden death academic probation" in *Rushmore* precisely because of his weakness in class. Any retro stylization in *Paper Moon* is dictated by its precise chronological setting (something Anderson films repeatedly deny the viewer), and Bogdanovich's monochrome cinematography is completely refuted by Anderson's dominant color palette.

Like *Rushmore*, Hal Ashby's *Harold and Maude* (1971) may use Cat Stevens's "The Wind" but (as with Nichols) for Ashby, this is a contemporaneous song. Max also yearns to be taken seriously as an adult, while unwilling to give up the essential childishness of his nature. There is also a swimming pool scene, where a main character's depression is signaled by apparently attempting to drown himself (but in both cases this is played for laughs). However, although there is bereavement in the film's backstory, Max, unlike Ashby's hero (played by Bud Cort), is not death-obsessed and does *not* take his attraction towards an older woman (the much, much older 79-year-old Maude, played by Ruth Gordon) to the point of a reciprocal physical relationship. Like inaccurate comparisons with Salinger's Holden Caulfield, Max's limiting of his life/sexual experience is a crucial difference. Ashby's *The Last Detail* (1973) may have inspired *Darjeeling*, with a similar premise of three males on a journey, in particular its attempt to interest an audience despite an apparent lack of plot. That said, Ashby's influence is ultimately more one of contrast than affinity. Anderson's work is unapologetically apolitical, at times resisting specific location in time and space and generically much more limited.

THE FRENCH CONNECTION (TRUFFAUT, GODARD, AND MALLE)

François Truffaut's *Les Quatre Cents Coups* (1959) has superficial similarities with *Rushmore* in dealing with the troubled schooling of a teenage boy, Antoine Doinel (Jean-Pierre Léaud), but as in many comparisons in this chapter, Anderson's narrative is only mildly transgressive by comparison. Unlike Doinel, Max does not have the courage to run away from school, and Max enjoys a much closer and more harmonious relationship with his father. Doinel is a reluctant accomplice to adult infidelity, whereas in *Rushmore,* Max exploits this for his own ends, or so he plans (splitting Blume from his wife). There is a small homage in the slow motion that closes *Rushmore,* but this is weakened by the appearance of a similar stylistic trope in all of Anderson's films whereas Truffaut's iconic zoom and freeze-frame on Doinel's face is memorable because it is *not* overused.

Like *Rushmore,* Truffaut's *Small Change* (1976) is an episodic portrayal of childhood, featuring a schoolboy with a crush on an older woman (the mother of a friend). Truffaut's film features a particularly comic but potentially tragic scene with a cat and a baby at an open windowsill, and this location seems important to Anderson too. We see characters at windowsills in *Bottle Rocket* (the sight of Anthony's initial "escape"), *Rushmore* (the means by which Max gains access to Miss Cross's house), and in *Tenenbaums* (Margot and Chas looking out across the street at Eli or Margot sitting, watching Etheline). Truffaut is a pervasive presence in Anderson's films, from small dialogue references like the "Not this one" from Zissou to Klaus in *Aquatic,* echoing Jules's line exactly in *Jules et Jim* (1962) to symbolic objects, like the gift of a music box in *Darjeeling,* where we see Jack's girlfriend and later his mother wind a music box, which evokes Thérèse, Jules's girlfriend, putting a coin in a mechanical piano. The love triangles at the center of *Rushmore* and *Tenenbaums* (at least in the problematic dynamic between Margot and Richie) may have been partly inspired by Truffaut's *Jules et Jim* (1962) and *Les deux anglaise et le continent,* or *Two English Girls* (1971), although the stunted emotional development of Anderson's characters preclude the kind of plot twists available to Truffaut.

It is important not to overstate the redemptive element in Anderson's work. Nearly all the examples that easily come to mind are actually more ambiguous than they appear at first (partly why Anderson's films repay repeat viewings). It is right to highlight the importance of rescues but we should not miss more specific parallels to French film of the nouvelle vague (the French New Wave), where redemption is also often bittersweet. Other more radical editing practices associated with the nouvelle vague, such as jump cutting, do not appear in Anderson's work. Location shooting occurs in *The Darjeeling Limited* because such a narrative would be very expensive and problematic to create on set and make believable to audiences. Handheld footage is used occasionally, where immediacy is important, such as the house robbery scene in *Bottle Rocket,* Eli's crash into the house in *Tenenbaums,* the landing and disembarking shots on Zissou's island, Eleanor's dramatic farewell, and the pirate attack in *Aquatic* but usually to imply movement, rather than rebellious spontaneity. The introduction to the *Belafonte* via a spectacular tracking shot suggests Anderson's preference for sound stages, and therefore directorial control, when available. Similarly, sea creatures are not portrayed via stock footage but stylized animation. Improvisation may occur in a very limited sense that Anderson's direction is often quite light-touch, and actors are encouraged to play the lines in ways that work for them. However, if this produces a take that Anderson does not like, he will reshoot until he sees something that he does. When it comes to locations and especially set design, very little is improvised. These aspects of production, like the writing of the script itself, are pored over for months. Improvisations have not been forced for budgetary reasons. If studios cannot or will not fund filming, Anderson is able and willing to pay for production himself (as in *The Hotel Chevalier*).

Anderson uses a sudden track up to an object or person at moments of dramatic climax, such as when Max approaches the desk to ask a librarian for a list of who has taken out the Cousteau book or when he expresses his wish to start a fencing team at his new school, when Anthony first spies Inez, and when Dignan comes closer to admitting his relationship (or lack of it) with Mr. Henry (that of sacked employee, not a central part of a criminal gang). It also appears in *Fantastic Mr. Fox* when Mrs. Fox delivers the punch line "It better not be" or when Fox suddenly instinctively realizes at the banquet that his sons are not there. It might show a weakness in Anderson, attempting to import drama into a situation which rarely merits it, but it does also convey the distorted values of the figure in the frame who sees greater importance in their situation, than we do (like Chas in his office or Eli lecturing on stage). They are very much the heroes in their own narratives. The zoom into Fox's face hidden behind cider bottles in *Fantastic Mr. Fox* is a similar basic effect but conveys real tension as he will be killed if he is found.

However, generally, the style of Anderson's films do not seem so disruptive of norms that it seems shocking or even incomprehensible (as some of Godard's films are), but he uses conventional devices in unusual ways. Except for rare examples like the shot of Chas's weights bench in *Tenenbaums* or the séance montage in *Darjeeling,* there are no radical, disorientating jumps in time and space, so that, for example, Anderson's use of text on screen usually has a suturing effect. We are told where we are (think of the montages in the opening of *Tenenbaums*) or what we are being shown (the montage of Max's clubs in *Rushmore*) by on-screen captions which do not obscure the main part of the image. Nonetheless, such devices are still intrusive and remind us that we are being told a story by a reliable narrator, by implication (since we have no specified narrator in any Anderson film, even in *Tenenbaums*) the director. Narratives are mostly linear, without major chronological leaps, with only a few clearly signaled exceptions (such as the report of the private investigator in *Tenenbaums*). Characters may not address the audience in terms of speech but often look directly at the camera, sometimes motivated from within the narrative (like the mirror shots in *Tenenbaums'* credit sequence or Richie shaving) but elsewhere placing us directly into the scene (as in the siblings interviewing Royal). Via the use of pictures and on-screen text, Anderson is quite prepared to challenge the notion of "show rather than tell" by showing *and* telling. Zissou and Eleanor talk about Esteban, so we cut to a shot of his portrait on their wall.

Jean-Luc Godard provides the third element in a triangle between Anderson and Tarantino, who also was strongly influenced by the Frenchman in making *Reservoir Dogs* (even calling his production company A Band Apart after one of Godard's films). Certainly Godard's *Bande à part* (1964) has some superficial similarities with *Bottle Rocket,* but there is very little genuine melancholy in Anderson's film and no real loss suffered. The general tone is closer to Woody Allen's early work in its absurdity, made all the more powerful as none of the characters seem aware of it. Unlike Godard's use of intertitles, breaking the dramatic illusion, forcing viewers to read text rather than images, and overtly reminding viewers of the presence of the director, Anderson adopts a more subtle version of this technique.

What is distinctive about Anderson's use of text on screen is the extent of his use of Futura as the dominant typeface. All signage, especially text denoting ownership, appears in Futura, a typeface particularly dominant in global printed material from the 1940s to the 1970s (including the credit sequences of European feature films, especially from Italy). This adds to the sense of an anachronistic time frame, suggestive of an era when decisions over typeface were made by printers rather than brand managers. Anderson's first release was in 1994, definitely part of the age of personal computing, where typeface can be changed at will. The sedate pace of the plane carrying an advertisement for "Boggis, Bunce and Bean International Supplements" across the screen almost makes it look like a banner on a computer screen. Futura was also a favored typeface of Stanley Kubrick, a director infamous for the totality of his control of the filmmaking process, although in films like *The Shining* (1980), he is primarily using text on screen to give situational information (time and place), a function only really appearing frequently in *Fantastic Mr. Fox,* made using Helvetica. For *Fantastic Mr. Fox,* some posters and trailer material do still feature Futura but some posters do not, preparing audiences a little for the break with Futura in the body of the film.

Designer Mark Simonson has usefully identified examples of Anderson's use of Futura typeface in *Tenenbaums,* not just for the credits but all text that appears within the film, including lettering on signage at the hospital, buses (italicized to suggest movement), and even Mordecai's cap. A rare exception to this is the more curvaceous Helvetica type used for Etheline's book, which signals it as slightly anachronistic within the narrative (although that is quite a subjective notion since there is no specific chronological time frame here). Although we have actors delivering scripted lines in a way that might perpetuate the dramatic illusion and the suspension of disbelief, the set is constantly screaming at us via this obsessive lettering that we are inhabiting a purely fictional universe. Futura is not unique to Anderson, but his wholesale deployment of it in all his films most definitely is. The effect, if not the purpose, is to author the text as if with a literal signature.

In *Fantastic Mr. Fox,* Anderson's use of text on screen is more conventional than usual in its use as purveyor of information, including time passing, which of Fox's criminal plans we are watching, or character backstory (such as Kristofferson's label around his neck, describing his family circumstances). We might realize there is a link between human and fox years, but the ratio is less important than the sense this creates of pressure on Fox; his biological clock is ticking. We do not need captions for the farms themselves as they have signage denoting ownership. Characters are identified by being labeled, sometimes via literal name tags like our first sight of Kristofferson or to denote possession like on Agnes's lab goggles, Petey's banjo, or Dudley's hat in *Tenenbaums.* As part of Badger's expository montage, we also have a series of three posed shots of the farmers in front of their farms with Bean's particularly powerful pistol held Sean Connery–style across his chest (as used on promotional posters for Guy Hamilton's 1964 *Goldfinger*). Such a device, with the characters directly addressing the camera, suggests this is how they see themselves in what could be termed a "Little Britain" shot (as used at the end of David Fincher's 2008 *Benjamin Button*). The montage of the three farmers condenses narrative information and impressions. Three skeletons, placed before a *Rushmore*-style blackboard, underline Bunce's status as an evolutionary freak (but possibly worth studying).

The self-absorbed, bourgeois lifestyle of the protagonist of Louis Malle's *Murmur of the Heart* (1971), 14-year-old Laurent (Benoît Ferreux), is reflected in the privileged backgrounds of virtually all of Anderson's characters—in *Rushmore*'s elitist status, the Whitman brother's argument over a $10,000 belt, or Zissou's life-as-expensive-hobby bankrolled by Eleanor. Jazz scores by Charlie Parker and Dizzy Gillespie and ubiquitous references to Marcel Proust, Albert Camus, and Georges Bataille give Malle's film a similar literary feel to *Tenenbaums.* However as with Salinger, Laurent experiences a much more transgressive side to his sexuality (here involving his own family). Anderson only touches lightly on incest in *Tenenbaums* and leaves it at a platonic level. A closer link to Malle is his documentary on India, *Calcutta*

(1968), an influence on *Darjeeling,* and his early work with Cousteau, *Silent World* (1956), part of the inspiration behind the film Max watches in *Rushmore* and that Zissou is seeking to capture in *The Life Aquatic.*

HEAVYWEIGHT AUTEURS (SCORSESE AND WELLES)

Martin Scorsese clearly admires Anderson, with Scorsese possibly giving his junior the kiss of death by suggesting he is his cinematic heir, shortly after seeing *Bottle Rocket.* Kevin Conroy Scott cites Anderson as saying that *Bottle Rocket* was intended as a gritty drama like Scorsese's *Mean Streets* (1973).[1] Even though it was not Scorsese's debut, it also features a group of aspiring criminals and, like *Bottle Rocket,* was the film that brought the director to public notice. Perhaps it is Anderson who is the true innocent as his relatively comfortable upbringing, reflected in the domestic situations of Dignan, Anthony, and Bob, makes such a venture hard to imagine. Scorsese, who also directed a concert film of *The Stones* (*Shine a Light,* 2008) shares a similar musical heritage with Anderson (Dignan is accompanied by the Stones' "2000 Man") and a use of its juxtaposition with slow motion. Dignan's walking back to jail is given dignity and status by its slow motion, linking him in our minds (and possibly his) with Robert De Niro as Johnny Boy moving down the bar to "Jumping Jack Flash" in *Mean Streets.* There is even the same slow forward movement up to "the watcher" (in this case Harvey Keitel) looking at the object of affection, shown in a reverse dolly shot.

Anderson has never used slow motion to dramatize (and some might say fetishize) violent action, as in the work of Sam Peckinpah, but like Scorsese, he does slow action down to underline the emotional power of a scene. Strangely, this does not seem to apply to Scorsese's exact use of the same technique, also with forward and reverse tracking shots, possibly because in Scorsese's case, he is cinematically idolizing examples of stylish excesses of masculinity. He creates real monsters, capable of killing; Anderson is only portraying pseudo-transgressors as Dignan walks away at the end of *Bottle Rocket* or a self-congratulatory Max emerges from an elevator in *Rushmore,* not after a well-planned "hit" but after delivering some bees to Blume's room. In the 1994 version, Dignan starts to chat to a uniformed cop about his training in a scene oddly reminiscent of De Niro in Scorsese's *Taxi Driver* (1976) in which Travis Bickle shows his idolization and admiration of a secret service man, and thereby his complete unsuitability for that kind of job. Via a clumsy attempt to ingratiate themselves, both characters lead the authority figures to what they are searching for (for Scorsese, Travis Bickle and for Anderson here, it is Bob's secret marijuana patch). In many ways, Anderson is underlining how the delusions of his characters derive precisely *from* such cinematic representations of being a tough guy (we see Max producing his own nakedly derivative version of *Serpico* and later a thinly veiled version of *Apocalypse Now*). However, like optical illusions that contain two pictures, viewers have to choose between a dramatic engagement with a character or assuming more distance and seeing a scene as a parody. The responses of laughing at and laughing with a character can be close, and we might switch from one to the other in close succession, but they are mutually exclusive at any specific given time.

Seitz also draws attention to Scorsese's use of tight overhead shots, with an example from *Taxi Driver* in Betsy's office. However, their use and frequency is very different in Anderson's films. In *Taxi Driver,* such a device underlines Travis Bickle's assumption of a God-like view of events, a narrative in which he casts himself as the agent of divine justice, bringing judgment and order to the streets of New York. In Anderson's work, this overhead shot is everywhere and seldom related to the agency of one particular character. On the contrary, it underlines the agency of the *director,* who has meticulously placed objects within a frame in such a balanced and orderly way, like a place setting at a formal dinner (which is exactly what we have in *Rushmore*). The shots, often act almost as intertitles held for several seconds, introducing a change of scene and a protagonist who is clearly a proxy director figure (not part of Scorsese's aesthetic), such as Zissou's map in *Aquatic,* with the on-screen title "Hunting Esteban's Killer."

Tight overhead shots are used for precise contents of containers like the jewelry box in *Bottle Rocket,* or more often written texts such as Blume's speech to the boys, a page of *The Rushmore Yankee,* stamp albums, Max's petition over Latin, and his grade C paper showing improvement in *Rushmore;* the book covers in *Tenenbaums,* or Ned's letters in *Aquatic.* Desktops are also favored subjects, such as Max's desk in the math lesson and drinking receptacles like the coffee cups shared by Blume and Miss Cross at the final production or Kristofferson's trick with the acorn. In *Darjeeling,* such a shot shows the tray of drinks that Rita brings with pink petals, lime juice, a snack in a blue packet, and a pot of red dye with which she marks each of their foreheads recording payment but also to provide a kind of anointing ritual. They are now marked as changed—travelers in an alien culture. We see Francis going through Jack's case and Francis later lying on his bed from such a bird's-eye view. The constricted nature of space on board the train motivates many of the tight two- or three-shots in the film, including a sense of forced intimacy among characters who might choose to be farther apart.

The whip-pans that Seitz notes are also much more prevalent in Anderson's work and significantly different from the work of Scorsese. In Anderson's work, they are nearly always 90 degrees, and Seitz manages to find an example that problematizes point of view between third and first person, which gives us a sudden glimpse of a situation through the eyes of a given character in the scene, such as Chas at his weights bench in *Tenenbaums.* However, this is extremely rare. There may be changes between the owners of these viewing positions, but they are always clearly subjective and motivated from within the scene (such as Margot and Chas looking down at a taxi and then up at Eli opposite). It can economically generate sympathy for a character but through overuse it can also quickly become the kind of stylistic trope that critics of Anderson find annoying. The camera movement that Seitz describes at the beginning of *Rushmore* is actually motivated and not a whip-pan. The example of Chas is an interesting one. We cut from a shot of him tying a tie, looking up, and then cut to a self-drawn (we assume) exercise chart from which we suddenly tilt down to Chas on the bench. Either the view of the charts was omniscient or we are meant to have the impression of a character who is so dynamic, he can move within the screen space in the blink of an eye.

In *Rushmore*, we momentarily share the point of view of a student in the class panning suddenly left to the impossible math problem on an adjacent board and then back to the main one. In *Aquatic,* 90-degree pans signal the sudden appearance of a character, such as a brief exchange between love rivals at the opening premiere or the man calling out from the crowd. In *Darjeeling,* there is the sense of Anderson playing games with his trademark 90-degree whip-pans. Anderson uses this typical shot to take in the inspector's pointing at a "No smoking" sign and then back to the reaction of the Whitmans, before cutting to all three crowded round an open window, smoking. However, what initially seems to be a rebellious act is then cast as the behavior of naughty schoolboys as we cut back to the inspector who is still standing there (an effect repeated after the snake episode when they are grounded in their compartment). Later, in the second bus departure scene, we have a three-shot of the brothers looking off-frame right as before but now a pan takes us to the father and we pan back and forth, each time revealing more well-wishers in a visual gag. As the brothers eat, Anderson pans back and forth between Paul and Francis rather than cutting, almost taking a midpoint position of a third figure watching the exchange like a tennis match.

In *Fantastic Mr. Fox,* the typical 90-degree panning shots, possibly due to the time required to produce them, possess a slightly more thoughtful purpose. When Mr. Fox and Kylie reach the last stage of the first break-in, Fox describes a complicated and dangerous course past numerous obstacles, which Kylie has to undertake. Reflecting his more straightforward approach (and underlining failings in Fox's own egotistical planning), Kylie suggests a different route just off to the right which is much easier. The sudden whip-pan right when Fox, Kylie, and Ash enter Bean's farm is motivated by the sudden revelation of the dog. Similarly, as Mr. Fox is chased by the rabid dog, sudden changes of direction are directly motivated from within the scene.

Recommended to Anderson by Scorsese, Jean Renoir's *The River* (1951) has a strong influence on *The Darjeeling Limited*. Anderson follows its location shooting and parallel character groupings (three teenage girls are replaced with three adult brothers) but interestingly perpetuates its view of the country as a source of the incomprehensible and the exotic. Anderson's film is not really about travel as the brothers do not learn anything specific about the culture they pass through, safely packaged behind the glass of a train carriage.

Their experience with the drowned boy appears to give them insight, but it is of a purely emotional kind. They still do not understand what is going on around them at the boy's house, on the bus, or at the funeral. None of the brothers are suffering any real pain. The blocking of Jack's limited writing ability hardly seems tragic; Peter and Francis argue over the trappings of their father; and Francis's apparent depression that led to his attempted suicide has no more status than Anthony's opening situation in *Bottle Rocket*. In both cases, Owen Wilson's bandaged face reflects the absurdity of his micromanaged schedules (one for 75 years, the other laminated). The country only provides any sense of healing in that it briefly forces them not to be quite so self-absorbed. Although they finally toss their suitcases away, they do carry them throughout the film up to that point.

Orson Welles, an auteur well before auteur theory, like Anderson was largely self-taught in filmmaking technique, meaning that he repeatedly watched those films he liked. Inevitably, this produces an element of imitation before it leads to originality. What is perhaps amazing in the case of Anderson, armed with a degree in philosophy rather than film, is that *Bottle Rocket*, his first feature, is as original as it is. Like Anderson, Welles also used a familiar pool of actors, drawn from his Mercury Theater Company, and third-person voice-over, although Anderson uses an actor (Alec Baldwin) rather than himself (Welles's preferred method), thereby not quite stamping his authorial mark as strongly as Welles. Both directors use wide-angle lenses but for quite different reasons. Welles produces great depth of focus and thereby allows connections to be made between planes within the frame, as in *Citizen Kane* (1939), connecting the mother inside the boarding house and the young Charles playing outside in the snow in the background, but for Anderson, it allows him to pack the frame with more objects or character in a static sense, like a family portrait. There might seem another similarity in bravura camera shots but *Kane*, for example, has a number of these involving forward movement and inventive transitions, such as the skylight lightning cut or the rising opera house shot. Anderson's equivalent, introducing us to the *Belafonte*, focuses not so much on the camera but *the set*; it is a marvel of set dressing rather than camera movement. Anderson can take partial credit for this of course, but it is an element in preproduction rather than shooting (logically finding its apotheosis in *Fantastic Mr. Fox*). The low-angled shots of the animals trapped in the sewer also evoke Welles's role in *The Third Man* (Carol Reed, 1949).

The interview with Royal isolated in long shot at one end of the table evokes the breakfast table montage of growing marital distance between Kane and his wife, and later wide- and low-angle shots within the house evoke more extreme low angles in *Kane* with visible ceilings. With illustrated chapter headings, *Tenenbaums* seems to be straining for a sense of dynastic decline as in *The Magnificent Ambersons* (1942), with its talk of two decades of "failure, betrayal, and disaster." However, the interiors of the Tenenbaum residence hardly seem spartan, and there is little sense of community outside the family passing judgment upon them (except Cash who still wishes to join their select club). The characters are in retreat, not decline. Celebrity does not equate with greatness. Of Anderson's heroes, only Zissou has actually achieved anything from which a decline might be measurable. *Rushmore*'s Blume is still a rich businessman, albeit unhappy in his personal life, and no one in *Bottle Rocket* or *Darjeeling* has achieved anything of significant note in their adult lives.

In *Fantastic Mr. Fox*, like *Citizen Kane*, there are a number of deliberately extremely low angles, also showing the ceilings, for example, in the tree house Fox buys, Ash and Kristofferson emerging into Bean's kitchen, and in the supermarket at the end. The dying words of Rat (echoed earlier by Kylie) are not profound or enigmatic like Kane's "Rosebud" but relate to an alcoholic drink. Bean's smashing up of his caravan in a violent rage parallels Kane's rage, but here Bean is seen as ridiculous, with a bike thrown out of the frame, towards the viewer, and he kicks a drum, inside which someone seems to be hiding (judging from a muffled cry). Although not quite on the same scale, Fox shares Kane's profession ("Now I'm a 'newspaper man'") and the camera movement back through a window into the Fox's new home reverses the famous boarding house sequence in *Kane*, and the rising shot up through the tree house construction past workmen evokes the opera house sequence in the same film. Like Welles's creative use of sound perspectives in *Kane*, the agent in *Fantastic Mr. Fox* is seen and heard in the background, speaking into his phone, before showing Fox round the new property. At a greater extreme, Anderson cuts sound almost completely at key moments, to convey a moment of personal trauma, like Blume underwater in *Rushmore* or Dudley finding Richie with his wrists slashed in *Tenenbaums*, where we see Dudley's screaming face but hear no sound as Richie is rushed to the hospital.

BUÑUEL

Anderson often mentions Buñuel's name when asked about his influences but rarely goes into specifics. Buñuel's work falls into a number of periods, but it is not really the surrealism, for which he is best known, that links him with Anderson but the Spaniard's so-called second French period (roughly 1964–1977). At this time, Buñuel especially used wide shots, which followed characters, sometimes including a shift of subject without cutting, such as in the restaurant scene in *Belle De Jour* (1967). On the *Tenenbaums* DVD, Anderson mentions Buñuel's use of movement, *The Discreet Charm of the Bourgeoisie* (1972) in particular, but his comments are quite vague, especially the notion of groups of people in rooms having conversations. The poolside party scene in P. T. Anderson's *Boogie Nights* (1997) is a clearer example of this as we follow one character for a few seconds and then transfer to another and follow them for a while as if the camera is restlessly looking for its subject. This appears in Anderson's Softbank and AmEx commercials (see chapter 9), the long take at the end of *Tenenbaums*, the camera following Dirk in *Rushmore* after the final production, or with Jorge on the boat at the party as a linking device between all the assembled characters.

However, there are as many differences as similarities. There is a slight logistical problem of movement, especially through large spaces, when Anderson prefers not to cut, so there is a reverse tracking shot of Bob through his house in *Bottle Rocket*. The specific Buñuelian camera movement just described is not quite the same as the introduction to the *Belafonte* in *The Life Aquatic* or the tracking shot through the train in *Darjeeling* (using a camera running along the ceiling) up to the bearded steward with Rita in the storeroom and then back to return to Jack. Anderson mentions on the *Tenenbaums* commentary that Richie's line "I'm going to kill myself tomorrow" is from a Buñuel film, but it is actually from Louis Malle's *Le feu follet*, or *The Fire Within* (1963). Perhaps it is the line itself or the camera movement that is more important than the specific source, but it is debatable on this evidence how well he knows Buñuel's work.

Anderson seems to express quite a selective view of Buñuel. Buñuel may follow an actor with a pan or a zoom, but Anderson's style explicitly uses one character as a linking device and draws attention to itself in a way quite alien to Buñuel. Like the example from *Aquatic*, there is an inherently demonstrative element in this camera movement (reflected in the dialogue "Let me show you…"), which foregrounds the work of the director (and often the production designer too) as in the opening robbery sequence in *Fantastic Mr. Fox*. There may be a childishness in Anderson's protagonists but there are no dream or fantasy sequences, whether signaled conventionally or not. Overtly surrealist imagery and political or religious subject matter have no parallel in Anderson's work. Buñuel's whole cinematic aesthetic, which was designed to provoke, is diametrically opposed to the balanced symmetry of Anderson.

CONCLUSION

In *The Anxiety of Influence: A Theory of Poetry* (1973), Harold Bloom discusses the power of previous artworks and identifies a number of potential options open to any aspiring artist. He is talking about poetry, but his ideas can be usefully applied to film, especially since Anderson is such a literary figure, at least co-writing his own scripts, which frequently use literary allusions. Put very simply, a "clinamen" designates a swerving away from a creative influence; a "tessera" is an element or fragment used to complete a precursor; a "kenosis" is a self-deprecating inability to follow in a person's footsteps, leading to the erasure of a predecessor; an "apophrades" is the idea that a successor is so in tune with a precursor, they could have produced the earlier work; and an "askesis" is a break with the past, a drawing a line in the sand.[2] However, none of these terms work in relation to Anderson's films. A "clinamen" would be too radical, a "tessera" too arrogant, a "kenosis" completely wrong (exactly the opposite holds true, nothing is forgotten); an "apophrades" seems difficult at best, as it is hard to imagine someone else making an Anderson film, and he has no direct precursor that he is completing, and an "askesis" is definitely inappropriate (musically and filmically, he is very backward-looking).

In essence, Anderson is not evoking previous films in order to subvert, deny, critique, or complete them. He is gently riffing on previous work, in a tone of polite homage rather than irony, which may deepen our appreciation of his films if we spot the references but will not interrupt our understanding of them if we do not (a little like the relationship of *The Hotel Chevalier* to *Darjeeling*). Such allusions seem placed for personal pleasure and for true Anderson fans to spot, a process described by David Bordwell in relation to the European art film.[3] Sometimes there is little other meaning other than an allusion to something outside the text. Kylie's outburst, when the Foxes are arguing, "You say one thing, she says another and it all changes back again," is purely a reference to *Rebel Without a Cause* (Nicholas Ray, 1955), little more than a gag for cinephiles to spot. The greatest amount of meaning is generated through a relation to other previous texts, in this case by the same author; that is, Anderson's films work like a palimpsest, a rewriting over the same text. In this, Anderson's films are not only recognizable but form one large super-text, a key tenet of auteurism, discussed in chapter 10.

The Discreet Charm of the Bourgeoisie: Anderson's Portrayal of Race and Class

ANDERSON AND RACE

White people love Wes Anderson movies more than they love their kids.

—Christian Lander

The fact that Wes Anderson movies merit their own entry (at Number 10, out of 150) in Christian Lander's *Stuff White People Like* (2008) does not represent an uncontestable reality, but the fact that it appears at all suggests that, for some viewers, the presentation of race is a recognizable element in Anderson's work. Jonah Weiner claims that Inez from *Bottle Rocket* and Rita in *Darjeeling* are "service-industry (hotties) with whom...depressed Anderson hero(es)...become obsessed,"[1] overlooking that Rita is more assertive than Jack realizes and later rejects him; that is, she uses him as much as being cast in the role as exploited sex object, and that Inez is engagingly shy and perhaps realistically looking at Anthony as her only escape from a life of menial labor. However, that said, Anderson's portrayal of race can be problematic.

Weiner portrays Sherman in *Tenenbaums* as a ridiculous bumbling, minstrel-like figure, played for laughs (misreading the kitchen scene with Royal). A counterargument might suggest that the role of Sherman is far from passive, that an actor of Danny Glover's stature would hardly take it if it was, and that the Coltrane remark was actually suggested by Glover himself. Furthermore, the key to the tone of this scene is not racial. That is the focus of Royal's comments because he is trying to rile Sherman. What we are watching is two older adult men jockeying for position as to who is the alpha male in this particular family; that is, the real focus is gender, not race. Royal's actions in (inexpertly) playing the race card are important as it is a reason for him to forfeit sufficient sympathy from viewers for his displacement by Sherman to work. Weiner's portrayal of Sherman as a butt of slapstick and racist comment misses the point. He is not provoked and calmly goes about the business of unmasking the illness scam. Sherman would have every right to pursue this with anger and deliver the knockout punch with some relish, but he does not. He represents the forces of order and logicality to Royal's chaos, but if that were all, Eleanor's attraction to him would be less persuasive. Sherman possesses real dignity and integrity, less showy than Royal's vitality, but in relationships over time, of greater value. As for the fall at the archaeological dig, if we laugh, it is due to the choreography of the scene and the accomplished acting by Huston and Glover. We are not laughing at a pretentious character here but actually, quite the reverse, since Sherman is protesting his unworthiness at the time.

Anderson's films are certainly poles apart from the work of Spike Lee but that is not necessarily a weakness. Anderson writes about what he knows best. An upbringing in middle-class Huston, Texas, and adult homes in affluent parts of California, Paris, and Rome may not make interracial tensions seem the logical material for his work. To readily ascribe racial representation to fictional characters is a fairly reductive critical approach and assumes the characters are nothing more than ciphers. It is certainly worth considering, but those who react in this way to Anderson's films are often missing the subtleties in the dialogue and performance. Just because a character has few lines, it does not preclude that these might be intended ironically. The name of Richie's final tennis opponent (Gandhi) is designed to be absurd.

> ANTHONY: God, this is great. Sitting here in the laundry room. You working on your vocabulary and we're sharing these tamales. It's...just how unexpected.

Where Weiner's comments carry more weight is in the area of minor characters. The characterization of Inez in *Bottle Rocket* is inherently limited by her speaking solely in Spanish. We either need to give Anthony credit for showing greater emotional depth than we see elsewhere or this relationship seems unsatisfactory, only serving as a white, middle-class casting of otherness as inherently exotic (symbolized by the elevation of fairly ordinary foodstuff). On asking her what part of Mexico she comes from, she answers bluntly "Paraguay." It is debatable whether Anthony really knows enough about her to be able to fall in love with her or whether he represents anything more for her than an escape from low-paid, menial work. On first viewing she is playing with her hair, perhaps suggesting a slightly coquettish nature, using her attractiveness to ensnare him. Anthony's compliment of how great it is that she can "bring a room to life like this" simply by pulling back the curtains is delivered without any visible sense of irony as if he has never thought of doing this. On the other hand, there is something quite endearing in his pup-pyish following of her into rooms, although this might be motivated as much by boredom as by interest in her specifically. His gesture of helping push the janitor cart or putting a freshly laundered towel to his face hovers between expressing a new sense of wonder at the world and just plain absurdity. Like Dignan, he is casting himself in his own narrative, here of a romantic rather than a criminal nature, but both are essentially ridiculous. His attempts to help tidy up, later following her to the laundrette, may seem sweet or verging on harassment. Like an apprentice stalker, he takes a picture from her locker, assuming it is of a younger self, only to be informed it is her sister at which point, he *asks to keep it anyway*. He seems in love with the idea of being in love as much as interested in one particular girl.

The linguistic difficulty the pair has might suggest the inability to ver-balize deep-seated thoughts and feelings, but the incongruity is more often played for laughs. Later when he calls Inez from the party, he punches the air just because she recognizes his voice. When an angry Inez says (via Rocky who translates) that Anthony is just "trash" and "like paper floating by," his only response is that "it doesn't sound that bad in Spanish." Inez's declara-tion of love appears comic when delivered (again via Ricky) to Dignan. and it is not completely clear whether Dignan deliberately conceals Inez's love for Anthony or literally thinks Rocky is addressing him (as he tells Anthony later). It makes more sense that he does know and just uses this apparent mistake as a way of explaining the delay in passing on the information, but it could also be explained by his emotional insensitivity.

The rapid seduction of Rita (Amara Karan) in *Darjeeling* seems quite taw-dry, with sex in a cramped toilet hardly representing a grand passion. When Rita later sits next to him, listlessly smokes and declares, "I gotta get off this train," it feels more like her sexual exchange with Jack is a means of escape than a meaningful relationship in itself. When he later asks if he can kiss her, she refuses fairly bluntly. Her speedy acquiescence could be seen as a pre-paredness to use her sexuality to improve her position, but she does not gain much by the exchange, and we see very few engaging qualities in Jack, which reflects poorly on her. Also, when Jack finally leaves the train, she thanks him, without sarcasm, for using her and cries. It is hard to see her as much more than a Western fantasy of available exoticism. The brief appearance of Mandeeza (Melanie Gerren) in *Aquatic* after the premiere also reflects an attitude of women as props, which is appropriate within the context of that narrative but could be a tendency some viewers might come to associate with the director.

Margaret Yang in *Rushmore* is a slightly different case because she pursues the hero, who seems oblivious to her charms, and her fakery with the science project also suggests she has something in common with the reconstructing of the world as his creative fantasy. Max Fischer's Jewishness is present but hardly foregrounded in *Rushmore* and perhaps it is wrong to emphasize Margaret's ethnic origin, which only Dirk mentions in the film itself, correcting Guggenheim that she is Korean. Max's interest in Vietnam (probing Blume a little about his experiences), reflected in his choice of spectacular final play, is engaging and understandable largely due to Max's naïveté. Structurally, Anderson uses the characters of Sherman and Margaret and the cementing of their relationship with Etheline and Max respectively to provide some narrative resolution at the close of the film (echoed in Margaret's kiss for Max in her role as Vietnamese villager Le-Chan in the school play). This may be unsatisfactory in character terms (part of us may prefer Royal and Miss Cross as more suitable partners), but as in Shakespearean comedy, structural consolation overrides romantic resolution. The difficulty with Inez, Rita, and Margaret is that Anderson repeatedly uses female characters from nonwhite, ethnic backgrounds as a catalyst in the development of the white male hero. In a single film, this might not be such a problem, but there is a series of ethnic minority characters, which only remain subsidiary or outline in their function.

In *Aquatic,* Anderson seems prepared to draw on stereotypical notions of Germans as literal-minded and humorless, reflected in the name Klaus Daimler with cliché suggestions of precision and efficiency (perhaps also the Luftwaffe Automotive garage in *Darjeeling*), and the cliché appearance of Werner in lederhosen. However, this is lightened by what Dafoe brings to his performance (for which Anderson must also receive some credit). Dafoe, in a rare minor role, adds great weight to the character of Klaus, muttering to Jane that Ned is Zissou's son "supposedly," like a sulky schoolboy, and whose seniority in the group is threatened by a new arrival. He pops up in front of Ned as he is taking out the trash and warns him that "this is *The Steve Zissou Show,* not *The Ned Show.*" After some macho posturing, Klaus slaps him and Ned threatens that if he touches him again, he will kick Klaus's teeth out. However, what could be just a childish exchange of threats turns comic when Klaus replies unwittingly with a different idiom, itself expressed negatively, "Not if I don't see you first." Such linguistic slips make Klaus more a pitiable figure of fun, picked up later when Ned does hit him and Klaus shrieks that he deserved a warning first. This is picked up again as Klaus is the first one to step over the line that Zissou sets out as a gauntlet, thinking it shows his support for the captain. He stands up for Zissou against the discontent of the interns, matching Marie's fiery rhetoric with laid-back hippy-speak: "I hear what you're saying but I think you misjudge the guy." After his tantrum during the raid to rescue Bill, Zissou tries to placate him by saying he and Esteban always thought of him as a baby brother, in a parallel to the Ned subplot. The notion of absent or errant fathers is thus partially subdivided between Ned and Klaus, both looking for some form of paternal recognition.

In the process, the initial rivalry between Ned and Klaus melts away. In a moment that is quite touching, Ned and Zissou reaffirm their mission and in the middle of the frame in the background, unseen by the other two, Klaus also participates in the musketeer-style hand gesture.

It is not perhaps that Anderson's films condone overt racism but that in a series of films, nonwhite roles are often subordinate and for sexual/comic relief only. The undistinguished pirates that attack the *Belafonte* in *Aquatic* represent pure cannon fodder in their inability to subdue the lone white hero, despite having many automatic weapons to his single pistol. On the other hand, Jorge's role in *Aquatic* adds stature to the traditional role of minstrel by endowing it with elements of Greek chorus, fused with Anderson's retro-pop sensibility (using David Bowie as a spine through the narrative). However, letting Jorge sing in Portuguese may intrigue or alienate viewers in equal measure. Jeff Goldblum's Hennessey may seem purely cartoonish, but there is more depth there than might seem the case at first. He is an anti-Zissou character, representing everything Zissou is not (financially secure, calm in manner, and most tellingly, the partner of Zissou's ex-wife). Hennessey's success is a visual image of Zissou's failure, professional and personal. However, it is a mark of the charisma of Zissou that we feel more warmly towards him and see the acts of theft from Hennessey's laboratory as comic rather than morally reprehensible. The way in which Hennessey exploits the situation after the piracy episode, knowing Zissou has no choice but to be towed to port at great expense, also means we view the subsequent loss of Hennessey's ship via an iceberg as poetic justice (possibly with a note of divine punishment for some Titanic-like hubris). As a contrast to Zissou, Hennessey's crew are dressed in pristine white with almost fascistic overtones, particularly Hennessey's second-in-command, the blond-haired Hugo. There is at the same time a contradictory throwback element as if beneath this veneer of scientific credibility, Zissou and Hennessey are just battling over money, women, and status akin to the style of Zissou's mentor, Lord Mandrake, as colonial hunters. Hennessey orders Hugo, on hearing about the break-in at his lab, to fetch his elephant gun and some buckshot, resolving to hunt down the criminals. However, despite Hennessey's air of sophistication, reclining on a couch in the middle of the deck in a white suit and sipping wine, his obtuseness in not realizing that Zissou was responsible for the break-in at his lab and somehow managed to persuade him that it was the pirates, marks him as a buffoon. Villa Hennessey is a reflection of his narcissistic personality, filled with pictures of himself and Eleanor together. Similarly, his first reaction after asking the question to Zissou, "Are you rescuing me?" is to declare "Fold" in the card game with the pirate who just shoots him.

In *Darjeeling*, given that country's colonial past and ongoing economic inequity, an element of servility is at least dramatically feasible (unlike Pagoda in *Tenenbaums*). Although the Royal-Pagoda relationship seems satisfactory to each side (it has endured for 30 years after all), the gag about Pagoda stabbing his master twice does not completely obscure the fact that Royal has a personal servant. If Pagoda owed Royal his life, culturally that might work, but the sense of obligation is the other way round. *Tenenbaums* is a film full of eccentric behavior but no one questions the anachronistic nature of this bond.

Anderson repeatedly casts Waris Ahluwalia and Deepak and Kumar Pallana, but it is the nature of their roles, even reflected in their character names, which is disappointing. As Vikram in *Aquatic*, Waris Ahluwalia has a few lines and is an important element of the ensemble crew, but despite having an important role in terms of plot in *Darjeeling*, he remains a nameless steward and an unnamed security guard in *The Hotel Chevalier*. Deepak Pallana appears in a series of unnamed, generic roles: a doctor (*Tenenbaums*), a bookstore employee (*Bottle Rocket*), or a fellow passenger (*Darjeeling*). In *Rushmore*, although he is named as Mr. Adams, a math teacher, this is an absurd fantasy sequence. Kumar Pallana's roles seem to be either literally anonymous, as "old man on train" in *Darjeeling*, or as in *Bottle Rocket*, where he operates under his own name or one which is clearly signaled as comic (Pagoda and Mr. Littlejeans). In all his roles, he is seen as bumbling and incompetent (a safecracker with no discernible touch in *Bottle Rocket*) and distinctly servile. Even where he has a name, as in *Rushmore*, he has little dialogue and his main contribution is the visual gag of being pinned up against a wall by a car driven by Blume. Kumar's vaudeville act of magic, juggling and a range of activities including chair-balancing, was given free rein in a scene in *Bottle Rocket* but was ultimately deleted. On the one hand, there is something endearing in Kumar's cluelessness in asking who Applejack was in *Bottle Rocket*, echoing Royal's lies about cancer in *Tenebaums* or simply stating, "Best play ever, man" when asked his view of the performance in *Rushmore*. He almost functions as an Anderson version of spot-the-dog for true die-hard fans who can exchange short phrases with each other as a code (like "try this it's very tasty" to a drug-fuelled Eli Cash as he is pursued through the house by Chas at the end of *Tenenbaums*). However, these tiny snippets of dialogue also relegate him to playing essentially the same character each time, almost as a personal favor to the friend who would regale Anderson and Owen Wilson as students with colorful stories while he worked at the Cosmic Cup Café.

Conversely, at times, Kumar might even be seen as a small-scale version of the hero, a kind of extra antihero. In *Tenenbaums*, like Royal's shooting of Chas, Kumar's act in stabbing Royal with a penknife and then helping him into a cab and later stitching him up could both be read as extreme examples of "tough love." In *Bottle Rocket*, although he appears hopeless, at least his incompetence is clear, while Dignan still harbors delusions of criminal grandeur, despite the robbery failing because of the thing he prides himself on the most, research.

In early drafts of *Bottle Rocket*, both Applejack and Rowboat, a Japanese-speaking "heavy" of Mr. Henry, are described as "black." Rowboat is played by Caan's real karate teacher, Takayuki Kubota, although Caan felt it was disrespectful for Kubota to be shown in just his underpants. It is true that in early drafts of the 1994 version, Applejack had more lines, explaining how he met Dignan when he intervened in a fight to help him. However, in *Tenenbaums,* we see the same tendency in the casting of the public notary that Royal calls upon to witness his divorce papers (Sanchez), Chas's driver (Anwar), and Royal's Asian masseuse (Sing-Sang), who cannot apparently speak English. In *Bottle Rocket,* although Applejack and Kumar are seated at the table at the country club, the waiters who serve them are black. The basic problem is that the features of anonymity, servility, and absurdity these characters display (often reflected in their names) are shown by nonethnic characters too, but the ethnic characters (apart from Danny Glover's Sherman) *all* show these features in some measure, repeatedly, remaining peripheral and subservient to white male heroes.

Ari and Uzi, the twins in *Tenenbaums,* are close to interchangeable Jewish caricatures. However, Ronny and Donny Blume in *Rushmore* are also virtually interchangeable and are clearly white. It seems the twinness is the prime factor rather than race here (although in both cases, it does raise the question of what kind of parents name their twin offspring with such similar names). When asked about which of his sons gave him a black eye, Blume admits, "I can't tell the difference anymore."

Darjeeling is probably the most troubling example of this weakness in Anderson's aesthetic in that he has made a conscious decision to set his narrative within a non-American, English-speaking context, and yet we learn virtually nothing about it. Emily May makes an interesting schematic contrast with the idealism of *Easy Rider* but misses the extent of the Whitman brothers' shallowness.[2] They continue to seek spiritual enlightenment by ironically failing to show enough curiosity about the culture they are passing through to interact with it. The only things they learn (or seem to be interested in) relate entirely to themselves. On the train, Jack thinks about his writing (even tearing up as he reads his own work back to himself); Peter frets about his wife; and Francis babbles on about his schedule. It is tempting to see the opening as emblematic, an apparently aimless race through a landscape without connecting personally with the people and culture itself. Without English-speaking lyrics, Satyajit Ray's music, to an audience unfamiliar with his work, may evoke little more than a sense of exotic otherness (like the talk of a man-eating tiger). The tea and cookies that Rita brings feel like a strange blend of British colonialism and American cultural imperialism. Peter's generalizations about the country are incredibly inarticulate: "I love the way this country smells. I'll never forget it. It's kind of spicy." Renoir's *The River,* although cited by Anderson as part of the inspiration for *Darjeeling,* surpasses Anderson's film in its portrayal of life *as it is lived in a different culture.* It is only when the Whitmans are literally brought near a river that something starts to break loose in the narrative, but it is hard to imagine Anderson emulating Renoir in using nonprofessional actors with the lack of directorial control they bring. We do see the brother's instinctive imperative to help a fellow human being as the Indian boys fall in the water, but just prior to the accident, Francis mutters, "Look at these assholes."

The brothers present stereotypical Americans abroad, all simultaneously producing medicines at the dining table, as if this is fully normalized behavior, like a kind of picnic (although it draws suspicious stares from the table opposite). Later, we see Jack knocking back cough medicine, which Francis describes as "a dumb way to get loaded." They themselves disturb other passengers, and yet Peter asks some Germans to quiet down.

There is an overtone of colonial superiority here. Most of the passengers seem to be white, and bells are rung for Indian servants to bring refreshments or other services. Jack's reaction on seeing the Indian girl is fairly primitive ("I want that stewardess") and suggests that this new, unknown culture is just like an exotic sweetshop for their pleasure alone and a romanticized backdrop viewed through a window.

Their first steps away from the train are a brief visit to a temple. Camera movements—tilting down from a tower, panning round the rooftops of the town, and a rapid zoom into a taxi as the brothers get out—in combination suggest the sudden immersion in a culture that is almost overwhelming in its difference so that like the protagonists, the camera does not know where to look or exactly what it is looking at. Rapid tilt shots of birds in cages are cut with incomprehensible signs (to English speakers) for frogs and fish and a close-up of a snake in a cage. Their choice of purchase is telling. Peter wants shoes; Jack looks at food; and Francis searches in vain for a power adaptor. From their clothes, language (they never attempt to speak anything other than English), and actions (attending a religious ceremony uninvited), the three remain firmly alien to this culture. There is no sign they understand what is actually going on at this ceremony, the fevered camera movement continuing inside the temple with a shot directly up at the bell followed by a vertical 90-degree arc from the roof to Francis. Even here, despite this lack of understanding, Francis still orders Jack to put some coins in front of the deity.

At a second temple, the trio adopt absurdly colorful headscarves (that they keep wearing into the next shot back by the train). Francis bows his head, but Jack is more interested in a picture at the back of a bloodied white man, before we cut back to the three supposedly praying. Even if this is based upon a real event that happened to Anderson, there is no sense that the brothers really know what they are doing here or that they have any real spiritual belief. Francis seems to expect some kind of wisdom simply to descend upon them. The three-shot, used on DVD covers and posters, may appear to suggest the brothers are devout and respectful but in context, they are faintly ridiculous. What is actually going through their heads is more material concerns as Francis demands Peter return his belt, which seems petty as well as a strange time to bring up the subject. Stereotypical elements of Indian culture are played for laughs, such as the snake which escapes from Peter's case.

The Westerners are all in a state of melodramatic panic, with Francis waving a stick around. By contrast, the Indian steward phlegmatically fetches a fairly small spatula and deals quickly with this minor irritant, popping the creature in a container held by the girl. Peter's patronizing declaration that children are playing cricket with a tennis ball obscures the fact that in such a crowded urban environment, they could hardly play with a real one (even if they could afford it). Francis exoticizes the people and culture, and talks about finding a peacock feather and going off to meditate, declaring, "I love it here. The people are beautiful." This pontificating is immediately undercut by Jack pointing out that some of these so-called beautiful children are laughing at them.

It might seem that using Satyajit Ray's music shows a greater response to Indian culture, but we still have the Kinks' "This Time Tomorrow," "Strangers," and "Powerman" (all from 1970) and the Rolling Stones' "Play With Fire" (1965); in other words, Western retro music is still used at will. Furthermore, by using tracks not by Ray but from Merchant-Ivory films, like the title music from *The Householder* (1963) and *Bombay Talkie* (1970), as well as one of Ray's own tracks, "The Deserted Ballroom" from *Shakespeare Wallah* (1965), like the presence of Peter Sarstedt, himself an Anglo-Indian, there is the sense of Indian culture packaged for a Western audience. The use of nonwhite characters largely in peripheral roles seems also to underestimate their talent. Casting Irrfan Kahn as an unnamed villager hardly seems fitting for the actor who played the title role in Asif Kapadia's *The Warrior* (2003). The final sequence in which the brothers board a different train to be served by a very similar steward and stewardess combination suggests they will be little more individualized than the previous pair.

There seems to be a casual, almost lazy approach to matters of racial stereotypes within the fictions themselves, like Anderson's use of cyclists and a *deux chevaux* to signal Frenchness in his Softbank commercial. In theory, *Aquatic*'s multinational crew should represent a sense of balance, but apart from Klaus, most operate at the level of a one-dimensional gag. This is not to suggest Anderson himself is insensitive (although the use of an Indiana redneck explanation for Margot's missing finger in *Tenenbaums* comes close), but certainly many of his characters are. Max refers to Magnus at least twice as a "mick," a term of abuse for the Irish. Although here there is the clear possibility that Max is doing this to rile the Scottish boy, this also occurs in scenes where Magnus is not present. Guggenheim's question "Who's the Chinaman with Fischer?" referring to Margaret, seems strangely blunt, but after Dirk's clarification (a role he also fulfils in connection with Magnus), Guggenheim states, "I know the Koreans. They're good people." Generalizations are bluff and insensitive rather than malicious. The name of Pagoda, although theoretically possible in an Indian context, seems more likely a misnomer based on ignorance of Asian culture. His presence in the background of the scene with Etheline, apparently peeling potatoes, would suggest he is not bound to Royal alone; that is, he is a family servant, whose main role, it seems, like Kylie in *Fantastic Mr. Fox*, is simply "to be available" (to Anderson as director as well as the Tenenbaum family). The secretary at the garage in *Darjeeling*, although she has a few words, is crudely denoted in the script simply as "Black Girl."

In *Fantastic Mr. Fox*, the exchange of a Black Power salute with a wolf is an odd digression. It constitutes the sole overtly political gesture in the whole of Anderson's oeuvre (apart from Mr. Bean bearing a striking similarity to media magnate Rupert Murdoch). Anderson claims the wolf episode "became the whole theme of the movie," which may be intended ironically, but this belittles any political point being made.[3] It is an overtly dreamlike, surreal moment, the wolf appearing off to the side of the road in a mountainous area, featuring ice amidst the film's dominant orange-colored landscape. The wolf does not speak, although Fox addresses him in English and French and calls out the strange element of small talk that he has a phobia of wolves. It seems that we are meant to see the episode as demonstrating that Fox has faced one of his phobias and matured as a result, but he hardly faces this deliberately. Kylie is the one who spots the wolf and although Fox tears up in close-up, exactly what he learns here is unclear. It is Kylie, not Fox, who keeps chattering on about wolves during their nighttime raids. It is perhaps a slight move towards the dreamlike quality that is more associated with Buñuel's early works, but it is still light years away from the surrealism of *Un Chien Andalou* (1929) with juxtaposed images, the meaning of which the viewer has to decipher himself. There is clearly supposed to be a meaningful relationship between the two animals here (signaled by the high-pitched, single voice singing), but if it is intended as a moment of epiphany, its precise nature remains ambiguous. Bearing in mind Anderson's largely apolitical aesthetic and the privileged nature of the protagonists in *Bottle Rocket* and *The Darjeeling Limited*, as well as the elitist backdrop of *Rushmore*, in this context, the gesture to the wolf seems flippant rather than cute.

However, Anderson's repeated restricted use of actors drawn from nonwhite origins should also be placed in a wider context of his work. Virtually all his white characters are deeply flawed and dysfunctional; that is the kind of universe in which he operates. It could even be said that the ethnic characters' position on the periphery of the narratives is partly their choice, and they look on in polite disdain (such as the Steward in *Darjeeling*) at the white heroes who blunder through the main plot. It is the absurd obtuseness of Anderson's *fictional* heroes that portrays people of color in a limited light rather than any pernicious agenda on the part of Anderson himself. It is also worth making the point that if the actors concerned felt that they were in some way playing roles that demeaned them or particular racial groups with which viewers might associate them, one assumes they would not keep working with Anderson, which plainly they do.

ANDERSON AND CLASS

ZISSOU: Let me tell you about my boat.
FOX: Tell me about them (asking about Boggis, Bunce, and Bean—three rich farmers)

Let me tell you about the very rich.

—F. Scott Fitzgerald

Weiner's criticisms would perhaps have more power if directed towards Anderson's narrow portrayal of class. Although Anderson tends to mention Buñuel in general rather than refer to specific films, Buñuel's 1972 *The Discreet Charm of the Bourgeoisie* at least could be used to describe the focus of Anderson's films. *Bottle Rocket* explicitly raises the question of class but does so via a gag that obscures this aspect of the film. When Dignan asks, "How does an asshole like Bob get such a great kitchen?" a line suggested by producer James Brooks, the answer is clear: from his rich parents. He does not have any visible means of financial support. Dignan may like to cast themselves as a rebellious, antiestablishment group "on the run from Johnny law." However, they have nothing really to run from or rebel against. Their lives, Bob's especially, are extremely comfortable. It is the ultimate irony, not only that they are tricked by Mr. Henry, who cleans out Bob's house, but also that they fail to see (unlike a professional criminal) that their own homes represent a great source of wealth. Mr. Henry calls Bob "the rich kid" from the outset, but the other two fail to see the connection. Bob is a member of a country club but does not play golf or tennis. The joke about his "interview" for the role of a getaway driver is not that he is the only one with a car but that the car is a Mercedes. The 1994 version also mentions parked on his driveway a brand new BMW and a Lexus that his parents will not let him use, and Dignan describes Futureman (Bob's brother) as coming from "a prominent family." Bob lives in a house that is worth looking after, and in the 1994 version, Bob nags Dignan to use a coaster on the table for his drink. When Dignan challenges Bob to a fight, he mentions a "backyard," a term that Bob does not immediately recognize in connection with his large garden. In a Spanish exchange between Inez and Julio, he may be "the rich guy" who is described as stupidly dropping his car keys in his own gas tank.

However, they are more than just a group of three rich young men. There is a subtle sliding scale of wealth between them. When Anthony feels stressed, he has the financial means to be able to check into an institution. He only leaves for Dignan's sake, not due to financial pressures. In the 1994 version, Anthony is carrying a credit card for emergencies from his mother. Dignan loses his temper with Anthony, not only because the car breaks down and the adventure comes to an end but also because Anthony gives Inez $500 as if it were nothing. As he says shortly before this, "What is broke to you? You're so spoiled man." It is worth remembering that they do not rob Dignan's house apparently because his family have nothing worth stealing. In the 1994 version, Anthony tells Bob that Dignan used to wear cowboy boots for phys ed. Anthony, whom we are told by Grace has never worked a day in his life, does not suffer in the mental institution at the opening, referring to the therapists as "understanding" and saying good-bye to people during his escape. The catalyst that propels Royal Tenenbaum back to his family is not guilt but the fact that he is broke. However, this should not obscure the fact that he has been living in what looks like a fairly expensive hotel for 22 years, and Richie (whose name reflects his privileged background) has been cruising the world aimlessly on a luxury ocean liner for seven months.

Inez and Rita offer two white men a brief distraction from their self-obsessed lives, but it is more the case of wealth and class that allows Anthony and Jack respectively to see these women as available for their pleasure. In *Rushmore*, Blume's sons are very much reflections and products of the system and a life of privilege, loutish, brutish, and exclusive (they do not want Max at their party). Max comes from a modest background—his father is a barber, and Max only gains a place at Rushmore through a scholarship. However, when he addresses his new classmates at Clover High, he does so across a linguistic chasm, reflective of class difference. His suggestion to set up a fencing club may be intended as a friendly gesture, and he may protest that he "was not born with a silver spoon in his mouth," but he has been surrounded long enough by those who have to adopt their culture and mannerisms. In *Fantastic Mr. Fox,* Kristofferson's difference from those around him is not just his embracing of yoga and karate but in language too, failing to understand Beaver's reference to a "wet sandwich." Kristofferson may have a sick father but in his perfectly accessorized swimwear and preference for meditation over tantrums, he is marked as a cultured, *middle-class* misfit.

Max's failure at Rushmore is created by his mistaking the tokens of social engagement (his plethora of clubs) for the real thing. Indeed, the film could be read as a cautionary tale about what happens if you try and escape your class origins. In an early version of the script, Max says that he disagrees with Blume's comments about the rich since "we don't choose who our fathers are." Anderson replaces this kind of realism with a more solipsistic sensibility in which characters do seem to be able to choose their offspring or parents (Ned in *Aquatic,* Margot in *Tenenbaums,* and even Max here as he reinvents his father as a neurosurgeon). Matters of class are overcome (or swept under the carpet) by the imaginative power of denial of Anderson's heroes. The fact that Anderson could film at the actual school where he himself was a pupil might suggest a growing climate of openness or a reflection of the fact that this institution and others like it still exist.

Blume's speech, apparently inciting rebellion, effectively against himself and people like him, could be seen as just a pose and doomed to failure. He can literally afford to be flippant as his life of privilege, symbolized by his

Bentley and large house with pool, rests on his social position as a steel tycoon. He can say what he likes due to his philanthropic gestures. The whole institution of Rushmore is based on the money of such parents, as indeed is his own considerable personal fortune. There are some suggestions that some of Anderson's male characters married into money and therefore struggle when the relationship breaks down, either being forced to pursue their ex-wife and beg for cash, like Zissou, or hole up in a hotel, like Royal or Blume. Max's later introduction of Blume to his father might be taken to signal some emotional growth, being prepared to acknowledge his humble origins (except our focus is on Blume's near-breakdown and his envy for the family closeness Max seems to have with his father). Maybe Max really does have it "all worked out."

The manner in which Zissou addresses the viewer echoes F. Scott Fitzgerald. Anderson shows us a character who has his own boat (a huge floating film studio/playboy's playground) and even his own island. The Whitmans in *Darjeeling* argue over a $6,000 belt and $3,000 loafers, and Francis drags a laminating machine around a country where millions struggle to eke out a living. Max may be in Rushmore on a scholarship and come from a more modest home than his peers, but he is still attending an elitist institution. Far from using his critical energies to bring this down (as Blume's speech might suggest), Max does not "set dead aim on the rich boys"; on the contrary, he seeks to join their ranks. Max's one-act play that gave him access to Rushmore may have been about Watergate, but he hardly personifies political subversion. Max later mentions that he "gets to do odd jobs" but whether this is an opportunity or expectation remains unclear. His only criticisms of the institution (reinstating Latin) or attempts at change (building an aquarium) are motivated by his delusional attempts to impress Miss Cross, not to bring about real change. *Bottle Rocket*'s aspiring criminals are not rejecting their social reality; they are indulging Dignan's fantasy of being on the run and being accepted by an alternative family, a criminal fraternity. The robbing of Anthony's house is not a blow against the notion of family or even one particular family; it is just a marker of their criminal amateurism *and* demonstrates that their family is rich enough to replace any loss. By the time the Whitmans have reached a station, they have moved back into a world of Western tourists and Eastern servants, with Sherpas to carry their cases. They ride into the frame on a moped in a further variety of the staple three-shot, which seems like an iconic, rebellious *Easy Rider* style image (ideal for a poster or trailer), except they are followed by a taxi weighed down by their cases. It is their material wealth that allows them to indulge in these fantasies of spiritual journeys. Jack has been staying an indeterminate amount of time at a very expensive Parisian hotel. When they disembark from the train, we see that the carriage is marked as a first-class sleeper, and their father's car, which they later try to repossess, is a red Porsche. The luggage they dispense with at the end may be intended to show a shift in perspective towards a less materialistic view of life, but it remains the case that these have been carried through the body of the film (often by porters), and the slow motion jettisoning of their emotional baggage may only serve to underline that these items were specially made by Louis Vuitton.

Mr. Fox's actions could be reads in class terms, in which he acts primarily in defense of his livelihood and, by extension, his family. He acts along with his other downtrodden comrades to liberate the produce derived from the land from the exploitative bourgeoisie (here, the farmers) and distribute it among the lowest of his particular society. The giant supermarket that looks set to feed them at the end is revealed as owned by Boggis, Bunce, and Bean. However, to read Anderson's work as politically engaged requires quite a distortion of the material we have. The Rolling Stones' "Street Fighting Man" (1968) accompanying Rat's predatory dance is an explicitly political song, describing student protest in the late 1960s, particularly in France. To place this in a children's animated film to accompany the posturing of a ridiculous character serves to parody and depoliticize the lyrics. Fox claims to buy the tree house because he does not want to feel "poor." However, the film is most effective when such clichés are questioned as when Fox's pep talk and challenge (paralleling Blume's call to arms in *Rushmore*) "Will you join me?" are met by only mumbled general and unenthusiastic assent. Overriding any political reading there is the palpable sense that he acts out of the selfish pursuit of adventure, putting his own life at risk (and again by extension, that of his family). His decision for just one more job has the feel of a career criminal, who needs the euphoria of danger, the thrill of the chase, as much as any material benefit that theft might bring.

However, part of the difficulty here, in considering questions of both race and class, is the problematic relation (or arguably nonrelation) between the whimsical and the typical. Attempting to read representative statements into Anderson's characters is difficult because the characters really do not relate to the real world but to other figures within this fictional world. Anderson is not presenting us with a slice of life but a highly stylized slice of one specific group. The characters we see on screen may be engaging, but it is unlikely we meet them in our everyday lives. Unless we accept Zooey's notion that "we're all freaks," Anderson is not talking about the human condition as much as the condition of a small group of humans (who just happen to be born into fairly privileged, white, upper-middle-class American homes). Characters have little to rebel against except their own privileged upbringing which they can run back to whenever real life becomes too threatening (like Bob in *Bottle Rocket,* the three siblings in *Tenenbaums,* or Max who transfers his Rushmore mentality to a new school, rather than leaving it behind).

Man with a Movie Camera:
Anderson's Use of the Frame

Increasingly, in Anderson's films, it is the composition within rather than between the frame that is paramount. Complex editing takes second place to elaborate mise-en-scène, careful juxtaposition (often based around a symmetrical notion of balance within an individual shot), and occasional set-piece long takes. This can be considered in the specific light of his use of paintings, the style of his commercials, which constitute a condensed version of his aesthetic, and his stylistic relation to early silent film.

Anderson frames and composes his shots so carefully almost any still frame can be used as a promotional poster. In general, Anderson seems to work up to a cut, at which point we have a defining image of that scene or sequence. There might be very rare examples of an effect like a crash zoom, a sudden and rapid zoom towards a subject, such as Richie and Eli during the rifle game, which creates the sense of an amateurish home movie, or when Royal is at the playground fence, trying to befriend the twins. However, transition devices, which draw attention to themselves, such as dissolves, are something Anderson never uses. Therefore, the mise-en-scène, shot composition, and the proxemics of performers are very important, and stylistically there are longer-than-average takes, often with little or no camera movement, achieved with frequent use of a rostrum camera and wide-angle anamorphic lenses that capture a greater amount of on-screen detail.

PAINTINGS

Anderson often creates frames-within-a-frame, most obviously in connection with paintings. Early scenes often include a framed painted image as part of a public performance, such as the backdrop to the opening lecture in *Aquatic* where the Naples opera house setting suggests an epic adventure, or *Rushmore,* where the state of Blume's marriage is depicted in his family portrait. He is sullen and smoking in contrast to his pale, redheaded family, and this shot appears later as an insert, almost like a flashback, in the pool sequence. Paintings are used to suggest the state of a character's fortunes, such as how far Zissou matches up to his mentor Mandrake in the Explorer Club scene, and in *Rushmore*, the fight between Max and Guggenheim over incriminating pictures of Blume and Miss Cross is conveyed via shadows played out over a portrait of Churchill, suggesting an excess of misplaced aggression.

In *Tenenbaums*, Eli Cash casts a fairly absurd figure, dressed in a pretentious hat, a tasseled jacket, and smoking with a long cigarette holder. The artwork he chooses for his study reflects this pseudo-sophisticated persona, but these pictures go much further than that. The motivation behind them and the scenes they depict are extremely perverse, like a nightmarish combination of John Boorman's *Deliverance* (1972) and David Lynch's *Blue Velvet* (1983), casting his relationship with Margot in a much more sinister light. The paintings, by Mexican artist Miguel Calderón, part of an exhibition piece entitled *Aggressively Mediocre/Mentally Challenged/Fantasy Island (circle one)*, include a lengthy shot of one picture in particular, *Bad Route* (1998). This features a group of shirtless young men, riding a range of different motorbikes and aggressively looking directly at the viewer. There is a sense of stylization about the images that might appeal to Cash but possibly like his final kamikaze drive into the Tenenbaum house, there is something quite dark and unsettling beneath the surface of his character, of which he seems unaware. If we are intended to see the pictures as reflective of artistic pretentiousness, then the same charge might be leveled at their actual owner and the one who wrote their presence into the script: Wes Anderson. It hangs in Anderson's own office, but his explanation for putting it in the scene (that both Cash and the figures in the painting seem to be on some kind of drug) seems unconvincing.

There are a number of levels of artifice, some readily visible, some less so, about the pictures themselves. They were inspired by genuine horrific crimes, involving rape and attempted murder, which the police then reconstructed, raising the whole question of the appropriateness of reenactments of real crimes as entertainment. Furthermore, Calderón then mimicked this process with his own actors, posing for photos. However, like controversial American artist Jeff Koons, Calderón did not actually paint the work himself but instructed a lesser-known artist to paint the picture. Anderson only discovered the full process after purchasing the picture in question, but the fact that he and Wilson considered at one point having the twins and Royal play similar kinds of dressing up games seems quite disturbing. It is true that Calderón's actions are similar to that of a director placing his characters in a scene, but it is the nature of the actions themselves that Anderson seems to pass over.

Like typical Anderson characters, *Bad Route* has a similar interest in symmetry and balance with several figures who look straight out at the viewer packed into the frame. Although both he and Anderson have been dubbed enfant terribles, Calderón's art seems driven by a desire to shock, almost completely absent in Anderson's work. Like Jack in William Golding's *Lord of the Flies* (1954), there is something strangely liberating and potentially dehumanizing about the wearing of a mask. In such a sexually depraved context, the pose of the bare-chested males, astride motorbikes, as representing cliché monsters, has a much darker suggestion of sexual violence (both real and fictional) to which the film and Anderson's comments about it seem strangely oblivious. The Rushmore Academy Web site even features a version of the picture with five different Steve Zissous on the bikes instead. It may represent the edginess that Eli can only dream about (the reality is closer to the clippings he still sends Etheline), but just for a few seconds, there is a darker world just beyond the frame here, which is the nearest that Anderson has so far come to the more deviant underworlds of Lynch or David Cronenberg.

In *Aquatic*, we are shown, via Zissou's explanation to Ned, a series of paintings of key figures in the backstory of the Explorer's Club and in Zissou's own history. The iconic Lord Mandrake, Zissou's apparent mentor, is shown alongside the colonial trappings of elephant tusks and stuffed leopards, placing him closer to a 19th-century adventurer, in which the natural world is more playground than laboratory to be observed and understood. Cousteau himself was a hunter before he was a conservationist, and there is something of this ambiguity in Zissou's initial comments about hunting down the Jaguar Shark. His own painting—sporting the ubiquitous red cap, which Jane notes in her report as "contrived," and prominent medals—does make him look ridiculously self-congratulatory. However, he is unhappy with the portrait, which seems more camp, implying perhaps not that he is effeminate per se but that the role of rugged, macho adventurer is not one he is fully comfortable with.

In *Fantastic Mr. Fox*, Mrs. Fox's accomplished hobby signals her as a more rounded, almost bohemian character, and she repeatedly paints one particular view of the landscape that surrounds them but with the addition of a lightning bolt, which later becomes a tornado. This might suggest the danger she feels overhanging the safety of her family—a danger created by her husband's nature, which once satisfied becomes moderated into fantasy (the quintessential Oz image). All the farmers manage to find after their unsuccessful attempt at digging out the foxes is one small painting, which might be one of the many that Mrs. Fox paints, or it might be intended as a sight gag about scale, but this would not really work as the animals come face-to-face with the humans later and are of similar size. Her huge landscape picture seems an indulgence until we see it used as a means of battle planning in the sewer, which is translated into a Situation Room, complete with plastic cups and string as communication devices, from which they can conduct operations.

The painting in Badger's office is also a little ambiguous. Initially it is centrally framed but largely obscured by Fox's head. In a subsequent shot, Fox stands up and reveals a group of what appear to be uniformed badgers standing on a hillside. Later, as Fox and Kylie steal away from the house at night on the final part of their master plan, they pass Badger's house, and we see this hillside in the background in greater detail with the remnants of felled trees. The Lascaux-style cave paintings that miraculously appear in the deepest space the foxes dig to escape the farmers (and upon which no one comments) suggest the caves are incredibly old or possibly the foxes have waited so long, they have done the paintings themselves, a neat visual irony with animals painting humans.

A further effect of all the paintings mentioned here is to keep another Anderson presence before us, that of brother Eric (over and above his presence on the soundtrack of *Fantastic Mr. Fox* too as Kristofferson). Eric Chase Anderson's *Chuck Dugan Is AWOL* (2005), subtitled *A Novel with Maps,* is the kind of book you would imagine Wes writing, a fully realized fictional world, where forward narrative momentum takes second place to wallowing in the detail of illustrations, planted clues, and a richness of detail that is as much visual as literary. Eric Anderson's interest in maps began as family Christmas presents, including Wes as an actual subject, and his book includes tight, overhead shots with several (apparently) random documents or points of interest, foreshadowing the beagle documentation shot in *Fantastic Mr. Fox*.[1] The prose reads in places like exposition from a screenplay, and the annotated drawings evoke the logoization of *Aquatic* (hardly surprising since he designed this too).[2]

ALTERNATIVES

Anderson sometimes makes other more self-conscious framing and editing choices. For example, in *Rushmore* when Max inspects Margaret's plans for her project, Anderson focuses on the space through which Max's arm reaches and brings the paper into focused close-up. Rather than following the subject, here the camera chooses a space and waits for the subject to move into it. Like the nighttime car scenes in *Bottle Rocket,* Anderson very occasionally uses an extreme oblique angle for his subjects so that they are not centrally framed. In *Rushmore,* as Blume and Max walk out of the elevator in separate scenes, they both invade the focal distance of the shot so that it blurs slightly, underlining the destruction of Blume's inner life (he is looking disheveled and is smoking and drinking to excess) and Max's Pyrrhic victory with the bees respectively.

In *Fantastic Mr. Fox,* the third robbery is conveyed purely by consecutive shots on surveillance cameras. As all four are displayed on screen at the same time, effectively we have a visualization of continuity editing with Fox exiting frame right and then entering frame left in moving from Camera 1 to 2. The scene therefore becomes a kind of editing studio, in which we see Fox and his helpers pick the lock, run into the farm, appear in close-up, and then steal away in longer shot, just as silhouettes, carrying their haul. At times, Anderson adopts more static framing, having figures move partly out of sight and then move back in, such as Bean walking up to Fox's tail before bending to pick it up and a similar action later with the beagle and drugged blueberry.

In *Fantastic Mr. Fox,* there is some distinctive subjective camera positioning, such as the shot across and over the head of a character whose back is to us to see the face of who they are looking at, such as when Fox squares up against Rat. This condenses the conventional shot/reverse-shot pattern by keeping the prime viewer (if not showing their reaction) in the frame. This is taken a stage further in the rabid dog chasing first Fox and then later Bean and his men, when we inhabit the point of view as if from a camera strapped to the dog's back, seeing the quarry from between his ears. The demonstration of how to lace the blueberries, involving hands entering the frame, conveniently skips over exactly where one might procure sleeping powder. A similar device is used when we occupy Fox's subjective point of view more exactly, as he approaches the dog and we see his outstretched arms, and a tempting bone comes into the frame. Such effects put us in the scene but also make us aware of our viewing position being manipulated by the director.

COMMERCIALS

Anderson was criticized for agreeing to make commercials at all as if his quirky individuality was forever compromised. However, several high-profile directors have made commercials with artistic credibility (like David Lynch, and Michel Gondry), and it is more productive to judge Anderson on the work rather than prejudge him about the medium. Unlike directors such as Tony and Ridley Scott, Wes Anderson has not moved into feature films from a background in advertising or commercial design (although his father did work in this field at one time). Unlike directors such as David Fincher, Anderson does not seem to be interested in trying out new technical aspects of filmmaking. His attraction to commercials would seem to be the speed with which they can be made, and clearly he does not work for free. A more persuasive rationale is that it helps him add to the myth of his own public persona. He is happy to give interviews in print and online, where his eccentricity and attention to detail nearly always surface as givens. What follows are some thoughts on a range of his commercials, restricted to those which are accessible for public viewing.

Avon (2003)

Anderson's little-known spot for Wieden & Kennedy, "Meet Mark," to promote Avon cosmetics, uses the same device that he would use in the AT&T commercials of a camera position revolving past different sets. Here, there is no single talking head, but each separate set features a girl who speaks outwards towards the camera. There are nine different sets featured, including work and home environments and some camera "drift" tracking across and slight zoom in on one section. Clearly there is intended to be some ambiguity as to who Mark is with the implication of a friend whom every girl should know, but there is the less positive impression of a chain of pseudo-sexual relationships, which with minor alterations, might be used in a safe sex campaign. Anderson carries some of his filmmaking aesthetic into such commercials, securing the services of key personnel, such as Bob Yeoman as his director of photography and using noncontemporary music. "Love Is All Around" from *The Mary Tyler Moore Show* can be heard in the background (possibly a nod to its creator, James L. Brooks, who helped Anderson at the start of his career). An apparent one-take shot, there are some postproduction special effects, which help to bridge transitions, and a slight feeling of aspiring to an ideal or an idea that still requires a technical fudge to make it happen.

Dasani (2005)

"Bear," "Hamster," "Dog"

Perhaps, after the lukewarm reception of *Aquatic,* Anderson was tempted by a project on dry land that he could complete in days rather than months. This series for Dasani bottled water has the typical Anderson 90-degree whip-pans, the camera following a figure through the scene, the blend of childish game-playing with adult knowingness, but viewers' reaction may be similar to Royal's noncommittal feelings on watching Margot's play in *Tenenbaums.* Working with the Anomaly agency and particularly copywriter and creative director Ernest Lupinacci, Anderson creates a series of 30-second spots around the same basic theme.

In "Bear," a bear emerges from hibernation to deliver his sales patter straight to the camera, from which we whip-pan to the same bear earlier, shaking off water after being in a mountain stream. The juxtaposition of a very conventional commercial register (an ordinary guy speaking in relaxed colloquial language) with an amateurish bear suit, with faces left uncovered, may not seem stark enough to create much of an impact. It does seem quite a compromise creatively and a world away from more imaginative uses of the same basic idea, such as the Aardman Animation film *Lip Synch* (Nick Park, 1990) which later became the *Creature Comforts* series (2003–present, Richard Goleszowski) and which used claymation figures interpreting real (but initially unrelated) recordings of various vox pop interviews about housing problems. There is a second spot featuring the same bear in which the dialogue features the observation that supposed clean mountain water contains salmon spawning so that this product comes with the final recommendation that it is "salmon-free."

There is slightly more wit in "Hamster," which features an oversized *Honey I Shrunk the Kids* style set and more colloquial language, such as the idea of selling the water in 80-ounce bottles (huge to this character), which the hamster describes as "fierce." However, the cliché patter of a busy fitness expert (played by Robyn Cohen from *Aquatic*), even involving the ironic presence of an exercise wheel, is not rendered more interesting by being delivered in a hamster costume.

"Dog" features the main character, a cocker spaniel, flopping into a huge kitchen with a giant stove, and discovering the joys of Dasani water. He drops the paper on the floor, wanders around the set with a huge table and chairs, sniffs the unappealing food, and enthuses about how great the water is, before delivering the nearest thing the series comes to a punch line: "It'll knock the taste of tennis ball right out of your yap." The dialogue is a little overwhelmed by a bass line, which feels like a nod to the Bloodhound Gang's "The Bad Touch" (2000), the video for which featured the band all dressed in unconvincing animal costumes.

The idea of animal testimonials seems a little ambiguous. Just because an animal recommends something, it may not necessarily be that great for human consumption. Most animals will eat or drink just about anything to survive. The budget (around $1 million) might not sound like a problem, but the speed of production (two days), simplicity (one might say banality) of the concept, and the limited sense of Anderson's own creativity here restrict the impact of the finished product. Anderson was not involved in the second wave of Dasani commercials a year later, suggesting a lack of interest on his part. One point to note here is the use of whip-pans, not so much to another location at the same time but to a previous experience by the character speaking at a different time; in other words, it is a kind of flashback, which Anderson has not used before.

American Express—"My Life, My Card" (2004)

> What is a film director? A man who's asked questions
> about everything. Sometimes he knows the answers.
>
> —Ferrand in Truffaut's
> *Day For Night*

With Dasani, and AT&T, Anderson is working around the narrow concept of a series of related 30-second spots. In theory, this allows for an element of progression but in practice that can be lost if the commercials are watched out of sequence. With this American Express commercial, Anderson has a less restrictive format. It is a two-minute mini film in its own right (its duration reflective of a substantial investment of time and money) for the Ogilvy and Mather agency. The timing of the release of the commercial links Anderson's directorial brand with the Tribeca Film Festival, which seeks to position itself as celebrating artistically valid independent film, especially in an archival function (its association with Scorsese adding to this) and reflecting popular taste. In his first appearance in front of the camera, Anderson, in safari suit and carrying a viewfinder, is both mocking the popular image of a megaphone-wielding director, a perfectionist in control of every area of production, at the same time as ironically adding to it.

The whole concept is clearly an allusion to Truffaut's *Day for Night* (1974), complete with characters named François and Jean-Pierre, chronicling the interrelated dramas behind the scenes of a film set, with the director as the God-like central figure, expected to have answers for questions about relationships and personal trivia as well as the making of the film. The exploding car is both a reference to a climactic event in Truffaut's film and an allusion to Orson Welles's *Touch of Evil* (1958), where the opening long take ends with a similar effect. Anderson is placing himself in a tradition of European art movies, in which directors effectively play themselves, such as Truffaut's Ferrand and Fellini's Guido in *8½*. The setting with fake snow (drawn attention to in Anderson's own dialogue) and the absurd dialogue about the gun ("Can I get a .357 with a bayonet ?"), refer directly to Truffaut's film. The allusion is aural as well as visual, using Georges Delerue's "Le Grande Choral" (also used later in *Fantastic Mr. Fox*). Delerue, who produced a number of scores for Truffaut, Louis Malle, and Jean-Luc Godard, is therefore closely associated with a whole group of directors, who directly inspired Anderson. *Day for Night* seems a clear influence on *Zissou*, where the creation of a fiction, the shooting of a film, threatens to overwhelm the lives of those involved in it. We also have a director struggling to hold a production together, a problematic pregnancy, a nervous breakdown from a British actress, and towards the end the death of a central character, Alexandre (Jean-Pierre Aumont), in an accident. The AmEx commercial was released around the time of *Aquatic,* effectively acting as a trailer for Team Anderson.

Other Anderson works are referenced, particularly *Tenenbaums,* from which we have Richie's tennis racket and pigeons (let free at the end) and Anderson's assertion that the performance of his actors sounds fake (evoking Royal, judging his adopted daughter's play and Jane on Zissou's miraculous escape from the Jaguar Shark in *Aquatic*). Stylistically, we have diegetic music as Anderson hits the play button on a stereo system; several 90-degree whip-pans; a narrative (and by implication, a directorial) concern with tiny details (the question about the origin of a pen); the use of Futura for the on-screen caption introducing him; the symmetry of the framing of the opening trio; the presence of Anderson regulars Jason Schwartzman, Waris Ahluwalia, and Wally Wolodarsky (hidden slightly better); and his usual cinematographer, Robert Yeoman, on the crane at the end. Anderson makes fun of his own reputation, asking for an impossibly precise kind of gun, which is miraculously sketched out moments later and his public reputation as perhaps being more critically fêted than actually liked, in the shrug of the little girl presented by her father (the man who loaned them the sports car) as a big fan. It is also of course a nod to *Bottle Rocket*. Always be nice to the guy with the car.

Anderson claims, "My life is about telling stories," but it is debatable to what extent this is really true. There seems an odd contradiction between Anderson's sensibility and the genre depicted here (a form of Bond-like action movie). Anderson's actual use of the product to pay for a helicopter shot (a reference to his difficulty in funding Max's stage show in *Rushmore* and Murray's subsequent offer of a blank check), coded in handing over his wallet, and his call to save the receipt would suggest he is a spontaneous kind of filmmaker, prepared and able to put his own money into projects to make them happen. The latter part of that is true (as in *The Hotel Chevalier*), but the kind of flexibility the client would seem to desire is not really a large part of Anderson's filmmaking aesthetic (even parodied in Bean's response to Petey's song in *Fantastic Mr. Fox*). Anderson asking for a snack that he has just been given or the explosive sound effect that is let off late underlines the *lack* of real improvisation in his filmmaking. In his work, action and dialogue do not fall out of sync like this. There may at times be the appearance of chaos, but like the explosions in *Fantastic Mr. Fox*, this is all tightly scripted and planned.

The question that he poses ("Making movies—how do you do it?"), only to be interrupted, is ironically answered by those same interruptions. It is the obstacles, the digressions, the apparent "nonbusiness" that make up the business. So it is with Anderson's movies. Those viewers looking for conventional notions of plot are usually disappointed. This is most often secondary to the business of creating a fiction, both within the narrative itself and in Anderson's own aesthetic. In a sense all Anderson's films, including his commercials, are about the processes by which fictions are made. He is both parodying the director as the solver of all problems (creative, logistical, and of course given the context, financial) at the same time as perpetuating it. This is a highly crafted piece of art, which, at his instigation, alludes in some detail to another self-reflexive narrative, constituting a self-aware meta-text, like his behind-the-scenes DVD extras.

AT&T (2007)

"College Kid," "Reporter," "Mom," "Architect," "Actor," and "Businessman"

Anderson may be credited with overseeing these commercials for BBDO, but his exact level of involvement with some of the series is a little vague. "Reporter," for example, is credited in some sources to Dan Baker. Anderson's AT&T advertisements, like the IKEA series, all use the same basic idea, like a running visual gag. Here flyaway scenery or a rotating director's chair transports the central character to various carefully crafted fictional locations.

In all of them, the central character directs his comments directly to the camera but also throws comments over his shoulder to the film set behind him. In "Actor," he briefly dons flight goggles so he can address the pilot of one location and tell him to "set me down over there." Although the one-dimensional gag about blending names for where the main character works tires quickly, it does actually reflect Anderson's own globe-trotting lifestyle.

"College Kid" and "Architect" also use Robert Yeoman as director of photography and credit Roman Coppola, son of Francis Ford Coppola, as on-set sound designer. The kid in question addresses his parents over his shoulder and exchanges a hand greeting with his brother. There is a slightly differently configured set here, so the focal character is rotated twice through 90 degrees and then back in the same direction, with repetition avoided by a slight forward track into the first change of scene. This seems perhaps unnecessarily complicated and (perhaps like the detail of the set dressing for "Actor," only visible for a couple of seconds at most) more of an Anderson party piece than strictly necessary.

"Reporter" suggests what happens if Anderson drifts too far from content that he feels comfortable with. It seeks to blend a light ironic tone (a missed phone call leading to the death of a journalist in an explosion) with a real-life setting. The Beirut context seems in retrospect to be at least naive, if not outright insensitive. The key quality of Anderson's movies, the creation of a fictional bubble, is missing here and with it, protection from the real world. Public apologies were necessary from AT&T and BBDO after complaints by Lebanese American groups, especially in the light of the assassination of Lebanese politician Antoine Ghanem in September 2007, and the commercial was removed from transmission.

Perhaps more interesting is the choice of Anderson to be the visible face of an attempt at rebranding a 130-year-old company often associated with dull companies and government agencies, as hip and fashionable. As with Avon, it seems that Anderson himself as much as his films is perceived by the advertising community (and one assumes their clients and potential customers) as representing those qualities of cool hipsterism that companies with relatively staid public images would like to be associated with their products.

In the work for Dasani, Avon, or the AT&T series, we are not being encouraged to see each setting as realistic but the exact opposite. We are directed to its representative quality and the technical ingenuity of the crew (and by implication, its director). There is no attempt at realism; we are viewing highly theatrical sets, filled with tokenistic props. Although we might expect the "Actor" commercial to feel more fake, it is actually typical. The whole series presents us with a series of quick-fire theatrical scene changes (one of the scenes in "Actor" literally involving a curtain and an actress receiving applause). This is the world of Max Fischer who, given limited space but almost unlimited budget, might ultimately produce such a product.

IKEA (2003)

"Living Room," "Kitchen"

The attraction of this series of advertisements is perhaps less clear. A firm, linked in the popular imagination with the continent of Anderson's fore-fathers, seems to offer limited creative potential and, on first viewing, a narrative one-trick pony. Each commercial begins in a tight shot of an argument or intense discussion between a couple, only to pull back after 15–20 seconds to reveal that the characters are actors in an IKEA show-room. The notion of Anderson still as director, demystifying the filmmaking process, with an ironic twist, links with the AmEx commercial, but here there is also a slight attempt to develop and distort the kinds of filmmaking that Anderson has actually pursued up to this point. Each commercial shows intense domestic and overtly realistic exchanges without stylization. They become almost little audition pieces for the actors concerned and involve the kind of acting style, heavily leaning towards the realistic and psycho-logically motivated, usually associated with heavy directorial intervention, which Anderson normally eschews. What the commercials rely on is giving the bubble of the tight shot before shifting to a wider context, from a scene of drama into a scene of fiction-making, and it is this wider context (literally the wider shot) that many Anderson films deny us.

These 30-second spots for Crispin Porter and Bogusky draw upon the considerable talents of Harris Savides, one of the most respected names in cinematography and regular collaborator with Gus Van Sant on films like *Gerry* (2002), *Elephant* (2003), and *Last Days* (2005). Anderson works almost with a single camera with some discernible handheld camera move-ment circling round a mother-daughter pair, initially framed in a two-shot. The off-frame voice is soon identified as the father (not the point of view of the camera), and we follow the father as he angrily paces past the camera and starts an argument with the mother. Suddenly, there is a 180-degree whip-pan as a voice off-frame asks the characters, now identified as IKEA customers, what they think of the product, before we cut to a retreating long shot with people walking past, the set now categorized as a furniture store, and close with the parents, smiling at their purchasing decision. The tone, however, is a little dark here as the subject of conversation, a daugh-ter admitting a pregnancy, hangs over any neat sense of closure. As in the introduction to the *Belafonte* in *Aquatic* or the shot through the train in *Darjeeling,* we are introduced to a setting by following a character moving through it. The set already exists and customers are implicitly invited to come to the set and audition in a similar fashion; that is, come and try out the goods by placing themselves as the stars of their own fictions. The act of acting, imagining themselves in another life, is conflated with their role as consumers.

Softbank (2008)

Brad Pitt shot a number of commercials for Softbank and whereas his work for David Fincher focuses on a single protagonist oblivious to the destruction around him, rendered by CGI, Anderson's approach is very different.[3] There are familiar Anderson tropes (a couple of 90-degree whip-pans and some text on screen) among more derivative elements. He uses an explicit homage to Jacques Tati's *Les vacances de Monsieur Hulot* (1953), complete with a hotel setting, a party of hikers, and cyclists. Pitt blends an Anderson sensibility (a hideous yellow costume evoking Dignan's jumpsuit) with props more associated with Tati (he carries a pipe but wears a hat that is not quite Tati's telltale homburg) and stumbles from one awkward situation to another. First he is offered a peach with a bite taken out of it, then seeks to push a stranded car only to lose his bag, is nearly run down by a group of cyclists, and finally takes a photo, which turns out to be inappropriate as a girl is being painted while posing topless.

The actual impossibility of the scene (a high-tech product placed in an anachronistic setting) draws attention to the creation of the image itself. Pitt acts as a proxy director of found images, framing a shot, whose significance then changes by an alteration to the context. In *Les vacances de Monsieur Hulot,* Hulot creeps up behind and kicks a man whom he thinks is spying on a girl, only for the context to reveal that he was bent over a tripod, taking a photo. An innocent, perhaps even childlike intent has a comic (but potentially darker) outcome. What links Hulot and Anderson is that their hapless heroes rarely initiate the gags and that we, the audience, are complicit in their misreadings of situations. As Phil Powrie states, "Hulot gets into other comic situations that do not have any witness but the spectator."[4]

Like Anderson, Tati was from a fairly bourgeois family background, had no formal film training, and favored narratives that sometimes drifted into episodic digressions, evoking similarly divided opinions from avid fans and fervent detractors. Tati and Truffaut, both French, were true auteurs and would write, direct, and sometimes even act in their own films. Although specifically evoking Tati's film, Anderson uses a slightly later soundtrack, with a quintessentially sentimental (possibly cliché) sound which still is often associated with French culture—Serge Gainsbourg's "Poupée de cire, poupée de son," sung by French singer France Gall, and winner of the 1965 Eurovision Song Contest for Luxembourg.

CONCLUSION

Anderson once said in a moment of self-deprecation that he could "take a subject that you'd think would be commercial and turn it into something that not a lot of people want to see."[5] In a sense, his commercials take subjects that we might not want to see and turn them into something interesting. All of his work in commercials (so far) draws the viewer's attention to the fictional nature of what they are seeing as the filmmaking apparatus, and thereby the presence of the director, is made visible. One particular way in which this occurs is by use of a single shot (or at least the appearance of one with well-hidden cheat cuts). It seems like this has more attraction for Anderson than simply being a challenge or a bravura trick only really accomplished directors can pull off. He has done this so many times now (Avon, Dasani, Softbank, AmEx), it almost feels as if he is drawn to a Bazinian position on long takes; that is, they represent a closer approximation of reality than cutting between different camera positions. However, Anderson distorts (or extends, depending on your point of view) what constitutes a single shot by having multiple sets and camera movement linked to a spokesperson figure in the foreground. He ensures that key personnel are close by, especially in the area of cinematography, and it may be that only animation and commercials offer the possibility of controlling or capturing the movement of his characters to the extent he really wants.

ANDERSON—KING OF THE SILENT SCREEN?

It might seem strange to consider Anderson's work in the light of silent film. After all, the presence of retro pop/rock music and a commitment to primary colors form distinctive parts of his distinctive style. However, silent film often did have some form of musical accompaniment, and processes like hand-tinting could give an element of color. In Anderson's films, there is a common tendency to show *and* tell (especially with text on screen), the use of repeated actors/stock character types, slapstick humor, Georges Méliès–style animation, positioning character by a frame, and a tendency to frontality and palpably slowing slow motion.

Anderson's method of shooting commercials, although employing some state-of-the-art technology, is ironically at the same time highly redolent of the early silent era. He shoots fairly quickly (by modern standards) in a matter of weeks with very few retakes and uses the same ensemble cast of six actors but with different roles for each spot; in other words, there is not the time to dwell on individuals as stars whom we see in close-up. Meaning is constructed by changes in the background scenery or a slight alteration of context, *not* by cutting and editing. His meaning is constructed not after the event but in the performance at the time of filming *within a single shot*. All of the speakers address the camera/audience directly and like Jorge's songs in *Aquatic* seem quite reminiscent (the figure in the foreground of the AT&T commercials in particular) of the role in silent film of a barker, whose job it was to interpret the images on the big screen behind him, providing commentary and making sure plotlines are clear.

One reason Anderson lives in New York, rather than Los Angeles, is his love of the theatre. There is a strong theatricality in Anderson's work, possibly

due in part to his lack of formal training in film. His first three films in particular are fairly limited in terms of locations and focus on intense relationships within them. There is an abiding theatricality in *Tenenbaums,* not just
in Margot's status like Max Fischer as a playwright but in the introduction of
the narrative itself, described as a "cast of characters" after the introductory
sequence. The A-list cast, showing Anderson's growing stature as a director,
are seen mostly seated before a mirror, Gene Hackman sitting with a face
mask, Angelica Huston attending to her eyelashes, Ben Stiller shaving next
to the twins, Gwyneth Paltrow in a hairdresser's chair, Owen Wilson buying
a hat, and Bill Murray brushing his teeth while dictating notes. These could
be the actors preparing for their roles or the characters in the universe of the
film. There is high drama in the way that Sherman assembles the members
of the Tenenbaum family together before unmasking Royal's fraud with the
fake medicine, hospital, and doctors.

The stop-motion of Selick's work on *Aquatic* and the whole of *Fantastic
Mr. Fox* evoke the earliest forms of animation, and the latter film in particular allows Anderson to position characters and specifically block scenes as
you might in a theatrical production, with a clear sense of three-dimensional
space. The digging downwards sequence in *Fantastic Mr. Fox* is bizarrely
similar to Georges Méliès's rarely seen classic *The Nightmare of the Submarine
Tunnel* (1907) in its surreal depiction of characters comically excavating in
the manner of running.

There is a theatrical element in the opening of *Aquatic* with a stage, a
curtain, and an introductory speaker, in Blume's speech in *Rushmore,* and
Eli's reading in *Tenenbaums* from a raised stage. There are also curtain calls
in large ensemble final scenes, literally so in *Rushmore* and symbolically so in
the huge shot in the submersible in *Aquatic.* This extends to the creatures
that they see out of the windows too as an acknowledgement of unseen filmmaking talent in the teams supervised by Henry Selick. In *Rushmore* this
theatricality is combined with slow motion, when Max takes a curtain call
for *Serpico,* although here the frontality of the situation is played more for
laughs so that Anderson can show via a 180-degree turn his nose stuffed with
blood-stained tissue.

The sequence introducing the *Belafonte* in *Aquatic* (the actual boat
being an old World War II minesweeper, towed from South Africa to the
Mediterranean to film) is a stunning blend of theatricality with filmic nerve.
Zissou is framed holding up a model, while standing in front of a giant picture. We then effectively have a dissolve by physical rather than filmic means
as lights behind the picture allow us to see through it, and then it rises up to
reveal the huge set, masterminded by production designer Mark Friedberg.
Three levels of representation (model, painting, and theatre set) are inte-
grated and all of them are pre-cinematic and like *Dogville* (Lars von Trier,
2003) blend an overtly theatrical set within a filmic context. It is clearly non-
naturalistic. These are theatre lights and what we see is a literal cross-section

of the boat, showing the detail of those working inside and drawing explicit attention to the means by which the film drama is constructed. Animated dolphins and a diver appear beneath the boat, but we are looking at an effect *as an effect*; clearly the boat cannot literally sail in this form. We pull back from a shot of Zissou in typical pose, fishing off the back of the boat, to take in the whole boat, and as in a theatre production, the lights go out to signal the end of a scene.

Some of the most powerful sequences in Anderson's films are the montages, which gain their meaning and power through the juxtaposition of shots without dialogue (albeit with music and some sound), such as the opening montage in *Tenebaums* or the detective's report on Margot (both with text on screen, functioning almost like intertitles). In several Anderson films, notably *Bottle Rocket* and *The Darjeeling Limited,* the central dynamic is triangular rather than comprised of tension between a hero and villain or hero and heroine. The conventional shot/reverse-shot is present but at times is of less importance than tight three-shots, longer takes, and rapid pans between three figures, in a balanced symmetrical formation. The symmetry of picture composition is everywhere, particularly all the posed shots in *Rushmore* featuring various clubs, from Max right in the middle of 12 language lab cubicles and the Model United Nations to Max in the corridor looking for Miss Cross's room. In *Tenenbaums,* Chas is often framed with an identical twin on either side, each dressed in a red Adidas tracksuit, and there is also the three-shot of Richie, Raleigh, and Dudley (who seems to follow Raleigh everywhere like a spare limb) as they receive the investigator's report on Margot.

Darjeeling is largely a train movie, linking it by association with several works of early film, using the dynamic possibilities of this mode of transport. In film's early days, so-called Hayle's Tours were very popular with audiences, with a camera attached to the front of a train, providing a roller-coaster-like experience for the viewer and, of course, one of the most famous early efforts from the Lumière brothers is *L'arrrivée d'un train à La Ciotat,* or *The Arrival of a Train at La Ciotat Station* (1896).

Anderson's slow motion shots are often of human figures walking (Dignan returning to prison, Max dancing, the Tenenbaums walking past the camera, Zissou marching to his boat, or the Whitmans running to the train). The delight in human movement evokes early Lumière footage of individuals walking through the shot (such as the 1895 *La Sortie des usines Lumière,* or *Employees Leaving the Lumière Factory*). There is even something of Eadweard Muybridge's experiments in the late 19th century, particularly 1883–1886, inviting viewers to consider the amazing fact of motion by slowing it down to single frames, including human figures, but also its representation *on film;* in other words, Anderson's slow motion reminds us of the iconic misfits who people his movies but also the cinematic technology and, by implication, the guiding directorial presence that put them there.

There are quite a number of sight gags liberally sprinkled through the films, from the motorbike joke in *Fantastic Mr. Fox* to the slapstick of Bill Murray pushing a tree over at the end of the graveyard scene in *Rushmore*. Such gags are not always overtly comedic either, such as Murray lighting two cigarettes at a time in *Rushmore*, symbolic of his crumbling emotional life. In *Fantastic Mr. Fox*, the wealth of visual details, especially in peripheral areas of the frame, creates parallels with silent film. The high-angle shot of Fox at the bottom of a hole effectively creates an iris shot so that our attention is drawn to the figure in the light. The dappled lighting that falls on the animals from the grilles above after they have been flooded out of their homes, like the light through the bottles of cider in Bean's store, or the fantastic effect of Bean momentarily illuminated by the light of his own cigarette is the kind of chiaroscuro effect associated with German Expressionism, perhaps particularly Fritz Lang's *M* (1931). This also deals with furtive, underground movement, albeit of a much darker subject matter (also possibly parodied in the close-up on Kyle's hand later, similar to posters for the film with an *M* drawn on a hand). Strictly speaking, *M* is an early sound film, but it includes an opening with children singing a song, presumably made up by themselves about a child killer (a darker version of the song Badger plays perhaps). This may seem a strange connection to make, but it is worth remembering that while Boggis, Bunce, and Bean are mostly absurd, buffoonish figures, they are all in a ruthless pursuit to kill the foxes ("they'll kill the children" is Mrs. Fox's first response in realizing they are being dug out). Bean in particular has an inhuman streak (reflected in his diet), and his sitting out of the pool of light when he addresses his fellow farmers and his posing and firing of his pistol give him a fairly sinister air.

Anderson's films display an abiding tendency to frontality, an evolutionary link with theatre, present in the first 10 years of film's development at least, such as the siblings in *Tenenbaums* interviewing Royal and later at a press conference, Chas and Margot looking out of windows as Royal brings Richie back from an outing, or the main credit sequence where all the protagonists look directly at the camera. In *Fantastic Mr. Fox*, when Fox and his accomplices enter Boggis's shed, they spread out as if upon a stage, and each performs an individual dance (as if in time to Petey's song, although this is not literally possible). This frontality also extends to edited sequences, such as the exchange between Mr. Fox and his wife at the farm gate near the beginning, when we cut between close-ups as they look directly at the camera. The shot of Dignan looking straight into the camera in *Bottle Rocket* before firing the biggest and loudest gun evokes the final frame of Edwin S. Porter's *The Great Train Robbery* from 1903, in which the figure shown is also posing as an infamous robber.

Even Anderson's commercials, filmed in single shots with a strong tendency to frontality, form a link with the acting style of early silent film. In relation to his Softbank commercial, his Tati homage is clearly following in the footsteps of Charlie Chaplin and Buster Keaton. Pitt has no dialogue, gives a very theatrical gesture in tipping his hat and waving the cyclists past, and is held mostly in long-shot, allowing us to see his whole body in action. Anderson's precision in picture composition and absurdity of body movement (think of Sherman's disappearance into the hole in *Tenenbaums* or Fox's limbering up) have their parallels in Tati's work. Like *Monsieur Hulot's Holiday,* Anderson uses wide-angle framing, occasional 90-degree cuts, and an episodic plot (mostly constructed around visual gags). Tati's films also had very little spoken dialogue, using sound almost like a succession of sound effects. Like Tati's Hulot and Chaplin's Tramp, Pitt plays an empathetic Everyman character, trying to help others but repeatedly shown as creator of his own disaster (both in losing his bag and the taking of the final photo). Pitt might seem as if he is playing against type, but he has always played quirky, slightly comedic roles from Jeffrey Goines in *12 Monkeys* (Terry Gilliam, 1995) to Mickey O'Neil in *Snatch* (Guy Ritchie, 2000).

Tenenbaums especially features several characters who act as blank slates onto which we project some kind of emotional life. Margot in particular is a difficult role to play as she is clearly intelligent but can seem more a collection of mannerisms and associated objects (barrette, lost finger, cigarettes, loafers, and fur coat) than dramatically involving. The young Margot (Irene Gorovaia) even sports a version of the striped dress worn by her adult self, which also acts as a visual connection with the zebra costume from her play. A stronger example of this is Bill Murray, who has managed to shift from mainstream comedies, like *Ghostbusters* (Ivan Reitman, 1984) or *Little Shop of Horrors* (Frank Oz, 1986) to critically acclaimed indie, art house pictures, like *Lost in Translation* (Sofia Coppola, 2003) and *Broken Flowers* (Jim Jarmusch, 2005), and his work with Anderson has formed a key part of that process. There is clearly a deep artistic understanding between the two men, who seem to be able to find what they are looking for in each other professionally. Post *Bottle Rocket,* Murray has featured in every single Anderson film.

A deadpan acting style can be seen in comic performers, more recently Stephen Wright in the United States or Jack Dee in the UK, but the best examples come from the silent era. Harold Lloyd and, most famously, Buster Keaton established themselves as distinctive in large part by their lack of facial expressions, a tradition that Murray continues. Key elements of deadpan humor tend to be flat intonation, ironic or sarcastic verbal content, and lack of facial expression. This latter feature is particularly important and links such images with the experiments by Lev Kuleshov from the late 1910s and early 1920s in which audiences were shown a series of identical images of contemporary star of the silent cinema Ivan Mozzhukhin juxtaposed with frames showing objects, such as a bowl of hot soup, a girl, and a coffin. Viewers repeatedly interpreted the blank expression as suggesting emotions based on the frames around it (like hunger in the example with the soup); that is, they projected emotional states onto the blank canvas, so to speak, of an inexpressive face. Anderson achieves a similar effect with Murray, not so much through juxtaposition of frames— indeed, he resists rapid cutting—but he gives us lengthy shots of Murray's face onto which we project the emotion of the context, such as grief in *The Life Aquatic*. The element of emotional projection derives then from within the shot or sequence itself or from its emotional rather than its literal context with preceding scenes. Murray is the ideal Anderson actor, given to a style that embraces the quirky, low-key, deadpan and adept at both serious and humorous roles and complex combinations of the two.

With a preference for the theatrical and a preference for composition *within* rather than between the frame, as Jason Morris notes, there is "a nod towards the medium's first promise—to be an honest representation of reality."[6] Clearly such notions of "honesty" and "reality" may be simplistic, and there is naïveté in approaches that dismiss early film as primitive, but there is still a certain form of sincerity in Anderson's film form, albeit contradicted by the care with which it is crafted.

The Unbearable Lightness of Being Wes Anderson

There is a real-enough danger, I suppose, that sooner or later I'll bog down, perhaps disappear entirely, in my own methods, locutions, and mannerisms.

—J. D. Salinger

Pilot: I've got a fox on a motorcycle and what looks like an opossum in the sidecar...does that sound like anything to anybody?

—From Anderson and Baumbach's script for *Fantastic Mr. Fox*

The growing number of online Anderson parodies from homemade sources or even more earnest film school projects suggests a superficial filmmaking aesthetic which anyone can mimic, such as fake campaign ads from the 2008 presidential election or even trailers for *Lord of the Rings*. Partly due to the way in which Anderson foregrounds matters of style and because his films are so distinctive, his films generate easy generalizations with very little by way of precise analysis of its purpose or effect. These stylistic signatures might provide evidence for some that Anderson's work has not developed but remains frozen in its own quirky aspic. However, these stylistic devices have more artistic integrity in themselves than is often seen to be the case and in total, they do represent a specific visual aesthetic rather than just a collection of pretentious tics.

For Michael Hirschorn, as a cinematic culture, we are "drowning in quirk." He defines this mode as "an embrace of the odd against the blandly mainstream...mannered ingenuousness, an embrace of small moments, narrative randomness (and) situationally amusing but not hilarious character juxtapositions."[1] Anderson's critics often find the most unpalatable part of his films is an unrelenting focus on all that is whimsical and eccentric. This appears in little gestures, such as Zissou's warm-up routine, the development of the receiver to hear music while diving, his little dance moves that accompany this and the throwaway gags, such as the aside "Catch anything?" to a crew member, fishing off the top of Hennessey's lab during the raid, as if this was an entirely logical thing to do. Baumbach's hope that the commentary for *Aquatic* does not sound pretentious is undercut by the fact that Anderson presumably has agreed to being recorded in his favorite busy restaurant.

Part of effective portrayal of whimsy seems a certain innocence (key elements of the characters of Dignan and Max), which becomes progressively harder to sustain over time. Also, a central part of the two characters mentioned here is their youth. What may appear forgivable sweetness in someone of school-age just seems ridiculous in an adult. Quirk is a mode that cannot be easily sustained over time. What happens to an enfant terrible who is no longer an *enfant*? Is he just "terrible"? Charlotte O'Sullivan finds *Tenenbaums* weaker than *Rushmore* primarily because "non-cuteness is essential to whimsy (and non-cuteness is what Max Fisher had in spades)."[2] Elsewhere the quirkiness seems less coherently motivated. The battered nature of the cabs in *Tenenbaums,* all from the Gypsy Cab Company, could be meant to show the whole family (and possibly city) in a process of decline. However, this is not a *Fall of the House of Usher* style narrative in which the fabric of the fictional environment is supposed to suggest moral decay. As motivation for a sight gag (Dudley's obvious observation that the cab is dented, suggesting he is hardly an idiot savant), it might work, but its repeated use seems strange. Sometimes Anderson seems to be purposely courting the notion of himself as a hipster (his use of Jarvis Cocker in *Fantastic Mr. Fox* or Jorge's songs in *Aquatic,* for example).

What seems largely absent from Anderson's films is tragic depth of feeling and the realism of everyday life. This opens them to the charge of just being light and insubstantial but perhaps that is the point. Milan Kundera's *The Unbearable Lightness of Being* (1984) explores the philosophical dichotomy of life lived in the light of Nietzschean belief in eternal return, the notion that everything reoccurs infinitely or that life has no significance and events are only experienced once (represented by lightness). The relevance for Anderson is that his cinematic world is infused with a sense of this lightness but not necessarily in a hedonistic way (except for the actions of Eli Cash). His characters search for a meaning in life but without any sense of learning from experiences or that actions carry spiritual consequences. Thus, we can spend two hours in the company of characters who float in a childish realm, almost in their own amniotic fluid, detached from the real world, imposing through force of will an alternative world, which matches their self-image.

Dignan's plans to be a master criminal, Max's plays, the Tenebaums' creation of self-contained worlds, Zissou's films and his public persona as a celebrity adventurer, Francis's laminated schedule are all attempts to impose order on a deliberately small setting. The time that Anderson took in bringing *Bottle Rocket* to its fuller version raises the question of why he felt so strongly about a tale that is apparently so slight. This, however, is exactly the point. It suggests life is made up of such moments in which individuals become aware of the minutiae of life, like Futureman staring at a leaf picked from the pool, and that the challenge of art is to capture and celebrate them as effectively as possible.

MUSIC

Anderson's use of slow motion creates a series of memorable cinematic moments, when time is arrested, or at least slowed, and we are invited to contemplate the emotional lives of the characters at a calmer pace, such as Margot stepping from the bus, Dignan heading back to jail, or Max exiting an elevator. However, key in this is the use of music. Although Anderson has not produced any pop videos, his films express this guilty pleasure by default (including virtually whole songs in the tent scene in *Tenenbaums*). It is tempting to see such moments as mini-epiphanies, but Anderson's use of music varies in its effectiveness and over time can seem a progressively blunt creative tool.

Anderson's films are scored mostly with Mark Mothersbaugh and Randall Poster as music supervisor, and Anderson rarely uses contemporary music; yet the music also does not come from the given era of the fictional world being shown; that is, it is not used to establish a chronological period. Lyrical content is the key factor. Mothersbaugh's role as a founding member of Devo and extensive experience with children's TV soundtracks provide a useful background here. Both Mothersbaugh and Poster have been fixtures ever since the revamped version of *Bottle Rocket* (James Brooks brought them in after appalling test scores of the original version). Since *Rushmore,* they have sought specific music permissions *prior to* production so that actors can be given specific tapes that will accompany their scenes, giving them a stronger sense of how their characters might finally appear on screen. For *Aquatic,* Mothersbaugh was involved before filming began and the cutting of the tit-for-tat battle between Max and Blume in *Rushmore* was even planned out around the Who's "A Quick One While He's Away" before the scenes were filmed.

Reactions to Anderson's use of preexisting music often echo attitudes to processes such as sampling, with critical voices coming from those who see it as narrowly derivative and lazy and more positive responses coming from those who point to arguably powerful scenes where it is used creatively. Like Tarantino, it could be said that he brings artists to the notice of a wider public, although Anderson's favoring of British Invasion bands undercuts this as most viewers will have heard the Stones, the Beatles, or David Bowie. The notion of using preexisting music was there from the outset, but the budget of *Bottle Rocket* prevented Anderson from securing all the permissions he wanted (the Charlie Brown music would appear later in *Tenenbaums*). Also, Anderson does include original scores, such as Mothersbaugh's distinctive electronica in *Aquatic* and Alexandre Desplat's orchestral work in *Fantastic Mr. Fox*, albeit not to the extent of Satyajit Ray in his movies. In *Aquatic*, Zissou's progress towards the hotel is accompanied by a more dramatic, orchestral version of Mothersbaugh's previously tinny-sounding, synthesizer theme (produced on quite an antiquated, multitrack system with Casio-sounding instruments, which also accompanies the menu on the DVD).

Anderson's use of preexisting music that is even close to the era of a film's production is rare. New Order's "Ceremony" (1981) appears on the trailer for *Aquatic* but is dropped from the film, where it would seem out of place, being so specifically associated with the early 1980s. Where contemporaneous music does appear, it is usually retro in style ("Needle in the Hay" in *Tenenbaums* or "Petey's Song" in *Fantastic Mr. Fox*) or ambient in nature. Sigur Rós's "Starálfur" (1999) would seem the perfect melancholy accompaniment to the Jaguar Shark scene in *Aquatic*, but this only works if we see Zissou's tears are well earned, which given his attitude towards those around him, including his potential son Ned and his supposed noble profession, might seem to be an example of a soundtrack overreaching emotionally. With ambiguous time frames, the notion of contemporaneous is often unclear anyway, and such features contribute to the apolitical feel to Anderson's films in which characters relate primarily to the fictional world in which they operate.

Just as Sarstedt's song was the catalyst for *The Hotel Chevalier*, Jackson Browne's cover of "These Days" (1967) inspired the writing of the first scene in *Tenenbaums* and arguably blends the musical and literary iconography of Nico's blond beauty and heavy eyeliner with a semblance of Salinger's Franny (the raccoon element of her coat is translated into Margot's makeup). The lyrical and melodic sense of melancholy and missed chances complements the situation of Margot and Richie, and Browne, as a New York–based musician, reflects the film's supposed setting. It is also a highly theatrical entrance, a symbolic representation of how Richie remembers her (and possibly fantasizes about her). The slow motion lends grace to her movement and is evocative of the shot of Max as publisher of *The Yankee Review* in *Rushmore*. Characters walking forward, as they do at the end of *Tenebaums*, seem to be a favored subject for slowing motion in Anderson movies. It is also not a simple matter of suddenly cutting to a film running at a different speed—the film palpably slows *as we watch it*, reflecting Richie watching the progress of a figure for whom he has very strong and undeniable feelings. The effect of such visible slowing is to create a sense of an iconic image fixed in the memory of a character (and possibly the viewer). Richie has given up his career and tried to put thousands of miles between them, but he cannot forget Margot and this shot goes some way to convey the power she still has over him. Anderson uses a typical blend of forward and reverse tracking shots so that we share part of her point of view (the camera being placed just behind her) but also his in a wished-for closer shot and appreciate the spectacle that someone creates (for one character at least) in walking into a space.

There is a subsequent contrast with Eli in a later scene, also followed in slow motion in receiving the adulation of his fans but rather than genuine feeling, he is exciting the groupie-like admiration of legions of followers. It helps create the notion of a vacuous rock star of the literati and focuses attention on apparently minor details such as his signing books without even looking. For Eli, Anderson uses the Clash's "Police and Thieves" and later "Rock the Casbah" as he buys and later takes drugs, suggesting that he sees himself as a rebellious, bohemian figure. Margot's exploits diametrically oppose this. She keeps her whole life secret in contrast to his living in the public eye via lectures and TV interviews (and also sending clippings to a family friend, Etheline). Her backstory is actually more antiestablishment and thus accompanied by the harder-hitting "Judy Is a Punk" by the Ramones.

The retro rock is less intrusive in *Fantastic Mr. Fox,* possibly because there is also some original music (composed by Desplat), but also it seems to be motivated more strongly from within the action and from the time when it is set, that is, not sandpapering over emotional cracks. Instead, it signals hedonistic action, such as the dance at the end or Jarvis Cocker's "Petey's Song," an excuse for a gag about improvisation. Music is used a little more playfully than in other films, for example, Anderson pauses the music twice as Fox stops to listen while running through the wheat field en route to the first break-in. "Love" by Floyd Huddlestone and George Burns lightly accompanies the diving scene, which was also used in *Robin Hood* (Wolfgang Reitherman, 1973), in which the central couple, Robin and Marian, were both foxes. Desplat, recording some parts of the soundtrack at the Abbey Road Studios, made famous by the Beatles, uses a choir from the American Cathedral in Paris, giving the "Boggis, Bunce, and Bean" song, supposedly sung by village children, a fairly professional sound.

There is a feeling of Sergey Prokofiev's *Peter and the Wolf* (1936) in Desplat's composition of themes for different animal characters, which are then modulated according to circumstances. Rat's theme is full of bravado when he first confronts Fox with dramatic drums, Spanish-style guitar, pipes and whistles, all creating evocations of Ennio Morricone's score for Sergio Leone's Dollars trilogy, *A Fistful of Dollars* (1964), *A Few Dollars More* (1965), and *The Good, the Bad and the Ugly* (1966). As Rat's fortunes change and he is about to die, a more melancholy version is heard with glockenspiel and bells sounding his death knell, to be replaced by a single voice accompanied by a horn, effectively singing his requiem.

While directors like Tarantino frequently select retro tracks, they do so often with ironic intent. Anderson's dialogue is laden with deadpan irony but *not* so the relationship between visuals and the soundtrack. It is this which, alongside his heroes-as-solipsistic-dreamers, centrally lends his films an air of childlike innocence. However, there may be a difficulty for some viewers, familiar with pervasive irony in the dialogue, but who are not used to responding to the soundtrack in a more genuine sense at the same time. Unlike pop videos, a medium that would naturally occur to someone of Anderson's era, cuts are not made on lyrical content. Music tracks run for the duration of a scene, apparently at will (think of "Hey Jude" playing over shots of the rooftops as Richie releases Mordecai) and can bleed across scenes too (Richie's escape from the hospital or Mr. Henry's final scam in *Bottle Rocket*).

Carole Lyn Piechota attempts to read the soundtrack of *Tenenbaums* as eruptions of repressed feelings, which is an interesting idea but leads to a simplification of the characters in that narrative. She assumes that the three songs by Nico, Elliott Smith, and Nick Drake act "as both catalyst and translator of the siblings' emotion,"[3] observing in a footnote that all three would go on to take their own lives. However, one might also suggest that Anderson uses music in an evasive way. Rather than writing dialogue or action to convey complex emotional states, he selects a song from a particularly evocative era and expects that to carry the emotional weight of a scene. There is a further contradiction here in the apparent timelessness of the narrative and key musical elements which are bound to be associated with particular eras (such as "Hey Jude"). Piechota tries to construct a Freudian-influenced psychological reading of Margot's behavior as driven by a wish to bond with her adopted mother Etheline but attempting to see Margot as a fully rounded psychic entity is difficult since she is more a collection of unchanging props. She reads Nico's "These Days" as representing Margot's emotions although she then goes on to accept that it is *Richie's* point of view that we mostly occupy here, admitting "perhaps, one is seeing Richie's dream, his hope for Margot."[4] Trying to read Richie as a Christ figure overplays his relative openness to Royal (he too is manipulative) and claiming that he is prepared to die to save Margot and himself from their desires sounds heroic out of context, but we are talking about suicide here.

Elliott Smith's "Needle in the Hay" (1995) accompanies Richie's suicide but again casting this in purely psychological terms omits key absurdist elements like his whispered "I'm going to kill myself tomorrow" (the purpose in waiting is unclear as we do not see him plucking up courage) and despite this resolution, his failure to write a note until *afterwards* problematizes whether it was a genuine suicide attempt at all. The music, which begins as Richie leaves the detective's office, suggests the impulse towards suicide constitutes his reaction to the revelation of Margot's past. However, again as much as this might reflect his inability to accept that she has had a sexual life that has excluded him, it also presents him as an innately childish character for whom suicide is a grand gesture, an attempt to match the activity of Margot's life with the drama of his death. However, the idea that by using Nick Drake's

"Fly" Anderson "suggests that Margot is telepathically calling him home" is an interesting one, and the music moves from non-diegetic to diegetic as the song is heard as Richie leaves the hospital, climbs up to her window, and is then revealed on Margot's own turntable.[5] The final line of the song, "It's really too hard for [*sic*] to fly" reflects Richie's doomed attempt at a flight from the family (paralleling the actions of Mordecai), from mortality, and from his feelings for Margot.

In *Aquatic*, Santos (Seu Jorge) sings David Bowie songs in Portuguese, accompanied by his own guitar playing, within the context of the fiction. Anderson claims that he did not set out to have this odd linguistic mix on purpose but that having cast Jorge, he wanted him to make the songs his own. The notion of a sailor singing to pass the time at sea is suitable given the dramatic situation, and he only sits in a chair if not on duty. Effectively his role is that of a Greek chorus, standing close to the action, within the scene but slightly detached from it. This is also a role taken by Nat King Cole in *Cat Ballou* (Elliot Silverstein, 1965), where he too sings songs and plays the guitar (alongside Stubby Kaye). Cole sings one repeated song, a ballad about Cat, which gives coherence to the film. It is a clearly non-naturalistic convention, more familiar to musicals and usually delivered in English so that the commentary link can be made more clearly, but it seems that Anderson wants his audience to work harder, making sense of lyrics some of which they may already know.

The motif is first used at the party, where Santos sings "Ziggy Stardust" as he threads his way around the boat, acting as a linking device between groups of characters. Then, as Zissou walks through the boat to the very end, we hear "Life on Mars" as he lights a cigarette and the action slows in a moment of contemplation. Zissou does live on another world from most people, whether literally underwater, trying to find finance from reluctant backers or indulging in his pseudoscientific expeditions. On Zissou's island, we see Santos in his first location away from the boat, up a tower, but still with his guitar. The song, "Rebel Rebel," seems ironic here as Zissou is hardly a rebel, except within the scientific community. This style of performance also feels like an easy-listening version, with all the antiestablishment edginess stripped out. "Space Oddity" precedes the pirate attack, acting as a form of warning, and Santos performs "Starman" in the *Belafonte*'s sound studio as if recording a track himself or explicitly producing part of the film-within-a-film's soundtrack, which of course is also part of Anderson's soundtrack for the film as a whole.

The use of a single musical source for so much of the soundtrack, over 10 songs, is a departure for Anderson (although he had originally intended to use an all-Kinks soundtrack for *Rushmore*), and it may seem egotistical to indulge the director's personal musical taste to such an extent. It does provide some sense of unity for a narrative that is constantly threatening to fragment into episodic digressions. However, the choice of "Queen Bitch" for the final song at the premiere is less effective. This hardly refers to Eleanor, who is really only a peripheral character anyway, and there is no undercurrent of sexuality, deviant or otherwise. Perhaps, the track is intended to lend a sense of calm to the resolution (although it could be said that Ned's death, far from making Zissou grow up in any way, actually allows him to avoid facing the responsibilities of paternity). Even if this is so, it contradicts Anderson's general choice of music for its lyrical rather than melodic content (except for the mention of a "bibbedy-bobbidy hat" which also relates to Zissou's distinctive headgear).

Music is also a key part of rendering notions of time redundant. Anderson's films seem at times close to fable or fairy tale and a prime cause of that is the ambiguity around precise setting or time frame. Music is conventionally used as a chronological cue, and Anderson tends to focus on lyrical or tonal qualities, so that in *Rushmore* we have several examples from the so-called British Invasion bands of the late 1960s, even though in theory the film is contemporary. Although *Rushmore* takes place in a specific school (St. John's, where Anderson himself went), the exact timeframe remains ambiguous. In theory, *Tenenbaums* is set in the late 1970s, but the chronology of the film seems irrelevant, confused, or connected to playing extreme games of what might be termed "involution," swallowing itself so that events refer to something that has not yet happened in the narrative. The library book at the opening is only first checked out in 2001 and yet the film we see, a dramatization of its contents, includes a tennis tournament that seems placed in the late '70s, while the final date on the tombstones reads 2001. We find ourselves scrambling around for explanations like perhaps the book is a reprint but more persuasively strange is the notion that time, like geography in *The Life Aquatic,* does not matter. Relationships and feelings matter, not the precise order of Margot's marriage and other sexual liaisons.

Tenenbaums in particular creates a mythic sense of place with a strongly literary feel, beyond the influence of Salinger. The New York that Anderson is creating is a strange parallel city (there being no New York "Y," Green Line bus company, or Gypsy Cab firm). It feels like a New York of the imagination, celebrating creative possibilities, a version of William Burroughs's Interzone from *Naked Lunch* (1959), but without the motivating factor of hallucinogenic drugs. Names such as the Irving Island Ferry, Mockingbird Heights, and 22nd Avenue Express seem plausible but do not actually exist. The sequence in the opening where Margot and Richie run away and stay overnight in a museum (represented by the U.S. Customs House in the film) is fairly closely modeled on a brother and sister pairing, Claire (highly intelligent and only girl among other male siblings) and Jamie in E. L. Konigsburg's *From the Mixed-Up Files of Mrs. Basil E. Frankweiler* (1967). Like Anderson's male protagonists (Dignan, Max, and Francis especially) and Anderson himself, Claire shows a great attention to preplanning and minor details and, like Margot and Salinger's Franny, is bored with her life and acts in secretive ways to try and inject some excitement into it.

At times, there are no specific chronological signals and a deliberately anachronistic choice of technology. In *Bottle Rocket,* the props are big and clunky to evoke a 1970s feel, like Dignan's binoculars, LED watches, and jumpsuits. This creates a fantasy universe, closer to the era of *Starsky and Hutch* (1975–1979), in which Dignan and Anthony seem to dwell (judging from their dialogue in the 1994 version). In *Tenenbaums,* Chas's Apple II computer is placed in the extreme foreground to make it look huge, and we have several shots of rotary payphones, such as on the roof by the recreation area. In *Aquatic,* Zissou's commentary talks of "technically advanced equipment" in relation to the kitchen, but we see a character, dressed in regimental yellow T-shirt, piping icing onto a cake. The sound studio and the more important functional areas of the boat, such as the engine room, look fairly run-down. *Fantastic Mr. Fox* is full of anachronistic technology: Mrs. Fox's vacuum cleaner, Badger's large yellow phone and his large clunky tape recorder, Bean's walkie-talkie large like a house brick, the wristwatches with calculators that were briefly fashionable, and the pseudo-Walkmans rather than iPods. Bean's surveillance equipment looks like a 1970s TV studio, complete with a large reel-to-reel tape machine. The effect of this is to place the narrative closer to the book's original release date (1970).

ANDERSON THE AUTEUR

NICHOLAS: I don't care if it's his worst work. If it says "Moses Rosenthaler" at the bottom, then keep bidding.

—draft of Anderson's script for *The Rosenthaler Suite*[6]

A very narrow view of auteurism might accept the fallacy that if an artist is designated as a genius, then everything he produces must of necessity be a work of genius (a view attractive to Eli Cash certainly). Unlike Welles, Anderson came to filmmaking in large part through his enthusiasm for those filmmakers who are an intrinsic part of the auteur theory (as both filmmakers and commentators). In a sense, they are his mentors and his touchstones. It is the notion of a distinct, personal vision that drew Anderson to this particular medium in the first place. At the same time, he grew up with knowledge of it as an idea and is aware of it being applied to him. Further complicating the picture, he is very drawn to the culture and lifestyle of France, where the auteur theory has not fallen completely out of academic fashion and where, at festivals like Cannes, figures like Godard are still viewed by some with reverence.

Devin Orgeron recounts Anderson's visit to his creative mentor, veteran film critic Pauline Kael, ostensibly to seek her view on *Rushmore,* but Orgeron suggests this is part of an elaborate piece of theatre in which his youth is contrasted with her age and her inability to understand his eccentricity is cast as a badge of honour.[7] Anderson was closely involved in the production of a tie-in book, Angus Hyland's *The Making of Fantastic Mr. Fox: A Film by Wes Anderson Based on the Book by Roald Dahl* (2009), and wanted Hyland to use as his model *Truffaut by Truffaut* (1987; 1985 in French), a seminal collection of interviews with the French director, apparently presenting himself honestly as the author of the text. This tradition continues today with the long-running Faber and Faber series of interviews with directors using the same title construct. Anderson here is consciously linking himself not just with how famous auteurs made their films but how they presented themselves *as auteurs* to the public via interviews and publicity material.

Extra-filmic factors, such as the plethora of names across posters, his own comments in interviews, and meta-texts like his AmEx commercial suggest Anderson works as part of a collective. However, what we have on screen suggests the opposite, an individual with a particular way of visualizing the world, including the appearance of allowing the butterfly to flutter as it were, before being pinned on a stick in the way he wants. Limited improvisation (in so far as any performance is an improvisation), collaborative writing, the individual actor's reading of a line, all these undoubtedly take place to a greater or lesser degree but ultimately it is Anderson's view of a shot that prevails. On the *Aquatic* DVD, Dafoe focuses on Anderson's pragmatism, stating "he doesn't indulge people's personal fantasies unless they align with his." However, the fact that so many individuals, cast and crew, are content to work with him repeatedly (sometimes for little or no money, particularly Bill Murray) suggests this is a process with which they are happy.

Directors who have been to film school and written the obligatory essays about auteurism and its weaknesses, its inherent impossibility, and its associations with a particular style of European cinema may well view auteurism in a different light than Anderson does. Although he had a place at Columbia Film School, he did *not* go, due in part to the *Bottle Rocket* project taking off. Instead, he largely educated himself about film through key influential figures, such as Pauline Kael, and he has strong personal and cultural connections to Europe, France in particular, and therefore does not view auteurism as a flawed and old-fashioned concept. On the contrary, Anderson actively embraces it, overtly name-checking key figures in its development such as Truffaut. Anderson seems partly attracted to Satayjit Ray's movies, in particular because they represent individual personal expressions, largely based in one particular geographical region (around Calcutta) that, like Anderson, Ray sometimes scripted himself and funded without having to compromise his independence.

To take Orgeron's idea a few stages further, Anderson uses a wide range of strategies to signal his presence in a film in a way similar to postwar European art house film. Although not to the extent of Hitchcock, Anderson does appear in some of his films. In *Bottle Rocket,* he is sitting on the bus near the beginning of the film, behind Owen and Luke Wilson; he is the uncredited voice of one of the tennis match commentators in *Tenenbaums* and provides the voice of Weasel in *Fantastic Mr. Fox*. Even when he does not appear, his own possessions signal his presence (his Calderón artwork in *Tenenbaums* or his own personal clutter for the table in *The Hotel Chevalier*).

As in the work of Woody Allen (in the midsection of his career anyway) the repeated casting of the same actors (Bill Murray, the Wilson brothers, and Anjelica Huston among others) blurs distinctions between films, giving some viewers the sense that they are watching the same film over and over. There is even the possibility that individual shots can migrate between films, such as the killer whale feeding from Bill Murray's hand, cut from *Rushmore* but reappearing in *Aquatic*. As Anderson himself admits, "I do feel a bit like my characters from one movie could walk into another one of my movies and it would make sense, whereas people from other peoples' movies would probably feel a bit uncomfortable there."[8] Anderson's "family" typically includes, among others, Karen Patch (costume designer), David Wasco (production designer), Robert Yeoman (director of photography), Barry Mendel (producer), Randall Poster (music supervisor), and Mark Mothersbaugh (composer). His co-writers are more than just writers as seen from the succession of parts played by Owen Wilson. Anderson acts as producer for Noah Baumbach on *The Squid and the Whale* (2005), and Roman Coppola is a second unit director on *Aquatic* (a new experience for Anderson) for much of the footage involving boats and helicopters. This latter example reflects a literal family connection after Anderson's work on *Rushmore* with Schwartzman (Coppola's nephew) and Murray's work with Sofia Coppola on *Lost in Translation* (2003). Possibly part of the attraction of actors like Seymour Cassell is the cinematic baggage they bring with them. Cassell, for, example has a long career, including extensive work with John Cassavetes in films such as *Faces* (1968), for which he was Oscar-nominated.

Anderson's preference to work with the same group of people, actors and crew, also reflects the fact that up until *Fantastic Mr. Fox*, he had not adapted the literary work of another. The subjects of his films, of people struggling with relationships, are reflected in the means he chooses to make them. There is an emotional connection between the cast, not just professional colleagues but close, personal friends. The observation by producer James L. Brooks that there had never been a read-through of the script of *Bottle Rocket* despite the main cast all being readily at hand reflects a certain naïveté on Anderson's part and a sense that his fictional world exists very much in his head. On the DVD commentary for *The Life Aquatic*, Seymour Cassell notes that people do not always know what Anderson wants. This is not to say that he is a poor communicator but that his distinctive vision of a film can be difficult to convey to others. This is another reason perhaps why he persists in calling upon a small band of trusted collaborators both in front of and behind the camera. For some, this seems a little incestuous but as Royal says in *Tenenbaums*, taking a fairly relaxed view of a potential relationship between Richie and Margot, "It's still frowned upon, but then what isn't these days?"

As well as Hitchcock-like cameos, Anderson places other telltale elements in his films for fans to spot. It is not only actors in the main roles whose faces reappear regularly but extras, like Brian Tenenbaum and Stephen Dignan, who are cast as Clay and Bob in *Bottle Rocket* and paramedics in *Tenenbaums*. Asked by a stranger in *Bottle Rocket* if he is in the military, Dignan replies that he just has short hair in a small nod to Owen Wilson's experience at military school and a near-miss career choice when *Bottle Rocket* was met by commercial indifference. Andrew Wilson's hand was used for the close-up of a hand with BB pellets still in it, since such an accident actually happened to him. Other directorial proxy figures include Roman Coppola in *Fantastic Mr. Fox* as Squirrel, rapping out orders in the moving and renovation process (a certain style of dictatorial directing, diametrically at odds with Anderson's own) and co-writer Noah Baumbach has a presence on-set in *Aquatic* as Philip, Drakoulias's right-hand man.

Even when a member of Anderson's extended "family" cannot appear in person, they are often given a symbolic on-screen role. In *Rushmore,* although not in the main cast, Owen Wilson appears effectively as the ghost of Edward Appleby, in pictures in his bedroom, and is given a final credit as Appleby himself. In *Tenenbaums,* originally there was to be another neighbor, a child prodigy, dressed in a white suit, called Mordecai, who was to be played by Schwartzman, but his part had to be cut and his name (and possibly dominant coloring) is transferred to Richie's hawk. Absent fictional characters are also signaled by symbolic presences on screen. Max's ruination of Blume's marriage even extends to the calligraphy of the signage in the hotel lobby to "Enjoy your stay," which seems to mock Blume's desperate state, and Max's method of tormenting Blume, with bees, links him with Olivia's dead husband, founder of that particular club.

In Anderson's scripts, there are some very obvious biographical overtones. Both Max Fischer and Anderson went to an elite fee-paying school (specifically St. John's School in Houston); both feel isolated from their peers; and both put on plays (including, in Anderson's case, ambitious stage versions of *Star Wars* and *The Alamo*). As with Max, these were the product of deals made with teachers to stay out of trouble. *Bottle Rocket* uses an experience of Anderson and Owen Wilson, who broke into their own property to show a landlord how insecure it was. In *Tenenbaums,* Margot, a fellow playwright and outsider, acts as an alter ego for Anderson. Anderson seems drawn to groups of three male friends (*Bottle Rocket*) or siblings (*Darjeeling*). He himself, like Owen Wilson, is from a relatively comfortable middle-class background, with a father who worked in advertising, and is the middle brother in a group of male siblings. The body of the film of *Darjeeling* uses several experiences of the three writers (Anderson, Schwartzman, and Coppola) as they crossed India by train, such as stopping off at a temple and being forced to wear brightly colored scarves, thereby almost casting the three writers as the Whitman brothers. Like Jack's writing, which he claims is fiction but is actually all based firmly on his own experiences, this does not preclude great art but makes imagining outside one's own self much more difficult. Like Margot's final play that only has a short run and receives mixed reviews, the extremely personal nature of Anderson's films in terms of their content and how they are produced can make his work open to the charge of being self-indulgent. Certainly, with regard to *Bottle Rocket,* there was (and possibly still is) a problem with pace, with Anderson and Wilson only very reluctantly cutting scenes, which apparently contribute little to the forward momentum of the narrative, such as an incident in which Bob deliberately rams a car in front that is slowing them down in Dallas.

Fantastic Mr. Fox, the first book Anderson owned, is especially personal. The characters of Ash and Kristofferson are interpolated into Dahl's novel to represent Anderson and his older brother Mel (a doctor) by whom he felt overshadowed at times. As a proxy figure for Anderson (and dressed in suits of similar color and cut), Fox is highly egotistic, always having to direct events, failing to listen to anyone (as his wife points out in a resigned tone of voice), even later interrupting Badger's speech. All scenes were filmed first with Anderson as a template, so that he literally is Mr. Fox's alter ego in animation terms. The choice of Jarvis Cocker as Petey is hardly accidental. Here he has the look of a Beatnik guitar player but like Jorge in *Aquatic,* he is not American. Cocker is a rare example of an overtly contemporary musician to appear in an Anderson movie, playing his own music (Serge only plays Bowie tracks in *Aquatic*). At one point, Cocker was even going to appear as an on-screen narrator, but test audiences found this confusing. Slim, glasses-wearer, purveyor of a certain "geeky chic," he is another Anderson alter ego, a British hipster, reflective of a specific strand of 1990s Britpop.

META-TEXTUAL REFERENCES

Anderson's movies are full of references to their own workings. When Fox breaks into Bunce's farm, the music that Bunce is listening to is the audio book version of *Fantastic Mr. Fox.* When Mrs. Fox says she is pregnant, Fox says to her that she is practically glowing at which point we cut to shot of an internally illuminated puppet. The melody of Mothersbaugh's "Scrapping and Yelling" from *Tenenbaums* is played backwards under the introduction to the *Belafonte* sequence in *Aquatic.*

The sense of Anderson's films speaking to themselves and primarily created for his circle of friends is exacerbated by the number of in-jokes (the prison uniforms bearing "Wasco State Penitentiary" after David Wasco, the production designer), a further example of text on screen, and particularly the naming of characters. Anderson rarely chooses character names at random. Since the appearance of Futureman in *Bottle Rocket,* characters have had cartoonish names, signature actions, and catch phrases. Personal friends and regular extras, like Stephen Dignan or Brian Tenenbaum, may have provided inspiration (the latter when blended with Salinger). Zissou could well derive from the character name in a series of photos by Jacques Henri Lartique, one of which is the basis for the posed karting shot of Max in *Rushmore*. The significance of names extends to places. The *Belafonte* is clearly an allusion to Harry Belafonte, known for his versions of calypso music, and the name of Cousteau's iconic vessel is seen in many of his TV programs.

There is a circling self-referential element to some names. Anderson's close friend Wallace Wolodarsky, writer on *The Simpsons,* plays a wrestling referee in *Rushmore* and Brendan in *Darjeeling,* using his own surname, and then Noah Taylor uses Wolodarsky as a character name in *Aquatic.* In *Aquatic,* Jorge's character Pelé Dos Santos blends the name of Brazil's greatest footballer with the club where he made his name. The name Winslett-Richardson is a blend of two great English acting families and, along with Cate Blanchett's accomplished accent, makes the actress quintessentially (but possibly also stereotypically) English. There is a sense of Nabokovian game-playing here mixed with a child of the '70s, name-dropping literary heroes and friends within a social context where the construction of one's own "porn name" (apocryphally, your pet's first name plus your mother's maiden name or the street where you grew up) is just a passing fad.

Naming functions as a directorial signature at one remove. However, the problem with using names in this way is, as with Dickens, that they are very useful shorthand, especially effective for minor characters, but when used for major characters who are supposed to grow and develop or at least show the potential for this, the names become constrictive. There is a sense of cartoonish figures bumping into each other, delivering lines which might be witty, but struggling to contain little emotional substance when linked to such labels. Drakoulias's final speech on the boat might be quite touching but just becomes ridiculous, not just because he loses his train of thought but because he is still a vampiric producer. Names encompass Anderson's personal experience and taste. The name and character of Kylie is apparently based on a handyman who worked in Anderson's apartment in New York. Kristofferson, a clear allusion to actor and singer Kris Kristofferson (a favorite of Anderson and Baumbach), is more a cipher than a particularly well- developed character. His presence is to act as an irritant to Ash and his place in the family, especially in relation to his father. He seems calm, mature, finds it hard to lie, and can fight his own battles but is presented as a finished article. How he came by such wisdom is never explained.

One interesting feature of the DVD extras is Anderson's creation of a further level of fictionalizing, creating texts that appear to be independent documentary-style creations that comment on the events of the film but are actually carefully crafted fictions. For *Tenenbaums,* we have *The Peter Bradley Show,* a parody of Charlie Rose's program (on which Anderson has appeared himself and even subsequently hosted) that for many viewers may seem realistic enough to seem real. The host, played by Larry Pine, appears in the body of the film, interviewing Eli and later seen fondling Margot during a publicity tour. The guests, Stephen Dignan, Brian Tenenbaum, Sanjay Mathew, and Deepak and Kumar Pallana are all the genuine actors from the film but their parts are all so minor that they really do not have much to say and are faced with questions more appropriate for those taking leading roles. The questioning becomes increasingly desperate and digressive (he asks Tenenbaum, "How is steel sold?"); Mathew corrects the mispronunciation of his name; and the Pallanas seem offended by an ill-judged gag about nepotism.

Anderson also creates further meta-textual fictions for the *Aquatic* DVD extras package, including an intern video journal. In particular, there is another fake chat show, *Mondo Monda,* with questions posed in Italian (again by a character from within the film, played by Antonio Monda, a genuine NYU film professor) and answers given in English and where we are not sure if the translation is delayed, wrong, or just absent. The discussion of the difference between a "rhapsody" and a "symphony" becomes a satire of critical pretentiousness but once a tongue-in-cheek tone is adopted, the potentially serious comment by Baumbach that the structure of the film is closer to American epic while the characters are more typical of a European film struggles for credibility. Like the precise chronological setting of the film, we have a mixture of markers here. While the décor of the studio, the furnishings, the lack of an audience, give the scene a more 1970s feel, the host refers to the film as looking "back to the '70s" in one of his questions. Perhaps this whole program reflects Anderson's frustration with the machinery of publicity and promotion that directors have to go through to bring their work to the public and suggests that perhaps the only honest response to questions of meaning is through parody.

Even *Fantastic Mr. Fox* features *A Beginner's Guide to Whackbat,* a brief but informative introduction to Anderson's fictional game, shot with a deliberately anachronistic scratchy film effect to suggest this is an ancient game. The rules are run through with typical intertitles, introducing "The players," "The equipment," and "The game," each with an accompanying extract from the film. Noticeably, it is only a brief film and the rules are still run through at breakneck speed and include nonsensical elements, such as runners sprinting back and forth until the pinecone burns down.

In terms of literal authorship, Anderson has always been open to working collaboratively, most obviously in writing partnerships with Owen Wilson but more recently with Noah Baumbach. *Aquatic* and *Darjeeling* marked commercial low points in Anderson's career, possibly suggesting his need for Owen Wilson's input as co-writer. Conversely, although Anderson claims to have hated the process, *Tenenbaums,* which he produced virtually alone (Wilson is credited but actually wrote very little), is arguably his strongest and most original script (for which he was Oscar-nominated). So far, he is only writing the script for *My Best Friend,* possibly indicating a wish for a slight distance from directing for a while.

While Zissou disparages the validity of signatures and Eli signs them without looking, Anderson himself seems to feel their enduring value, asking for Kael to sign some first editions when he met her and making sure Mrs. Fox's paintings bear the name "Felicity Fox" as a reference to Dahl's widow (and thereby establishing his validity as Dahl's creative heir). Like Zissou's ubiquitous branding, Mr. Fox's distinctive whistle (possibly a nod to Alan Alda's Hawkeye from *M*A*S*H*), wink, and clicking noise he makes with his tongue mark him as an Anderson creation, another pseudo-director branding himself as well as orchestrating events. The implication is that such characters (and by extension, Anderson too) need telltale visual and aural signs to generate a sense of identity (even Richie has one, silently performed to an autograph hunter in *Tenenbaums*). Kylie's attempt to imitate Fox's trademark with his own kick-step and a clap is a personal reflection of the notion in the main plot that everyone has individual, distinctive talents and reflects too Anderson's belief in auteurism as a natural and desirable artistic concept to aspire towards.

"THE CINEMA OF SATURATION"

In comparing *Tenenbaums* to *Amélie* (Jean-Pierre Jeunet, 2001), Jonathan Romney posits a "hypothetical Cinema of Saturation" but believes Anderson's film to be superior because we are "uncertain whether to smile or to squint so as to make out what else an image might be hiding," making us work harder as viewers for a richer final cinematic experience.[9] Anderson has described a book of detailed drawings of fantasy houses as the first creative endeavor he can remember and there is still something in the enclosed but minutely organized interiors of the Tenenbaum house, the *Belafonte,* and the train in *Darjeeling.* Anderson's films are packed with detail, which other films would not include, especially around issues of set dressing. This is not to say, however, that they are an irrelevant distraction. Long before Anderson recreated Roald Dahl's house for *Fantastic Mr. Fox,* there was a dollhouse feeling to the fictional worlds in his films. This tendency could be seen to reward repeat viewings (especially on DVD) or represent a suffocation of the dramatic lives of characters.

Bottle Rocket establishes Anderson's preference for strong primary colors—Dignan's yellow jumpsuit, Anthony's red fleece, and the green fields where they practice with the guns all have the brilliance of a children's picture book. Even here though there is some ambition in giving the middle part of the film, Anthony's love story and the group's interlude as outlaws, greater color than the pallid first and third sections, which represent the reality of their lives more precisely. In *Aquatic,* the color palette of the scenes involving Zissou is distinctive, not just in the red Smurf-like caps but also the blue of the island house and his van, contrasting with the yellow of items like the submersible. In *Darjeeling*, there is a distinctive wood-brown of the train interior and lighter blues of the compartments (echoed in the temple headscarves, the shirt of the boy whom the Whitmans sit with, and the room where they sleep). A later rare shot beyond the train shows the blue of the carriages edge into a landscape dominated by yellow powdery dust.

Eric Chase Anderson, Wes's elder brother, produced the dozens of almost-identical paintings of Margot in *Tenenbaums*, supposedly created by Richie. These clearly show Richie's obsession, but the pose itself of her scowling over the top of a book also provides the equivalent of a counter-shot. On the DVD extras, we see the detailed murals drawn of the family backstory and that element of posed cartoon/caricature appears in several montage sequences, most obviously at the opening but also in the investigator's report on Margot. Anderson seems literally very "hands-on" adding detail to drawings of Royal's hair. The Dalmatian mice are also actually a creation of Anderson's; the animals were literally colored in with Sharpies. The care which Anderson, particularly in collaboration with his regular production designer Mark Friedberg, puts into his sets, especially domestic interiors, is reflected in *Tenenbaums'* 300 set-ups, some for a shot with only one line or even no lines. There is an incredible pursuit of the minor but significant detail.

This is an extreme example of Anderson's aesthetic elsewhere, in that literally everything we see on screen is created from scratch, it is a fully imagined universe. Anderson's usual color palette is stripped out. Gone are all semblances of blues and greens and in their place a range of glorious, autumnal orangey-browns. In this respect, Mrs. Fox with her landscapes is a stand-in for Anderson, re-creating the look and color scheme of the set. This makes exceptions, like the appropriately named blueberries, seem extremely blue.

At times, Anderson draws our attention to the set, foregrounding his artifice, such as the construction of the tree house in *Fantastic Mr. Fox* or the shot near the end that drops down, Kubrick-like, through the strata of ground beneath the farmer's feet to where the survivors are eking out a living. A related shot appears in passing through the wall into the crystal cave. Indeed, viewers' responses may relate very specifically to the notion of diminutive size and act as a litmus paper for their response to Anderson's films more generally. If they find dollhouses sweet, they may find the almost-obsessive detail in Kristofferson's pajamas, Agnes's spots, and the breakfast table (held in shot so we can see all the small details) all rather quirky and sweet. If not, they might just find it pedantic and distracting. It is debatable, perhaps, exactly how much of this detail (for example in *Darjeeling* the hand-made props or elaborate paintings on the outside of the train, depicting events that occur during the narrative) is even visible. If it was held in shot longer, this last effect might work like the library book in *Tenenbaums*, that is, creating a narrative that refers to itself as it actually unfolds. The tracking shot of Mr. Fox and his wife through the first farmyard does show their ingenuity, speed, and agility, but it also affords Anderson the opportunity to show the carefully crafted backgrounds and minor details. It evokes the tracking shot at the end of *Rushmore,* except here we pause with the characters as their progress (evoking a kind of *Mission Impossible* style obstacle course) is momentarily halted and our attention drawn to the set and by implication, the intelligence behind it, that of the director.

There are several tight overhead shots (in itself a device focusing on detail), like Mrs. Fox's paint box or the whackbat explanation (overtly referencing Disney's 1942 Goofy cartoon *How to Play Baseball,* complete with dotted lines). The montage of Mr. Fox's first plan involves a number of similarly positioned shots. We have a collection of documents about beagles, which we assume are either imaginary since they actually belong to Boggis or suggest a microscopic level of preparation. There is some inconsistency here as Fox's subsequent mistakes during the robberies or indeed his choice of Kylie as his prime helper makes it clear that he relies on luck and charm as well as planning (he does not tell us where exactly he procures "sleeping powder"). His insistence on recording their conversation seems more to foreground the ancient equipment rather than accurately reflecting his character. However, like the whip-pans, they tend to be slightly more motivated than in other Anderson films, such as the close-up on Kylie's hand, which has the single word "Blueberry" written and decorated with arrows and stars to help him remember, all in vain. Anderson often uses overheads to show food, and here we have the scale and repetition of Boggis's diet, stressed by a further split screen effect multiplying the image by four. The lacing of blueberries for beagles (evoking the drugging of sultanas for pheasants in *Danny the Champion of the World*) is shown in a typical overhead shot.

The scope of the set is emphasized from the opening when Mrs. Fox, walking towards the camera, briefly disappears from view, only to reappear over the brow of a low hill. The same shot is used later as a figure runs for cover from the setting of explosives. The lighting and shots across a broader landscape frequently remind us of the existence of a wider, larger space beyond the scene in question, particularly through windows (such as Kylie conspiratorially appearing to talk to Fox). Whereas a lot of stop-motion animation uses tighter shots, especially in interiors, it really does feel here like Anderson has a broader vision of a complete world. At times, Anderson uses a reverse tracking shot through an interior that only reveals character in the foreground on the edges of the frame, such as Fox looking round the tree house for the first time.

Anderson conducted much of the principal photography for *Fantastic Mr. Fox* via phone, webcam, and e-mail from Paris, causing some friction with Gustafson and Tristan Oliver, director of photography. It is debatable when attention to detail becomes control freakery and certainly the demands of stop-motion animation seem to exacerbate Anderson's tendency to micromanage, even ironically at a distance, which might seem close to Francis's laminated schedules. Scott alludes to *Bottle Rocket*'s soldier scene in suggesting that "it often seems it's how things are arranged rather than the drama that's important."[10] However, this misses the point that the drama is in the details. It is deeply ironic that critics like Scott and Gilbey especially see Anderson's attention to detail as "the defining, and deadening characteristic" of a Wes Anderson movie and yet both misspell "Dignan."[11] It is such attention to detail that makes Anderson's work exceptional.

CONCLUSION

In terms of Collins's notion of "the New Sincerity," the dominant use of retro rock and the deliberate placing of narratives in an ambiguous or "out-of-time" chronological period create an element of looking back in Anderson's films. Modern technology is eschewed in favor of something bigger and more "clunky." However, it is debatable whether this is part of a yearning for a purer time with an almost-religious fervor. This is a simplistic response to the sequences using slow motion, suggesting they carry a profundity some viewers might well reject. The Whitmans are yearning very hard for a spiritual meaning to their journey but that does not mean the funeral scene yields such subtext.

There are a few scenes that seem like they embrace such a spirit of joie de vivre, like Dignan waving fireworks out of a car window, Royal taking the twins on a series of rebellious activities, or Zissou jumping into an improvised pool in the ice. However, in each case, the complexity of the character and interrelationships and particularly the debatable nature of any narrative closure within that narrative can be seen as undermining such a reading. Dignan's playing with fireworks at his age might be seen as reflecting the lack of thought and substance in his 75-year plan and indicative of his desire for notoriety over accepting adult responsibilities. Royal's advocacy for hedonism comes after years of ignoring his family, is prompted by his financial situation, rather than a genuine change of heart, and takes place as part of a brutally insensitive scam, exploiting the feelings of those he claims to care about. The term itself, "sincerity," is a highly subjective concept. It embraces both the sense of wonder in "childlike" and the puerile connotations of "childish." Like the positive and negative readings of the key term in relation to Chaucerian satire, "indulgent," Anderson has created a Janus-like mode of filmmaking, looking both ways simultaneously. Grace's line in *Tenenbaums* ("I do like Dignan . . . but he's a liar") encapsulates this contradiction.

In terms of his actions and self-dramatization, Dignan might alienate audiences but the lying element is crucial. Like Max, Zissou, and Royal (and a lesser extent, Francis), it is this ability to fictionalize which Anderson celebrates. Eli is a ridiculous figure but there is also something audacious in his manipulation of facts ("Everyone knows Custer died at Little Bighorn. What this book presupposes is . . . maybe he didn't?"). In *Gulliver's Travels* (1726), Jonathan Swift introduces us to a group of talking horses, the Houyhnhnms.

What marks these creatures as special, apart from the gift of speech, is their ability "to say the thing which is not."[12] This makes them paragons of virtue, but it also makes them colorless and uninteresting. They cannot lie but they also cannot create stories or poetry. Subsequent readers often remember the adventures of Lilliput more powerfully because here we have the elements of a powerful story and (as it turns out) a fallible narrator. Anderson's heroes are also unreliable narrators but the more interesting for it.

There may be a lack of cynicism in Anderson's work but that is also because there is a lack of engagement with the real world. The reaction of protagonists to the challenges of life is to fictionalize it. Drawn almost exclusively from fairly comfortable backgrounds, these characters suggest that avoiding cynicism is also easier when your financial circumstances insulate you from the less pleasant elements of life. Anderson's scripts are filled with irony but often this is felt by viewers, not characters within the fiction; like Dignan, they remain resolutely "innocent." What seems undiminished is the heroes' drive to reinvent themselves. In Blume (the name itself suggestive of the character's latent qualities to develop), we have the quintessential example of an Anderson hero, both careless (in the sense of "couldn't care less") at the opening and carefree in his love for Miss Cross.

If the New Sincerity is supposed to represent an embracing of uninhibited feeling and action, even at the risk of looking uncool, then Anderson's movies are definitely not part of this critical movement. They accept the whimsical and the eccentric but to the point of lionizing a different kind of cool, which still takes great care over how it looks. The fact that *Aquatic* has acted as the catalyst for online merchandise only underlines the extent to which attention to detail morphs into a fully accessorized universe. In the montage sequences especially, if his films celebrate the spontaneous outpouring of feeling, paradoxically, they do so in a very carefully crafted, self-aware medium. Perhaps for the true hipster, style *is* substance, not so much in the ironic suggestion that we are leading empty lives driven by branded consumerism but that there is a certain beauty in that lifestyle. The signatures most commonly associated with Anderson (which are largely there right from *Bottle Rocket*) reflect his content, rather than standing alone. While Anderson may not be a cinematic poet akin to Andrei Tarkovsky or Pier Paolo Pasolini, he does share a concern for form, not necessarily at the expense of content but that one should reflect the other and above all, he expresses "a belief that the way something *looks* is what dictates how it will make you *feel*."[13]

Conclusion

Wes Anderson doesn't make movies anymore. He creates overly precious paintings inhabited by emasculated man-children...watching this film [*Aquatic*] is like visiting the Natural History Museum. It's a beautiful building, but most of its pleasures are filled with lifeless things.

—Robert Lanham

ANDERSON'S HEROES

ANTHONY (ABOUT DIGNAN): Say what you will about him, he's no cynic and he's no quitter.

Part of auteurism is connected with the notion of a personal vision so that there is often a blurring between the director's own life and what we see on screen. His sense of ownership is so strong, it seems hard to imagine someone else directing an Anderson script or the possibility of his directing a script written entirely without his input. Anderson's heroes show the same kind of tenacity in pursuit of their obsessive dream as a director needs in order to get a film made. However, there also seems to be an innocence in Anderson's appropriations. Like Etheline in *Tenenbaums*, Anderson's own mother was an archaeologist and during production he gave Huston a pair of his mother's actual glasses to use as a prop. As suggested by interviews on the DVD, when Huston pointed out the link between the characters, he seemed genuinely shocked.

Several films are based either wholly (*Darjeeling*) or partly (*Bottle Rocket* and *Aquatic*) around the structure of journeys. *Rushmore* is notable for its opposite sense of stasis. It is Max's lack of desire to ever leave school that is seen as unhealthy. These journeys, both literal and metaphoric, focus on a protagonist seeking an adventure. This is central to *Bottle Rocket*, where there is no indication that Dignan, Bob, and Anthony even need to go on the run and in *Aquatic*, Zissou is trying to rekindle his success as a filmmaker by setting himself the audacious challenge of finding a hitherto-unknown and dangerous species. In *Darjeeling*, this pursuit of a spiritual journey is central to Francis's laminated schedule. Characters appear to be results-driven but are actually in love with the process. For Zissou or the Whitman brothers, the journey is more important than the destination and how much Dignan or Mr. Fox get from the robberies is less important to them than the planning and the postmortem.

For some viewers, this marks Anderson's heroes as deluded fantasists, playing childish games, whereas for others this tendency represents an unquenchable pursuit of something greater than they are. The prime movers in these adventures are all dreamers, who cannot accept the prosaic reality of their lives. For some, this refusal to accept the less-appealing aspects of reality is infantile but for others it represents a stubborn resistance in the human spirit, to wish things were different than they are. In Anderson's filmmaking, typified by heightened stylization of music, color, dialogue, even shot composition, the suggestion is that such transformations are possible, albeit only in the realm of film. The accusations of childishness that might be leveled at delusional heroes might also be used of Anderson's cinematic art. It seems a natural progression for him to try animation as a fictional realm, where entirely fictional worlds can be created, where characters can perform physical movements impossible in the real world, and where the term "childish" denotes imaginative freedom. Mr. Fox is literally seeking the same thing that Dignan, Blume (especially underwater), Cash, and Zissou are all seeking, a form of escape. Like Mr. Fox's question to his wife, they appear to offer a choice but will always take us on the scenic route. From Dignan to Mr. Fox, all his heroes have a misplaced faith in their master plan, recording even the rituals of planning.

There is an almost Chaucerian tone to many of Anderson's films in that we are encouraged to laugh *with* rather than *at,* his flawed heroes. We are not allowed the luxury of emotional distance, to place ourselves above them. When Max declares that his recipe for a perfect life is to find something you love and then do it for the rest of your life and that his thing is going to *Rushmore,* we indulge this absurdity rather than feel superior to it. As Anderson says of Max in production notes for *Rushmore,* "There's something wrong with him. But in this case, it's a condition I tend to admire."[1] In the case of Max or Dignan, the younger the protagonist, the more easily we can accept such childish dreaming. Conversely for Zissou or the Whitman brothers, such behavior can seem just self-indulgent and childish in a negative sense.

As Dirk says in *Rushmore,* "With friends like you, who needs friends?" Centrally, Anderson is interested in the protean nature of family and friendship, particularly how ties of blood guarantee no emotional closeness and conversely how bonds of close friendship constitute a greater sense of family.

Margot and Richie are inhibited from a relationship because of their pseudo-familial ties, while Eli who has no parents of his own seeks to have himself adopted by the family he idolizes. The fact that Anderson works with many of the same cast and crew in his films means in effect that he is working with friends; that is, increasingly his creative life blurs into his personal life. However, what was once his territory alone, stylistically and thematically, has become increasingly crowded. One of his future projects, a version of *My Best Friend*, has been preempted to some extent by Jay Roach's *Dinner for Schmucks* (2010), also a remake of a French film (Francis Veber's 1998 *Le dîner de cons*, or *The Dinner Game*), in which a potentially distasteful middle-class game based on the social niceties of bourgeois living exploits unwitting lower-class victims for the purposes of entertainment.

In *Bottle Rocket* we have an alternative group in Dignan's pseudo "crime family," who actually have very little in common and start to fragment almost immediately (cynics might say like a real family). It is only the force of Dignan's dream that keeps them together. Neither Anthony nor Bob seems very committed to the idea of a life of crime. Bob does not seem to have thought through the consequences of breaking the law. The possibility that his brother might land in jail for possession of marijuana is a visible shock to him, and Anthony is immediately sidetracked by his romantic pursuit of Inez. Bob's return, although seen as a "betrayal" by Dignan, is for the greater good of Bob's family, and he sees it as a chance to prove himself to his brother, and perhaps Anthony matures slightly in falling in love with someone beyond his own class, race, culture, and language. Perhaps, in this respect, their attempt at being outlaws does create a greater sense of family, just not necessarily with each other. Anthony and Bob do visit Dignan in jail so they do not abandon their friend, but there is no sense in which they wish to follow in his footsteps. Ultimately, given their personal and financial circumstances, despite the robbery at Bob's house, both Bob and Anthony are far too comfortable in their lives to imagine suddenly jettisoning a life of relative luxury just to become felons. For them, crime was never a career path, just an adolescent phase, a way of creating a sense of belonging until something better came along.

More than dysfunctional families, Anderson is interested in one very precise area, fathers who struggle to accept and understand their responsibilities (Zissou, Royal, or Peter). As a slightly concussed Jane says in *Aquatic*, "I need to find a baby for this father." Like Royal Tenenbaum, Zissou is a man in late middle age, trying to win back the love of his former wife, fearing that this may be his last chance to do so. Typical of many reviewers, Ryan Gilbey refers to Murray's performance in *Rushmore*, describing both Blume and Zissou as showing a "midlife crisis," but actually genuine self-doubt is in short supply.[2] Zissou's questioning of himself is really designed as a self-deprecatory strategy to provoke compliments from Eleanor, rather than genuine explorations of the soul. Max in *Rushmore* also considers "What am I gonna do?" but for him it is almost a prelife crisis as his life has hardly begun.

Royal initiates his scam because of a shortage of cash, not due to introspective soul-searching. Either we find parents trying to reconnect with their children (*Tenenbaums*) or children trying to reconnect with their parents (*Darjeeling*) or a little of both (*Aquatic*).

The possibility of redemptive change, even if it is of an ambiguous nature in *Tenenbaums, Aquatic, Darjeeling,* and *Fantastic Mr. Fox* (both of Fox and Rat), seems like a repudiation of Fitzgerald's notion that "there are no second acts in American lives."[3] *Bottle Rocket* focuses almost entirely on a group of young characters but even here, there is the sense of Anthony maturing via his love for Inez and Dignan's irrepressibility suggests that his life, even one as an unsuccessful criminal, is far from over. *Rushmore* also deals mostly with the first act of Max's life, and it seems as if there is potential in Max and Blume to change the course of their lives. Anderson's films are more interested in a three-act structure, with the first and the last proving most interesting. *Bottle Rocket* and *Rushmore* would fit into the first phase (Dignan, Bob, and Anthony have never even had a steady job), *The Life Aquatic* and *Tenenbaums* into the third, and *The Darjeeling Limited* somewhere in the middle but still not representative of *midlife*.

A male protagonist comes to connect emotionally with offspring, who may not actually be related (Margot and Ned), but he is still finally accepted as kin. Both Royal and Zissou must confront the conflict between a character as others have constructed it and their own sense of self. In the case of Zissou, the hero dramatizes the problem of being overwhelmed by this constructed other, this public face, which he has worked so hard to create and now he cannot live up to. In a sense, all Anderson's films are really about filmmaking and what happens to characters when the fictions that they have constructed about themselves come into conflict, not so much with reality (this is in short supply in Anderson's films—none of Selick's creatures actually exist) but with an alternate and possibly contradictory fiction. The central characters are leaders, acting much as a proxy director, Dignan and Mr. Fox trying to be criminal masterminds, Max a theatrical director, Zissou a director/explorer, and Francis as savior of the Whitman family.

Brannon M. Hancock's attempt to read Anderson's first three films as celebrating the notion of communion in a religious sense ignores the flawed nature of the heroes and the potential irony in the denouements, for such interpretations to work.[4] When Royal says "me too" in relation to a wish to be a Tenenbaum, Hancock is skipping over the comic absurdity of such lines. It could be said that almost any fictional text requires an element of interaction with others for character development to take place. Overarching readings of Anderson's work are undermined by the fact that many of the commonplace assumptions about his films are open to question. For example, it is routinely assumed that his films are concerned with failure and yet the Tenenbaums have not really failed because they have not yet tried. Margot has stopped writing plays; Richie was successful until his self-imposed withdrawal from sport; and

Anthony has never worked. Max's final act can be seen as redemptive but perhaps he has not overcome his crush, just learned to live with it. Dignan's spirit is far from crushed, and he is already planning his next job but he is still in prison. The point about failure depends entirely on one's criteria for success. Anderson's characters are routinely described as failures or figures in decline but on closer inspection, it is often more a case of self-deprecation or the collision of adult reality with an immature ego. Both Zissou and the safecracker Kumar bewail their loss of talent but like Richie's supposed failure as an artist, it is unclear exactly how much talent they had to lose in the first place.

The films show the danger of pursuing the enticing maxim that Max finds in the library book ("When one man, for whatever reason, has the opportunity to lead an extraordinary life, he has no right to keep it to himself"). It legitimizes self-belief, but it also opens the door to egoism and feels quite close to Nietzschean ideas of will to power. Max, Zissou, even Mr. Fox all appear to be pursuing their dreams for noble ends, but there is a strong vein of egotism that runs beneath their motivation. For all Fox's speech about being a wild animal and wanting to make his children proud, it is literally the thrill of the chase that draws him on.

If characters are less fully rounded, psychological entities than collections of physical and verbal tics, deadpan comedy can be sustained but melodrama and farce require a level of character identification that not all viewers manage with Anderson's work. Sudden expressions of emotion, such as Anthony saying that he loves Inez, Zissou's attack on the pirates, or Charles's final tearful breakdown at Royal's gift of a dog, struggle to convince when characters have studiously avoided such an emotional range up to this point. Far from shifting tones as Seitz asserts, we might move from the romantic (Richie and Margot in the tent) to the melodramatic (Richie at the mirror, perhaps borrowed from Dustin Hoffman, contemplating suicide) but stylistically, the means are the same. There is a flattening, some might say a deadening, of tonal range. Admittedly, there is an increase in pace on Dudley's discovery of Richie, wrists slashed, but immediately afterwards as the family are sitting around his hospital bed, it is quirky deadpan humor, delivered in measured tones, that prevails. The romantic scene in the tent is carried primarily by the juxtaposition of music and the childish setting, precluding any great emotional (or transgressively incestuous) climax here. Anthony's passivity and Margot's panda-eyed lack of reaction, juxtaposed with Charles's perpetual anger-near-breaking-point, means *Tenenbaums'* emotional heart, if it has one, has to come from the roguish antics of Royal whose motives and sincerity are always suspect. Likewise, the tears that Zissou sheds at the beginning and even the end, are compromised by his charismatically manipulative character, typified by laconic throwaway remarks, that we see between these two points. When we do need tonal shifts, as when Zissou falls down stairs and starts talking about himself in the third person and how tragic his life is, the emotional leap seems strained and unconvincing. Feelings ultimately are implied rather than shown. A shot from Zissou's point of view lingers on Eleanor sitting on a balcony, but later there is no outpouring of anger or grief at Ned's death, and the final ensemble party still has Zissou wisecracking about what he thinks of others.

This difficulty is exemplified in scenes where there is a declaration of love. What could be a scene of great emotional weight can only be read comically. Like Terry (Lee Tergesen) in *Wayne's World* (Penelope Spheeris, 1992), in *Tenenbaums,* Richie repeating how he loves Charles only provokes him into storming off, snapping angrily, "Don't keep saying that." Richie and Margot go to extremes to avoid declaring their feelings for one another. In *Bottle Rocket,* a message of love is not passed on and is in a foreign language anyway, and in *Darjeeling,* Francis shouts "I love you" at Peter and Jack, neither of whom respond with quite the same enthusiasm.

The contradictory use of music (wanting audiences to pay attention to lyrics and to be led by the melodic mood of a piece of music and yet not wanting them to necessarily associate it with a given era) adds to the general sense of whimsy, which can be engaging in the short term but mitigates against passionate engagement with character. There is an inherent distance involved with the operation of whimsy. When we look at a character acting or speaking in a manner that is eccentric, it is unlikely that we ourselves normally act like this or know many people who do. These films offer escape from the real world rather than engagement with it, which works as long as Anderson can keep finding engaging characters, sufficiently detached from the real world to keep the balance of whimsy and credibility intact. Where this tips too far towards the real world, we have *Darjeeling*; where it moves too close to self-indulgence (in character, and possibly in Anderson too), we have *Aquatic. Tenenbaums* and *Rushmore* possibly work better because this mode of whimsy seems appropriate to the hermetic settings.

Anderson's protagonists are deluded in creating little worlds for themselves, in which they are the heroes. Dignan waves his thanks to the doctor, imagining he is a janitor who helped his friend escape. The key point here though, and what stops them for the most part from becoming merely egocentric, is that they create something. By sheer force of will, they imagine the world as other than the film audience perceives it to be. They seek to impose a sense of order on their lives (via Dignan's 75-year plan, Royal's cancer scan, or Mr. Fox's three-part heist). They aspire to be something greater than they are and pursue this dream with absolute devotion, bordering on obsession. Even at the end, Dignan has an escape plan. Charlotte O'Sullivan asserts, "It's only when Max and Royal give up their dreams (Max by resigning himself to the public school system, Royal by divorcing his wife Etheline) that they gain the affirmation they crave."[5] There is certainly an attempt at a resolution of character conflict and a drive for narrative closure of sorts but in neither case is it either convincing or satisfying. We much prefer the rebellious phases of both characters, and their sudden conforming to familial or social pressures, while edging closer to a realistic compromise, given their extreme positions, is not credible.

What you virtually never have is characters actually *trying* to be funny. What makes the dinner scene in *Rushmore,* where Max is drunk and tries to make jokes at the expense of Peter (Andrew Wilson), seem odd (and partly funny, it has to be said) is that it is relatively rare. Anderson's characters are written to be unaware of their own absurdities, although we as audiences can see them clearly. This produces a slightly goldfish bowl element to his films, which can almost seem intrusive or voyeuristic. We see characters when they are vulnerable and weak rather than strong, successful, and heroic.

Max is the quintessential Anderson hero, part rebel, part fool. It might take initiative and creativity to found and run quite so many esoteric clubs, but this is also a displacement activity from academic responsibility. Then again, this implicitly criticizes the school as an institution that fails to value Max's gifts for organizing others as well as for self-promotion. Far from lazy, he seems, on the contrary, to have an unusually high sense of commitment; the problem is what he is committed to. He embraces fully the notion of the well-rounded individual and the value of extracurricular activities but misses the main business of lessons. Almost every scene features Max and what we see is his solipsistic universe. In the pantheon of heroes-as-adolescents, Max may remain a favorite with Anderson fans perhaps because he fits this role best; that is exactly what he is. Dignan, the Tenenbaums, Zissou, and the Whitman brothers may all try to act like children at times *but they have left school. Fantastic Mr. Fox* provides a useful bookend along with *Bottle Rocket* for the main films considered in this book. The hero in *Bottle Rocket* is trying to be something he is not (a master criminal) whereas in *Fantastic Mr. Fox,* he is trying to deny what he really is. As a result, *Bottle Rocket* aspires to be a heist movie but is really a comedy, and *Fantastic Mr. Fox* seems like a children's animation but is really a philosophical caper movie.

Salinger's characters try to engage with the adult world and are disillusioned by it, but Anderson's characters retreat from it, fabricating their own alternative universe, like Dignan's life "on the run from Johnny Law," Max's plethora of clubs at Rushmore, the Tenenbaums' brownstone, Zissou's floating clubhouse on the *Belafonte,* or the Whitmans' cabin from which they can view the passing Indian countryside. Anderson is not concerned with unmasking the phoniness of adult hypocrisy because his characters are too busy playing roles themselves. Max, Royal, and Zissou are great actors, both in their own performance and in inspiring similar attempts in those around them, and are not beyond fakery to achieve a dramatic end—Max with fake blood, Royal with Tic Tacs, and Zissou advocating an autograph hunter forge his name.

Retreat is a very beguiling prospect. There is an innate element of escapism in viewing any film, and watching Anderson's movies can be an uplifting experience, but Orson Welles's metaphor about filmmaking being like the biggest train set a boy could have comes to mind. *Aquatic* gave Anderson some bigger more expensive toys and *Darjeeling* some from a different part of the world, but the same limitations apply. Perhaps there is the faintest hint of evolution in his style. *Darjeeling* was the first film not to use Mark Mothersbaugh, and in *Fantastic Mr. Fox,* we have some original music, no slow motion sequence, and no Futura typeface used in the film itself. Perhaps like IKEA, a former client, which changed its dominant typeface (also in 2009), Anderson is even ready to forsake the pleasures of Futura. However, perhaps we should not expect any radical change. Like the AmEx commercial, when he starts a project he goes back to particular film, literature, and music that he likes. Until his personal tastes change, his filmmaking style is not likely to undergo radical transformation. Conversely, perhaps critics should stop criticizing him for not making the films that they would like him to make and focus instead on what we do have: a distinctive body of work, which has kept its identity despite commercial and critical pressures to change. Like Woody Allen, Anderson has had to endure the standard criticism that his more recent releases are not as good as his earlier work, and yet the parallel is hardly fair. Allen is prolific with 42 features completed to date. To make a crude film-by-film comparison, by now Allen would only be at the stage of *Love and Death* (1975) in his career.

Anderson's next project, provisionally titled *The Rosenthaler Suite,* is Anderson's first overt remake, although it plays into the hands of critics who see his career as stalled or atrophied. His attraction to French cinema continues in an Americanized version of Patrice Leconte's *Mon meilleur ami,* or *My Best Friend* (2006). Anderson's title refers to a collection of paintings by a dying artist that the protagonist, Nicholas, tries to buy up. We still have an interest in framed images, here paintings (Leconte's antiques dealer becomes an art dealer), one of Truffaut's iconic performers, Daniel Auteuil, and Laconte's Paris becomes a New York with a particularly Jewish, Paul Auster–like feel (particularly his 1989 *Moon Palace* with the enigmatic artist not introduced until late in the narrative).

As Douglas Templeton notes, "Can the poet understand his life, if he does not fictionalize it?"[6] Apparent emotional distance, irony, and deadpan reactions (all aspects which some viewers and critics find annoying) are also key stratagems that people, especially when young, use as defense mechanisms to avoid facing difficult questions about themselves. Anderson's films are filled with characters avoiding truths about themselves, and it is their visible fragility in doing so which makes them empathetic. At most levels, Dignan should be laughable, but Anthony and Bob keep coming back to him (going along with the initial break-out and staying in the gang, respectively) because to do otherwise would crush him. They may have infuriating egos, but they are actually deeply insecure. Thus, Anderson's protagonists are indulged (Dignan talking up the professionalism of the raid on Anthony's house, Max drunk at the dinner table or claiming earnestly that "Harvard's my safety," and Zissou needing easy interview questions). It is this earnest naïveté that allows such characters to function and a key part of why they are charismatic.

The romance of the heroic act, a final shot at personal redemption, is partly admirable but also often egotistical and absurd. If we are swept along by empathetic identification and emotion, we too see them as redeemed heroes; if not, if we retain a sense of the wider context, they are sad, deluded, emotionally retarded individuals attempting to cast themselves as the heroes of their own narratives. A fox can outsmart humans with guns but only with a large dose of fantasy (Ash, like Zissou, running unscathed through an unbelievable hail of bullets), which we are also expected to indulge (not questioning Badger's ability to communicate with paper cups and string). Does Dignan go back to rescue Applejack out of a sense of loyalty and integrity or because it allows him to play the part of noble, self-sacrificing hero? In a sense, he has won because the arrival of the police and the failure of the robbery allow him to play this part. Anderson's heroes are allowed to be reintegrated with their family group (even Dignan with his fellow criminals). They do not die the lonely death of heroes from the French New Wave (Arthur [Claude Brasseur] at the end of Jean-Luc Godard's *Bande à part* [1964] or Michel [Jean-Paul Belmondo] at the end of *À bout de souffle* [1960]).

Anderson's heroes are given the dignity of a form of redemption within a peer group, because they are able to bring their self-image closer to how others perceive them. Dignan's description of his planned robbery involves a long list of exciting features, including dynamite, pole vaulting, and hang gliding. The reality, at a cold-storage facility, involves none of these. Dignan's idolizing of his gardening job included the simple pleasure of "listening to stories." It is Dignan's fictionalizing of himself, along the lines of his cinematic heroes, that draws in his accomplices and means that even when he is caught, he does not stop dreaming. However, this is not a selfless act. It is not a process of recognizing oneself in others but *imposing* oneself on others by creating an engaging cinematic fiction. Mr. Henry says, "The world needs dreamers" and in Anderson's films, populated by aspiring directors and creators of fictions, these dreams are of a specific *cinematic* kind. Despite showing the fragility and delusional quality of these dreams (symbolized for example in *Bottle Rocket* by the fact that Dignan's trousers are always slightly too short), Anderson does not take the dramatically easier path and destroy them. They may fail but without them, we have no cause for hope. They dare to do what we may not. They are our surrogate dreamers and we destroy them at our peril.

Relating to Anderson's films ultimately requires a positive view of dreamers, makers of fictions, and surrogate filmmakers. If we believe, as Anderson appears to do, that life is richer for them, we may indulge them their fantasies; if not, we may stand back, as some critics do, and laugh at their absurdity, unwilling to accept that it is shared by us all. The problem that Anderson has, and it is one entirely of his own making, is that in placing his characters in such hermetically sealed and stylized worlds, it becomes progressively easier to reject the sense of a shared bond with the characters. If we have never met anyone like the Tenenbaums, Zissou, or Dignan, the narratives remain fanta-sies, interesting, but ultimately temporary in their ability to involve us.

Novelist Sebastian Faulks describes human consciousness as "the ability to tell a story to ourselves...even if it is a misrepresentation—you can start to plan and visualise a past and future, and therefore causality."[7] In short, Anderson's solipsistic heroes may be extreme and obsessive in their desire to manufacture a reality, which matches their desired self-image, but this impulse is distinctively and uniquely *human*. Therefore as much as we are encouraged to laugh at Anderson's heroes as ridiculous, there is also a con-trary impulse running through his characters to celebrate them as fallible but clearly *human*.

Notes

INTRODUCTION

1. Robert Lanham, *The Hipster Handbook* (New York: Anchor Books, 2003), 2, 17, 29, and especially, 132–36.
2. Scott Tobias, "Olivia Williams," *AV Club,* http://www.avclub.com/articles/olivia-williams,38187/.
3. Jim Collins, *Film Theory Goes to the Movies,* ed. Jim Collins, Hilary Radner, and Ava Preacher Collins (New York and London: Routledge, 1993), 243.

CHAPTER 1

1. Mark Olsen, "If I Can Dream: The Everlasting Boyhoods of Wes Anderson," *Film Comment* (January/February 1999):1, 12–17.
2. Martin Scorsese, *Esquire* (March 1, 2000), http://www.esquire.com/features/wes-anderson-0300.
3. Ibid.

CHAPTER 2

1. Henry James, *The Art of Fiction and Other Essays* (Oxford: Oxford University Press, 1948), 11.

CHAPTER 3

1. Jonathan Romney, "Family Album," *Sight and Sound,* vol. 12, no. 3: 13.
2. Matt Zoller Seitz, "The Substance of Style, Part II," http://dialogic.blogspot.com/2010/06/matt-zoller-seitz-substance-of-style.html. "Tannenbaum" is husband of Salinger's eldest Glass daughter, Beatrice or "Boo Boo" Tannenbaum (née Glass). It also evokes the name of Brian Tenenbaum, a close friend of Anderson and regular actor in minor roles in his films.
3. Romney, "Family Album," 86.
4. Ibid., 123.

5. Ibid., 103.
6. Ibid., 121.
7. Ibid., 10.
8. Roald Dahl, *Danny the Champion of the World* (London: Penguin Books, 1975), 215.

CHAPTER 4

1. André Bazin, *What Is Cinema?* vol. 1, trans. Hugh Gray (Berkeley: University of California Press), 155.
2. Ibid., 158.
3. Ibid.
4. Ibid.
5. Dyalan Govender, "Wes Anderson's *The Life Aquatic with Steve Zissou* and Melville's *Moby Dick*: A Comparative Study," *Literature/Film Quarterly,* vol. 36, no. 1 (January 1, 2008): 61–67.
6. Ibid., 65.
7. Ibid., 66.

CHAPTER 5

1. Scott Tobias, "Interview with Wes Anderson," *AV Club,* October 10, 2007, http://www.avclub.com/articles/wes-anderson,14161/.
2. Ben Walters, "Fantastic Mr Fox," *Sight and Sound,* vol. 19, no. 11 (November 2009): 58.
3. Mark Olsen, "If I Can Dream: The Everlasting Boyhoods of Wes Anderson," *Film Comment,* vol. 35, no. 1 (January/February 1999): 12–17.

CHAPTER 6

1. Roald Dahl, *Fantastic Mr. Fox* (London: Penquin Books, 1970), 3.
2. Ibid., 70.
3. Ibid., 29.

CHAPTER 7

1. Kevin Conroy Scott, "Lesser Spotted Fish and Other Stories," *Sight and Sound,* vol. 15, no. 3 (March 2005): 15.
2. Harold Bloom, *The Anxiety of Influence: A Theory of Poetry* (Oxford: Oxford University Press, 1973), 14–16.
3. David Bordwell, *Narration in the Fiction Film* (New York and London: Routledge, 1985), 211.

CHAPTER 8

1. Jonah Weiner, "Unbearable Whiteness: That Queasy Feeling You Get when Watching a Wes Anderson Movie," *Slate.com,* http://www.slate.com/id/2174828.

2. Emily May, "*The Darjeeling Limited* and the New American Traveller," *Senses of Cinema,* http://archive.sensesofcinema.com/contents/08/49/darjeeling-limited.html.
3. Sam Davies, "Wild Thing," *Sight and Sound,* vol. 19, no. 11 (November 2009): 19.

CHAPTER 9

1. Eric Chase Anderson, *Chuck Dugan Is AWOL* (San Francisco: Chronicle Books, 2005), 6.
2. Ibid., 9.
3. Mark Browning, *David Fincher: Films That Scar* (Santa Barbara, CA: ABC-CLIO, 2010), 3.
4. Phil Powrie, *The Cinema of France* (London, Wallflower Press, 2005), 65.
5. Wes Anderson, "The Man in the Ironic Mask," *Independent,* February 21, 2010, http://www.independent.co.uk/news/people/profiles/wes-anderson-the-man-in-the-ironic-mask-1905792.html.
6. Jason Morris, "The Time Between Time: Messianism & the Promise of a 'New Sincerity'," *Jacket Magazine* 35 (2008), http://jacketmagazine.com/35/morris-sincerity.shtml.

CHAPTER 10

1. Michael Hirschorn, "Quirked Around," *Atlantic Monthly,* September 2007, http://www.theatlantic.com/magazine/archive/2007/09/quirked-around/6119/.
2. Charlotte O'Sullivan, "*The Royal Tenenbaums*: A Review," *Sight and Sound,* vol. 12, no. 4 (April 2002): 60.
3. Carole Lyn Piechota, "Give Me a Second Grace: Music as Absolution in The Royal Tenenbaums," *Senses of Cinema,* http://archive.sensesofcinema.com/contents/06/38/music_tenenbaums.html.
4. Ibid.
5. Ibid.
6. Wes Anderson, "Draft for *The Rosenthaler Suite,*" *The Playlist,* November 16, 2009, http://theplaylist.blogspot.com/2009/11/wes-andersons-latest-script-called.html.
7. Devin Orgeron, "La Camera-Crayola: Authorship Comes of Age in the Cinema of Wes Anderson," *Cinema Journal,* vol. 46, no. 2 (Winter 2007): 40–65.
8. Wes Anderson, Interview with Arnaud Desplechin, July 2, 2009, http://www.interviewmagazine.com/film/wes-anderson/.
9. Romney, "Family Album," 15.
10. Scott, "Lesser Spotted Fish," 14.
11. Gilbey, "*The Life Aquatic with Steve Zissou*," 59.
12. Jonathan Swift, *Gulliver's Travels* (New York: Books Inc.), 186.
13. David Amsden, "The Life Obsessive with Wes Anderson," *New York Magazine,* September 24, 2007, http://nymag.com/movies/filmfestivals/newyork/2007/38024/.

CONCLUSION

1. Wes Anderson, Rushmore Production Notes, http://rushmore.shootangle.com/academy/films/rushmore/library/rushmore_press_kit.pdf, 6.
2. Gilbey, "*The Life Aquatic*," 59.
3. F. Scott Fitzgerald, usually attributed to Notes attached to Edmund Wilson (ed.) *The Last Tycoon* (New York: Penguin Books, 1941), 31.
4. Brannon M. Hancock, "A Community of Characters—The Narrative Self in the Films of Wes Anderson," *The Journal of Religion and Film,* vol. 9, no. 2 (October 2005), http://www.unomaha.edu/jrf/Vol9No2/HancockCommunity.htm.
5. O'Sullivan, 60.
6. Douglas Templeton, *The New Testament as True Fiction* (Sheffield, UK: Sheffield Academic Press, 1999), 209.
7. Sebastian Faulks, *Human Traces* (London: Vintage, 2005), 454.

Bibliography

Amsden, David. (September 24, 2007). "The Life Obsessive with Wes Anderson," *New York Magazine,* http://nymag.com/movies/filmfestivals/newyork/2007/38024/.

Anderson, Eric Chase. (2005). *Chuck Dugan Is AWOL.* San Francisco, CA: Chronicle Books.

Anderson, Wes. (June 18, 2008). "The Director's Director," an interview with Jennifer Wachtel," *GOOD,* Issue 011, http://www.good.is/post/the_directors_director/.

Anderson, Wes. (July 2009). "An Interview with Arnaud Desplechin," http://www.interviewmagazine.com/film/wes-anderson/.

Anderson, Wes. (November 16, 2009). Draft for *The Rosenthaler Suite. The Playlist,* http://theplaylist.blogspot.com/2009/11/wes-andersons-latest-script-called.html.

Anderson, Wes. (February 21, 2010). "The Man in the Ironic Mask," http://www.independent.co.uk/news/people/profiles/wes-anderson-the-man-in-the-ironic-mask-1905792.html.

Anderson, Wes. Rushmore Production Notes, http://rushmore.shootangle.com/academy/films/rushmore/library/rushmore_press_kit.pdf.

Anderson, Wes, and Owen Wilson. (1999). *Rushmore* (classic screenplay). London: Faber & Faber.

Bazin, André. (1967). *What Is Cinema?* vol. 1, trans. Hugh Gray. Berkeley: University of California Press.

Bloom, Harold. (1973). *The Anxiety of Influence: A Theory of Poetry.* Oxford: Oxford University Press.

Bordwell, David. (1985). *Narration in the Fiction Film.* New York and London: Routledge.

Browning, Mark. (2010). *David Fincher: Films That Scar.* Santa Barbara, CA: ABC-CLIO.

Collins, Jim, Hilary Radner, and Ava Preacher Collins (eds.). (1993). *Film Theory Goes to the Movies.* New York and London: Routledge.

Dahl, Roald. (1970). *Fantastic Mr. Fox.* London: Penguin Books.

Dahl, Roald.(1975). *Danny the Champion of the World.* London: Penguin Books.

Davies, Sam. (November 2009). "Wild Thing," *Sight and Sound* 19:11: p. 19.

Faulks, Sebastian. (2005). *Human Traces.* London: Vintage.

Fitzgerald, F. Scott. (1926). "The Rich Boy." In *The Penguin Book of American Short Stories*. New York: Penguin Books.

Fitzgerald, F. Scott. (2009). *The Crack-Up*. Edmund Wilson (ed.). New York: New Directions.

Gilbey, Ryan. (March 2005). "*The Life Aquatic with Steve Zissou:* A Review." *Sight and Sound* 15:3: pp. 58–59.

Govender, Dyalan. (January 1, 2008). "Wes Anderson's *The Life Aquatic with Steve Zissou* and Melville's *Moby Dick:* A Comparative Study." *Literature/Film Quarterly* 36:1: pp. 61–67.

Hancock, Brannon M. (October 2005). "A Community of Characters—the Narrative Self in the Films of Wes Anderson." *The Journal of Religion and Film* 9:2, http://www.unomaha.edu/jrf/Vol9No2/HancockCommunity.htm.

Herron, Don (ed.). (1988). *Reign of Fear: The Fiction and the Films of Stephen King*. Novato, CA: Underwood-Miller.

Hill, Derek. (2008). *Charlie Kaufman and Hollywood's Merry Band of Pranksters, Fabulists and Dreamers: An Excursion into the American New Wave*. Harpenden, Herts.: Kamera Books.

Hirschorn, Michael. (September 2007). "Quirked Around." *Atlantic Monthly,* http://www.theatlantic.com/magazine/archive/2007/09/quirked-around/6119/.

James, Henry. (1948). *The Art of Fiction and Other Essays*. Oxford: Oxford University Press.

Lander, Christian. (2008). *Stuff White People Like*. New York: Random House.

Lanham, Robert (2003). *The Hipster Handbook*. New York: Anchor Books.

May, Emily. "*The Darjeeling Limited and the New American Traveller.*" *Sense of Cinema,* http://archive.sensesofcinema.com/contents/08/49/darjeeling-limited.html.

Morris, Jason. (2008). "The Time Between Time: Messianism & the Promise of a 'New Sincerity'." *Jacket Magazine* 35, http://jacketmagazine.com/35/morris-sincerity.shtml.

Olsen, Mark. (January/February 1999). "If I Can Dream: The Everlasting Boyhoods of Wes Anderson." *Film Comment* 35:1: pp. 12–17.

Orgeron, Devin. (Winter 2007). "La Camera-Crayola: Authorship Comes of Age in the Cinema of Wes Anderson." *Cinema Journal* 46:2: pp. 40–65.

O'Sullivan, Charlotte. (April 2002). "*The Royal Tenenbaums:* A Review," *Sight and Sound* 12:4: pp. 59–60.

Piechota, Carole Lyn. "Give Me a Second Grace: Music as Absolution in *The Royal Tenenbaums,*" *Senses of Cinema,* http://archive.sensesofcinema.com/contents/06/38/music_tenenbaums.html.

Powrie, Phil. (2005). *The Cinema of France*. London: Wallflower Press.

Romney, Jonathan. (March 2002). "Family Album," *Sight and Sound* 12:3: pp. 13–15.

Salinger, J. D. (1955). *Franny and Zooey*. London: Little, Brown and Company.

Scorsese, Martin. (March 1, 2000). "Wes Anderson." *Esquire,* http://www.esquire.com/features/wes-anderson-0300.

Scott, Kevin Conroy. (March 2005). "Lesser Spotted Fish and Other Stories." *Sight and Sound* 15:3: pp. 13–15.

Seitz, Matt Zoller. (June 3, 2010). "The Substance of Style, Part II," http://dialogic.blogspot.com/2010/06/matt-zoller-seitz-substance-of-style.html.

Simonson, Mark. (August 17, 2004). "*Royal Tenenbaum*s's World of Futura," http://
www.marksimonson.com/article/87/royal-tenenbaums-world-of-futura.

Swarup, Vikas. (2006). *Q & A*. London: Swan Books.

Swift, Jonathan. (1726). *Gulliver's Travels*. New York: Books Inc.

Templeton, Douglas. (1999). *The New Testament as True Fiction*. Sheffield, UK:
Sheffield Academic Press.

Tobias, Scott. (October 10, 2007). "Interview with Wes Anderson." *AV Club*, http://
www.avclub.com/articles/wes-anderson,14161/.

Tobias, Scott. (February 16, 2010). "Olivia Williams." *AV Club*, http://www.avclub.
com/articles/olivia-williams,38187/.

Walters, Ben. (November 2009). "Fantastic Mr. Fox." *Sight and Sound* 19:11:
p. 58.

Weiner, Jonah. (September 27, 2007). "Unbearable Whiteness: That Queasy Feeling
You Get When Watching a Wes Anderson Movie." *Slate.com*, http://www.slate.
com/id/2174828.

Index

About the Author

MARK BROWNING has taught English and film studies in a number of schools in England and was a senior lecturer in education in Bath. He has published study guides for film education and academic articles on the processes of adaptation. Browning currently lives and works as a teacher and freelance writer in Germany. He is the author of *David Fincher: Films That Scar* (Praeger, 2010), *Stephen King on the Big Screen* (2009), and *David Cronenberg—Author or Filmmaker?* (2007).